WILD EDIBLE PLANTS OF NEW ENGLAND

LOCATE, IDENTIFY, STORE, AND PREPARE YOUR FORAGED FINDS

FORAGE AND FEAST SERIES: COMPREHENSIVE GUIDES TO FORAGING ACROSS AMERICA

SHANNON WARNER

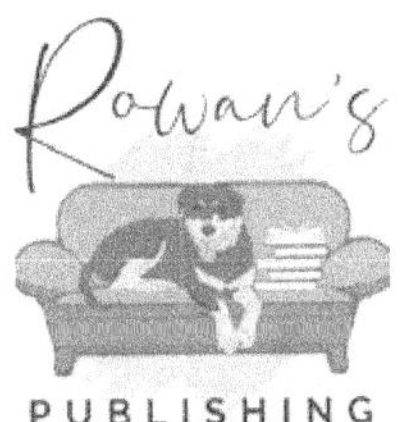

CONTENTS

PART FIVE
TREES AND NUTS

PART SIX
MUSHROOMS AND FUNGI

PART SEVEN
SEAWEED

PART EIGHT
POISONOUS

PART NINE
RECIPES

PART TEN
APPENDIX

ALSO BY SHANNON WARNER

<u>**Individual Books:**</u>

Wild Edible Plants of the Mid-Atlantic

Wild Edible Plants of California

Wild Edible Plants of the Pacific Northwest

Wild Edible Plants of Texas

Wild Edible Plants of the Great Lakes *(Coming Soon)*

Wild Edible Plants of the Great Plains *(Coming Soon)*

Wild Edible Plants of the Southeast *(Coming Soon)*

Wild Edible Plants of the Gulf Coast *(Coming Soon)*

Wild Edible Plants of the Upper Midwest *(Coming Soon)*

Wild Edible Plants of the Rocky Mountains *(Coming Soon)*

<u>**2-in1 Guides:**</u>

Wild Edibles of the West Coast (California & the Pacific Northwest)

Wild Edibles of the Northeast (Mid-Atlantic & New England)

Foraging the Wild South (Texas & the Southwest)

Foraging the Midwest *(Coming Soon)*

Foraging the Southeast *(Coming Soon)*

Foraging the North *(Coming Soon)*

New England has a harsh climate, a barren soil, a rough and stormy coast, and yet we love it, even with a love passing that of dwellers in more favored regions.

-HENRY CABOT LODGE

PART ONE
WHY FORAGE?

WANDER & GATHER
A FORAGER'S GUIDE TO NEW ENGLAND

Welcome to the enchanting world of foraging, where every step is a discovery and every plant holds a story waiting to be told. In the lush landscapes of New England, where verdant forests meet rocky coastlines and fertile fields stretch as far as the eye can see, an abundance of wild treasures awaits those with a keen eye and a curious spirit.

As you embark on this journey with me, imagine yourself stepping into a natural pantry, overflowing with nature's bounty. From the sweet tang of wild berries to the delicate fragrance of woodland herbs, each foraged find is a testament to the rich tapestry of life that thrives in this corner of the world.

In these pages, we'll delve into the art and science of foraging, weaving together ancient wisdom with modern knowledge to unlock the secrets of the land. Whether you're a seasoned enthusiast or a curious beginner, there's something here for everyone to discover.

But foraging is more than just a means of gathering sustenance; it's a way of connecting with the earth on a deeply personal level. It's about forging a relationship with the land that sustains us, learning to listen to its whispers and honor its gifts with gratitude.

Throughout this book, we'll explore the diverse ecosystems of New England, from the rugged mountains of Vermont to the sandy shores of Cape Cod. We'll learn to identify edible plants, mushrooms, and wild fruits, and uncover the hidden gems that lie hidden beneath the forest canopy.

But foraging is not without its risks, and it's essential to approach this practice with care and respect. We'll discuss the importance of sustainable foraging practices, ensuring that we leave behind no trace and harvest in harmony with nature's rhythms.

So, whether you're drawn to the thrill of the hunt or the simple pleasure of a stroll through the woods, I invite you to join me on this forager's odyssey through the heart of New England. Together, let's wander and gather, and let the beauty of the natural world be our guide.

FORAGING SUSTAINABILITY AND ETHICS

Foraging is rewarding, you can find some exotic and tasty things, but there are some basics you need to learn before heading out. Let's face facts, you can eat a tasty-looking mushroom if you don't know what it is, but you may only be able to do that once.

Your top priority is understanding the health and safety concerns of foraging and the "how-to" in Identify edible plants to avoid anything poisonous. In a survival situation, it's better to go without food than to eat something that makes you sick.

Let's take a second to talk about where these glorious plants come from; without Mother Nature, there is no foraging. The importance of responsible and sustainable foraging is something everyone needs to take into consideration before haphazardly going out and pulling up plants. It means you should know how to forage ethically and consider nature conservation.

Foragers have a responsibility to not only keep themselves safe but to look after the environment. If people don't look after the natural world, it's not just the plants and animals that will suffer. Humanity will suffer as well. It's not just a moral and ethical duty to take care of the land we forage from, but we have practical reasons for doing so. With this in mind, how can you forage ethically?

Some of the following tips and principles are obvious, while others are less so.

- Only harvest what you need.
- Never pick all of a plant. Take up to ⅓ of the leaves of a plant; any more than that risks the plant's health. Please don't take a plant in short supply; let it grow before Harvest.
- Rotate your foraging areas. Not doing so may stress a habitat too much.
- Leave an area looking at least as good as you found it, take any trash with you, and don't trample plants or other natural spaces. If you brought it in, you need to take it back out.

- Replant dislodged roots and plant seeds in similar areas. Avoid introducing invasive species to a site free of them.
- Use appropriate tools to avoid doing too much damage.
- Cut leaves and stems with a sharp object instead of pulling them and risking uprooting the plant, for example. It's also easier for a plant to heal from a clean cut than a tear or twist.

Ethical foraging primarily comes down to common sense. You've probably done a good job if you haven't left too much evidence of your presence. If you focus on Harvest invasive species over rarer ones, you might even be helping out nature. As well as respecting nature while Harvest wild edibles, responsible foragers must also respect the law.

Believe it or not, you can't simply wander wherever you like and take whatever plants interest you. Foraging is a surprisingly controversial activity, depending on where you are. Each state in the United States has different foraging laws and regulations and can even differ from National Park to National Park. Foraging may not be permitted in specific locations. Other areas allow you to harvest exact amounts of a wild harvest. Some places may let you take nuts and berries but not take mushrooms or any roots.

The best way to find out the rules where you plan to forage is to ask. Check with local wildlife authorities and park authorities for information. Signposts are also your friends, but you can often find this information online before you visit an area. You don't want to discover that you're breaking the law by encountering an angry park ranger.

Another potential legal pitfall when foraging is whether the land you're Harvest from is publicly or privately owned. Here's a funny story; see if you can spot my mistake. I once enjoyed a hike in the Appalachians, the views were stunning, and it was a beautiful day. I assumed that it was a public area, but guess what? It wasn't. I ended up being chased away from the site by an angry gentleman and his equally angry dogs. It wasn't the most pleasant end to my hike, but I learned an important lesson. If there are barbed wire fences or other signs of an animal pasture, then it's probably a privately owned area. Private owners rarely appreciate trespassing and appreciate people taking plants from their property even less. When foraging on private land, you should ask the landowner for permission and explain what you're doing. Some people won't mind foragers, as long as you're respectful. The worst they can do is say no.

In short, if you doubt whether you can legally forage in an area, then check. Even if you're relatively sure, then check. It's the best way to stay on the right side of the law and to avoid awkward encounters or, worse, a fine.

PART TWO
STATES

ONE
CONNECTICUT
THE CONSTITUTION STATE

Welcome to Connecticut, one of the original 13 colonies and the delightful heart of New England! It's often called the "Constitution State". It's known for its beauty, history, and unique charm. It's nestled amidst the rolling hills of the Berkshires and the sparkling shores of Long Island Sound, it beckons you with its irresistible blend of historical charm, vibrant culture, and awe-inspiring natural splendor. Immerse yourself in the allure of quaint colonial towns brimming with antique shops and cozy cafes, or embark on an outdoor escapade to discover lush forests, scenic hiking trails, and picturesque coastal panoramas. With its rich history, thriving arts scene, and genuine warmth, Connecticut invites you to savor the very essence of New England in one delightful package.

Yearly Weather Patterns

Connecticut enjoys all four seasons. Each one brings a new color to the state.

- *Winter* (December - February): The state gets pretty cold in the winter with snowfall common. The average high temperature is 34°F (1°C), and the average low is 18°F (-8°C).
- *Spring* (March - May): Spring starts to warm things up. The average high is around 60°F (15°C), and the average low is around 40°F (4°C). This is when the flowers start to bloom!
- *Summer* (June - August): Summers in Connecticut are typically warm and humid. The average high is 83°F (28°C), and the average low is around 60°F (15°C). Perfect weather for a trip to the beach!

- *Fall* (September - November): Autumn is absolutely beautiful with the trees turning red, orange, and yellow. The average high is around 65°F (18°C), and the average low is around 44°F (6°C).

Land Topography

Connecticut is home to a wide variety of landscapes, from gentle hills and green valleys to majestic mountains and serene coastal plains. Flowing through the center of the state, the Connecticut River holds the distinction of being the longest river in New England. It plays a crucial role in supporting the lives of both people and wildlife. The state is divided into two main regions: the Eastern Highland and the Western Highland. Both regions have rolling hills and mountains.

- *The Litchfield Hills:* situated in the northwest corner of the state, boast breathtaking landscapes adorned with delightful towns, shimmering lakes, and lush forests.
- *Farmington River Valley:* The Farmington River Valley, nestled in the central part of the state, is known for its tranquil beauty, winding waterways, and fertile farmland.
- *Eastern Highlands:* The eastern region of Connecticut is characterized by its rugged terrain, including the Eastern Highlands, where dense forests, rocky ridges, and pristine lakes abound.
- *Long Island Sound:* Along Connecticut's southern coast, you'll find the sparkling waters of Long Island Sound, a tidal estuary celebrated for its vibrant marine ecosystem and stunning scenery comprised of sandy beaches, rocky cliffs, and marshy wetlands.

I have traveled a good deal in Concord, and everywhere, in shops, offices, and fields, the inhabitants have appeared to me to be doing penance in a thousand remarkable ways.

-MARK TWAIN

Foraging Hotspots

The following list offers suggestions on possible foraging spots. Remember to check your local foraging laws before setting out. Here are some top spots:

- *Meshomasic State Forest:* This is the oldest state forest in Connecticut. You can find various berries, nuts, and edible mushrooms here.
- *Devil's Hopyard State Park:* You can find edible plants like fiddlehead ferns and wild garlic here.
- *Bigelow Hollow State Park:* This park is great for foraging wild berries and mushrooms.
- *Hammonasset Beach State Park:* Besides the beach, this park offers trails to forage for wild beach plums.
- *Paugussett State Forest:* A good place for finding wild berries, edible plants, and nuts.

Local Foraging Groups

If you're interested in foraging, here are some local groups you can join:

- **The Connecticut Valley Mycological Society**: Another group for mushroom enthusiasts. http://www.cvmsfungi.org/
- **The Connecticut Botanical Society**: A society for those interested in plants, including wild edibles. http://www.ct-botanical-society.org/
- **The 3 Foragers**: A group of people passionate about foraging and eating wild food. https://the3foragers.blogspot.com
- **Connecticut Foraging Club:** A group of people passionate about foraging. They offer foraging outings throughout CT. Facebook Group

Whether you're a resident or just visiting, there's always something to explore and discover in the Constitution State!

TWO
MAINE
THE PINE TREE STATE

Maine is known fondly as the "Pine Tree State" and was part of Massachusetts until it finally became its own state in 1820. The first people to live here were Native American tribes, like the Penobscot, who lived off the land for thousands of years. Its nickname comes from the tall, beautiful pine trees covering over 80% of its land. These trees are more than just beautiful—they're also important to Maine's history and economy. In the early 1600s, the first European settlers arrived, and Maine's forests have been a source of timber since. It's also been a center for shipbuilding, and fishing, helping to shape the United States as we know it today.

Yearly Weather Patterns

- *Winter* (December to February): Expect lots of snow! Maine winters can be very cold with temperatures often below freezing. Skiing, snowboarding, and ice fishing are popular activities during this season.
- *Spring* (March to May): The snow begins to melt, temperatures rise, and the state starts to bloom. This is a great time for hiking and bird-watching.
- *Summer* (June to August): This is when Maine truly shines. With mild temperatures ranging from 70 to 80 degrees Fahrenheit, it's perfect for exploring the state's beaches, forests, and mountains.
- *Fall* (September to November): Maine is famous for its foliage. Leaves change to stunning shades of orange, red, and yellow. It's also a great season for apple picking.

Land Topography

Maine's topography is rich in variety, with rugged coastlines, dense forests, gentle hills, and towering mountains. The state's landscape was heavily influenced by glaciers during the Ice Age, resulting in unique features like U-shaped valleys, moraines, and kettle ponds. Maine's bedrock is mainly granite, giving rise to its rocky terrain and supporting industries like quarrying and mining. Glacial erratics, massive boulders carried by glaciers and left in random locations, are scattered across the state, creating distinctive geological landmarks.

- *Appalachian Mountains:* The state is home to a significant portion of the northern end of the Appalachian Mountain Range, including the famous peaks of Mount Katahdin and the Mahoosuc Range.
- *Lakes and Rivers:* Maine is dotted with thousands of lakes and ponds, including Moosehead Lake, the state's largest freshwater body, and the Allagash Wilderness Waterway, a network of pristine rivers and lakes.
- *Coastal Beauty:* Maine's coastline stretches over 3,500 miles, featuring picturesque harbors, rocky cliffs, sandy beaches, and iconic lighthouses such as Portland Head Light and Bass Harbor Head Light.
- *The North Woods:* The vast northern reaches of Maine are dominated by the North Maine Woods, a sprawling wilderness area known for its remote forests, abundant wildlife, and network of logging roads.
- *The Downeast Region:* Located along the eastern coast, the Downeast region is characterized by rugged peninsulas, fjords, and islands, including the stunning landscapes of Acadia National Park.
- *Peatlands and Bogs:* Maine is home to extensive peatlands and bogs, including the expansive Aroostook National Wildlife Refuge, which provides habitat for rare plants and wildlife adapted to these specialized ecosystems.

"I would rather feel bad in Maine than feel good anywhere else."

-E.B. WHITE, AMERICAN AUTHOR

Foraging Hotspots

The following list is just suggestions on possible foraging spots. Remember to check your local foraging laws before setting out. Here are some top spots:

- *Acadia National Park:* Known for its diverse plant life. You can find various kinds of berries, mushrooms, and wild herbs here.
- *Downeast Lakes Community Forest:* A perfect place to forage fiddleheads, a local delicacy.
- *Baxter State Park:* Rich in wild blueberries and edible mushrooms.
- *Allagash Wilderness Waterway:* Great for finding wild leeks, also known as ramps, in the spring.
- *Debsconeag Lakes Wilderness Area:* You can forage for wild cranberries and mushrooms here.

Local Foraging Groups

- **Maine Mycological Association** - A group dedicated to studying and safely consuming mushrooms. https://www.mainelymushrooms.org/
- **Wild Food Gatherers Guild** - A group passionate about wild food foraging. https://www.wildfoodgatherersguild.org/

It's a treasure chest filled with history, fantastic weather, beautiful landscapes, and a unique tradition of foraging for natural foods. Happy foraging in Maine!

THREE
MASSACHUSETTS
THE OLD COLONY STATE

Welcome to Massachusetts, the heart of New England's charm! Tucked away in the northeastern part of the United States, Massachusetts is a vibrant mosaic of history, culture, and natural beauty. Whether you're exploring the historic streets of Boston, unwinding on the peaceful beaches of Cape Cod, or admiring the breathtaking peaks of the Berkshires, there's a little something for everyone to savor. Treat yourself to delectable seafood, delve into our colonial roots, or immerse yourself in the lively arts community of towns like Cambridge and Northampton. With its inviting ambiance and varied scenery, Massachusetts beckons you to discover, enjoy, and embrace the enchantment of the Bay State.

Yearly Weather Patterns

- *Winter* (December to March): Winters can be cold, with average temperatures falling from about 20°F to 30°F. Snow is common and can make the landscapes look like winter wonderland.
- *Spring* (March to June): In Massachusetts, springtime starts off cool but gradually gets warmer. The average temperatures range from 40°F in March to 70°F in June.
- *Summer* (June to September): Massachusetts summers are typically warm, with temperatures ranging from 70°F to 85°F. However, the ocean breeze might make coastal areas a bit cooler.
- *Fall* (September to December): Fall in Massachusetts is stunning, with beautiful colors of leaves changing from green to yellow, orange, and red. The

weather cools down, with temperatures ranging from 70°F in September to around 40°F in December.

Land Topography

Massachusetts offers a varied topography, with everything from coastal plains to rugged mountains. The state's coastline along the Atlantic Ocean is a visual treat, boasting sandy beaches, rocky shores, and scenic coastal marshes. Evidence of past glacial activity is visible in features like kettle ponds, drumlins, and moraines, all of which contribute to the state's unique terrain. River valleys such as the Connecticut River Valley and the Merrimack Valley provide fertile land for agriculture and stunning scenery. In the western part of the state, the Berkshire Mountains dominate the landscape, offering picturesque views, hiking opportunities, and especially vibrant fall foliage displays.

- *Cape Cod*: One of the most iconic features of Massachusetts' topography is Cape Cod, a sandy peninsula jutting out into the Atlantic Ocean, famous for its beaches, lighthouses, and quaint towns.
- *Mount Greylock*: Standing at 3,491 feet (1,064 meters) is the highest point in Massachusetts and is part of the Berkshire Mountains. It offers panoramic views of the surrounding landscape.
- *Boston Harbor Islands*: Just off the coast of Boston lies a collection of islands, forming Boston Harbor Islands National Recreation Area, providing opportunities for outdoor recreation and exploration.
- *Quabbin Reservoir*: Located in central Massachusetts, the Quabbin Reservoir is one of the largest man-made reservoirs in the United States. It supplies drinking water to the Boston metropolitan area and is surrounded by protected forests and wildlife habitats.
- *Martha's Vineyard and Nantucket*: These two islands off the coast of Cape Cod offer distinct topographies, characterized by sandy beaches, coastal cliffs, and picturesque towns, attracting visitors seeking relaxation and natural beauty.

"I have traveled a good deal in Concord, and everywhere, in shops, offices, and fields, the inhabitants have appeared to me to be doing penance in a thousand remarkable ways."

-HENRY DAVID THOREAU

Foraging Hotspots

The following list is just suggestions on possible foraging spots. Remember to check your local foraging laws before setting out. Here are some top spots:

- *Berkshire Mountains*: Known for their wild berries, medicinal plants, and various mushrooms.
- *Middlesex Fells Reservation*: A perfect spot to find wild greens, berries, and nuts in season.

- *Cape Cod National Seashore*: Foragers can find beach plums, rose hips, and edible seaweeds here.
- *Blue Hills Reservation*: A great place to find wild mushrooms, blackberries, and ramps.
- *Harold Parker State Forest:* Here, you can forage for fiddleheads, wild ginger, and morels.

Local Foraging Groups

- **Boston Mycological Club**: A club dedicated to the study and enjoyment of mushrooms. www.bostonmycologicalclub.org
- **New England Wild Edibles**: A group that organizes foraging tours and workshops. www.newenglandwild.org
- **Massachusetts Audubon Society**: While not a foraging group per se, they often host walks and programs that discuss local flora, including some foraging insights.www.massaudubon.org

Remember, foraging should always be done responsibly and sustainably. Always ensure you have correctly identified any plant or fungus before consuming it. Happy foraging in Massachusetts!

FOUR
NEW HAMPSHIRE
THE GRANITE STATE

Welcome to the beautiful state of New Hampshire, also known as the Granite State! Here, you'll find a delightful combination of natural wonders and charming small towns. Situated in the heart of New England, New Hampshire is blessed with stunning landscapes, ranging from the majestic White Mountains to the peaceful shores of Lake Winnipesaukee. As you wander through picturesque villages adorned with historic covered bridges, you'll be greeted by friendly locals who are always ready to welcome you with open arms. Whether you're an avid hiker exploring the Appalachian Trail, a skiing enthusiast conquering powdery slopes, or simply enjoying a delicious maple syrup treat at a cozy diner, New Hampshire has something special for everyone. Come and immerse yourself in our breathtaking vistas, vibrant fall foliage, and warm hospitality – you'll quickly understand why New Hampshire perfectly blends rugged adventure with serene tranquility.

Yearly Weather Patterns

- *Winter* (December to March): can be harsh, with temperatures often dropping below freezing. Snowfall is significant, making this the perfect time for winter sports like skiing and snowboarding
- *Spring* (March to June): is generally mild with temperatures ranging from 40°F to 60°F. Rainfall is frequent, and flowers begin to bloom.
- *Summer* (June to September): is warm and sometimes humid, with temperatures typically between 70°F and 85°F. This is a great time for outdoor activities like hiking and swimming.

- *Fall* (September to December): is marked by crisp air and brilliant foliage. Temperatures usually fall between 50°F and 70°F.

Land Topography

New Hampshire's geography offers a wide range of elevations, from sea level along the coast to over 6,000 feet in the White Mountains. This diversity creates a variety of ecosystems, each with its own unique plant and animal life. The state's landscape was shaped by glaciers during the last Ice Age, resulting in remarkable features like U-shaped valleys, moraines, and kettle ponds. The northern part of New Hampshire is dominated by the majestic White Mountains, with Mount Washington standing tall as the highest peak in the northeastern United States at 6,288 feet (1,917 meters). Apart from its mountainous regions, New Hampshire also showcases rolling hills and fertile valleys, especially in the southwestern part of the state. These areas are characterized by small farms, forests, and delightful rural communities.

- *The White Mountains:* This famous mountain range is renowned for its breathtaking beauty, featuring picturesque valleys, charming alpine meadows, and pristine lakes scattered across the scenery. It's a beloved spot for nature lovers, providing a wide range of outdoor activities such as hiking, skiing, and awe-inspiring scenic drives.
- *The Lakes Region:* Central New Hampshire's Lakes Region is known for its abundance of over 250 lakes and ponds, with the beautiful Lake Winnipesaukee standing out as the largest in the state. Tourists come here to enjoy water activities, fishing, and peaceful boat rides.
- *The Seacoast Region:* The picturesque coast of New Hampshire along the Atlantic Ocean boasts sandy beaches, rugged cliffs, and quaint seaside towns. Portsmouth, known for its colonial buildings and lively arts scene, is a standout attraction in this region. It's easy to see why visitors love this area.
- *The Connecticut River Valley:* Nestled along the western edge of New Hampshire, the Connecticut River Valley is a haven of fertile fields and breathtaking views. This enchanting area acts as a seamless barrier between New Hampshire and Vermont, creating a perfect setting for farming, outdoor adventures, and preserving the local wildlife.
- *The Great North Woods:* If you're seeking a slice of wilderness in northern New Hampshire, look no further than the Great North Woods region. With its dense forests, untouched rivers, and an abundance of wildlife, it's a dream come true for outdoor enthusiasts. Whether you're into hunting, fishing, camping, or snowmobiling, this region offers endless opportunities for adventure.
- *The Monadnock Region:* In the southwestern part of New Hampshire lies a region called Mount Monadnock, which takes its name from one of the most frequently climbed mountains worldwide. This area is a true gem, with its enchanting mix of wooded hills, fertile valleys, and charming villages. Nature enthusiasts and avid hikers are drawn to Mount Monadnock, as it provides them with an opportunity to immerse themselves in the beauty of the surrounding countryside while enjoying breathtaking panoramic views.

> "New Hampshire, with its scanty soil, still lures the farmer by its rugged beauty"

-JOHN STEINBECK, AUTHOR OF TRAVELS WITH CHARLEY

Foraging Hotspots

The following list is just suggestions on possible foraging spots. Remember to check your local foraging laws before setting out.

- *White Mountain National Forest*: Here, you can forage for berries, mushrooms, and edible plants.
- *Pisgah State Park*: Look for various types of mushrooms, fiddleheads, and wild leeks.
- *Bear Brook State Park*: Berries and nuts can often be found here.
- *Hampton Falls*: Foraging for seaweed and shellfish is popular along the coast.
- *Monadnock Region*: This region offers a variety of edible plants and mushrooms.

Local Foraging Groups

- **New Hampshire Mushroom Company**: They offer foraging workshops and mushroom identification services. https://www.nhmushrooms.com/
- **White Mountain Forager**: This group organizes guided foraging tours in the White Mountains. https://www.whitemountainforager.com/
- **New Hampshire Outdoor Learning Center**: offers classes on identifying wild edible mushrooms and plants common all over New England. http://nhoutdoorlearning.com/master-outdoorsman/flora/
- **Russ Cohen**: a naturalist and food enthusiast. Foraging walks and classes are being conducted in most parts of New England. http://users.rcn.com/eatwild/bio.htm

Remember, when foraging, always follow the principles of Leave No Trace, ensuring you leave nature as you found it for others to enjoy.

FIVE
RHODE ISLAND
THE OCEAN STATE

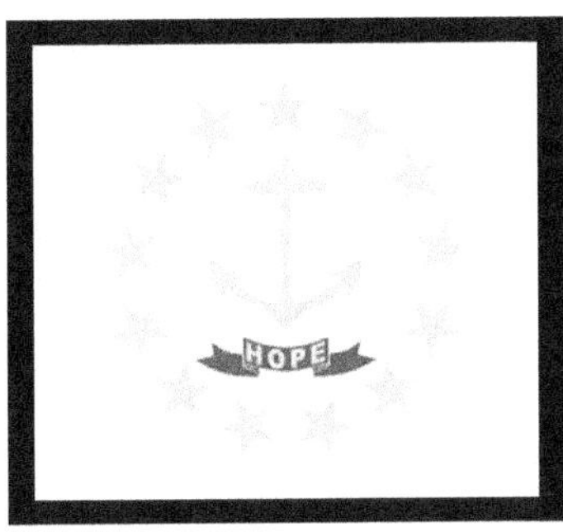

Welcome to the captivating coastal gem of Rhode Island! Tucked away between Connecticut and Massachusetts, this tiny state is bursting with character and endless surprises. With its picturesque coastline, rich history, and vibrant cultural scene, Rhode Island is a paradise for adventurers, food enthusiasts, and history buffs alike. Explore the charming streets of Newport, bask in the sun on the sandy shores of Narragansett, or indulge in the culinary delights of Providence's bustling food scene. Whether you're wandering through colonial-era streets or sailing along tranquil bays, Rhode Island's warmth and hospitality will make you feel right at home. So come and discover the magic of the Ocean State – where big adventures come in small, delightful packages!

Yearly Weather Patterns

- *Winter* (December to February): Winters are cold with average temperatures from 20°F to 40°F. RI gets around 34 inches of snow every year.
- *Spring* (March to May): Spring is a beautiful time to visit, with temperatures ranging from 40°F to 60°F. As the snow melts, Rhode Island bursts into a bouquet of colors with beautiful flowers blooming all over.
- *Summer* (June to August): Summers are warm and comfortable. The average temperature ranges from 70°F to 85°F, perfect for beach visits and outdoor activities.
- *Fall* (September to November): Fall is the perfect blend of comfortable weather

and breathtaking scenery. Temperatures range from 40°F to 60°F, and the state's trees put on a stunning show of fall colors.

Land Topography

Rhode Island, the tiniest state in the United States in terms of land area, spans a little over 1,200 square miles. Its landscape showcases a delightful mix of sandy beaches along the coastline and picturesque rolling hills and forests further inland. The western part of the state boasts charming rolling hills, with elevations reaching over 800 feet above sea level. Surprisingly, despite its urbanization, Rhode Island proudly preserves extensive forested areas, which encompass approximately 55% of the state's land. These lush green spaces serve as a haven for a wide range of wildlife and offer abundant opportunities for outdoor recreation.

- *Ocean State*: Despite its small size, Rhode Island boasts an impressive 400 miles of coastline, earning it the nickname "The Ocean State."
- *Coastal Plains*: Along the shoreline, you'll find low-lying coastal plains, characterized by sandy beaches, salt marshes, and estuaries.
- *Narragansett Bay*: Dominating the geography of Rhode Island is Narragansett Bay, a large estuary renowned for its scenic beauty and important role in the state's economy and culture.
- *Islands*: Rhode Island includes several islands within its territory, with the most notable being Aquidneck Island (home to Newport), Conanicut Island (Jamestown), and Prudence Island.
- *Glacial Features*: Evidence of past glaciation can be seen in the state's landscape, with drumlins, eskers, and moraines scattered throughout.
- *The Great Swamp*: Located in southern Rhode Island, the Great Swamp is one of the largest freshwater wetlands in the state, offering important ecological functions and recreational opportunities for visitors.

There is a sense of maritime history in Rhode Island that you don't feel in many places...It's everywhere, in the bones of the place.

- JOHN WILLIAMS, FAMOUS AUTHOR

Foraging Hotspots

The following list is just suggestions on possible foraging spots. Remember to check your local foraging laws before setting out.

- *Arcadia Management Area:* This area is well-known for its wide variety of wild mushrooms, berries, and edible greens.
- *Blackstone River Valley National Historical Park:* Here, you can find numerous wild berries and native plants.
- *Ninigret National Wildlife Refuge:* An excellent spot for foraging seaweed, shellfish, and coastal plants.
- *George Washington Management Area:* This place is great for foraging berries, mushrooms, and wild greens.

- *Beavertail State Park:* Known for its abundance of wild berries and sea vegetables.
- *Lincoln Woods State Park:* A haven for foragers, with a variety of mushrooms and berries.
- *Snake Den State Park:* Home to wild herbs, berries, and mushrooms.

Local Foraging Groups:

- **Rhode Island Wild Plant Society**: This group is dedicated to the appreciation and preservation of Rhode Island's native plants. www.riwps.org
- **Mushroom Hunting Foundation**: They offer foraging tours and classes in Rhode Island. www.mushroomhunting.org
- **Earth and Ocean:** Susan Clements is a herbalist and an educator. An advocate of using wild plants as medicine, food, and skin and body care. She offers foraging tours in various locations. https://www.earthoceanherbals.com/

Come and explore the smallest state with a big heart. Rhode Island is waiting for you!

SIX

VERMONT

GREEN MOUNTAIN STATE

Welcome to Vermont, where the air is crisp, the mountains are majestic, and the maple syrup flows like liquid gold. Situated in the heart of New England, Vermont is a delightful fusion of natural beauty, small-town charm, and vibrant communities. From idyllic villages scattered across the countryside to bustling cities brimming with creativity. Outdoor enthusiasts will be thrilled by the endless opportunities for hiking, skiing, and exploring the great outdoors, while food lovers will relish the farm-to-table cuisine and exquisite artisanal delights that abound. Come and discover why it's called the "Green Mountain State" – where the beauty of nature and the warmth of community converge to create an unforgettable experience.

Yearly Weather Patterns

- *Winter* (December to February): Winters can be harsh, with lots of snow and very cold temperatures. However, this also makes Vermont a great place for winter sports like skiing and snowboarding.
- *Spring* (March to May): In the spring, you can expect warmer temperatures and lots of rain. The snow begins to melt, and the landscapes become greener.
- *Summer* (June to August): Summers in Vermont are quite comfortable. Expect average temperatures in the upper 70s to low 80s Fahrenheit. The days are sunny and warm, perfect for outdoor activities.
- *Fall* (September to November): Fall is the most beautiful time of year in Vermont. The leaves change to bright red, orange, and yellow, creating breathtaking landscapes. Temperatures cool down to the 50s and 60s Fahrenheit.

Land Topography

Vermont's landscape is dominated by the majestic Green Mountains, a breathtaking range that stretches from north to south across the state. These mountains offer incredible views, fantastic hiking trails, and thrilling ski slopes. For centuries, Vermont has been renowned for its top-quality granite, which is extracted from places like Barre and Bethel. This granite has been used in the construction of iconic landmarks such as the Washington Monument and the US Supreme Court building. The state is crisscrossed by several river valleys, including the Winooski, Connecticut, and Otter Creek valleys, which not only provide fertile land for agriculture but also create picturesque scenery. Outside the mountainous areas, Vermont boasts rolling hills and charming countryside adorned with farms, orchards, and maple sugaring operations.

- *Lake Champlain*: Lake Champlain, one of the biggest freshwater lakes in the United States, serves as a boundary between Vermont and New York, offering numerous opportunities for boating, fishing, and waterfront fun. Vermont boasts a variety of stunning islands in Lake Champlain, such as Grand Isle, South Hero, and Isle La Motte, each with its own unique appeal, diverse scenery, thrilling outdoor adventures, and intriguing historical landmarks.
- *Appalachian Trail*: Vermont is home to a section of the iconic Appalachian Trail, where outdoor enthusiasts can hike through the state's diverse terrain and soak in stunning views from its peaks.
- *Lake Willoughby*: With the nickname "Lucerne of America," Lake Willoughby is a picturesque glacial lake encircled by towering cliffs. It's a great spot for swimming, boating, and rock climbing adventures.
- *Vermont's Tallest Peak*: Mount Mansfield, towering at an impressive height of 4,393 feet (1,339 meters), holds the title of being Vermont's highest peak. With its awe-inspiring vistas, this majestic mountain is a beloved spot for outdoor enthusiasts seeking adventure through hiking, skiing, and snowboarding.
- *The Taconic Range*: Vermont's western border with New York is adorned by the majestic Taconic Range, creating a dramatic and scenic setting. One of its notable peaks, Equinox Mountain, grants visitors the opportunity to soak in the awe-inspiring panoramic views of the surrounding landscape.

"I am as happy now as I ever expect to be, and that is saying a great deal."

- FORMER U.S. PRESIDENT CALVIN COOLIDGE

Foraging Hotspots

The following list is just suggestions on possible foraging spots. Remember to check your local foraging laws before setting out.

- *Green Mountain National Forest*: Known for wild berries, mushrooms, and many edible plants.
- *Champlain Valley*: Look out for wild asparagus and various types of berries during the summer months.

- *Marsh-Billings-Rockefeller National Historical Park*: A great spot to find nuts and various wild fruits.
- *Mount Mansfield State Forest*: Wild ramps, morels, and fiddleheads can be found in abundance.
- *Northeast Kingdom*: Abundant in wild berries, edible greens, and mushrooms.

Local Foraging Groups

- **The Mushroom Foragers**: They talks about wild and cultivated mushrooms and wild edible plants. They conduct workshops related to mushroom foraging and cultivation. https://themushroomforager.com/ourstory/
- **Vermont Foragers**: A Facebook group that offers foraging information. https://www.facebook.com/groups/vtforagers/

Vermont's beauty is unparalleled, offering year-round outdoor activities and an abundance of nature's bounty to forage. Explore its green mountains, shimmering lakes, and discover the joy of foraging in the wild!

NOTE FROM THE PUBLISHER

We completely understand the advantages of using color photos to identify plants. However, to make this book edition more affordable, we decided to use black-and-white photographs, which helped us reduce printing costs, and we passed that savings on to you. But don't worry—we have a solution for you! Scan the QR code below and download a complimentary printable PDF file that includes vibrant, clear, color photos of all the plants featured in the book. Happy Foraging!

FRUITS AND BERRIES

A merican Cranberry
Vaccinium macrocarpon [*V AK-SIN-EE-UM MAK-RO-KAR-PON*]

Did you know the American Cranberry belongs to the same family as blueberries and rhododendrons? It's often referred to as the large cranberry. The term "cranberry" is derived from the German word "kranebere," which translates to "craneberry," due to the flower's resemblance to the neck, head, and bill of a crane bird. Native Americans were the first to utilize cranberries for food and medicinal purposes, passing on their knowledge to European settlers.

Cranberries naturally thrive in boggy and wetland areas with acidic, sandy soil. Look for them in marshy locations, particularly those with low-lying, waterlogged conditions. In some regions of New England, wild cranberries can be found along the coast, particularly in sandy or peaty soils near salt marshes or tidal areas.

Identification:

GROWTH/SIZE: grow low to the ground in a trailing or creeping manner, forming dense mats. They can reach up to 6 to 8 inches tall.

BARK/STEM/ROOT: The stems are slender and woody, often reddish. The roots are fibrous and spread horizontally, anchoring the plant to the ground. The bark is smooth and may have a reddish tint.

LEAF: The leaves are evergreen, small, and oval-shaped, with a glossy green color. They grow alternately along the stem and have finely toothed edges.

FLOWER: The flowers are small and pinkish, resembling tiny bells. They bloom in late spring to early summer, usually around June, and grow in clusters at the ends of the stems.

FRUIT/SEED/NUT: The fruits are round, red berries with a tart flavor. They mature in the fall and are ready for harvest around September to November. The seeds are small and numerous, embedded within the flesh of the berry.

Non-toxic look-alike(s): *Lingonberry (Vaccinium vitis-idaea)* and *Bilberry (Vaccinium myrtillus)* are low-growing, perennial shrubs that flourish in acidic soils across forested, boggy areas. While cranberries are typically found in wet bogs, lingonberries and bilberries often grow on forest floors, each adapting to slightly different moisture levels. These plants bear small, glossy berries—cranberries in deep red, lingonberries in bright red, and bilberries in dark blue or purple-black.

Toxic look-a-likes: *Bittersweet Nightshade (Solanum dulcamara):* This plant produces small, bright red berries that can look similar to cranberries. However, the berries of bittersweet nightshade are toxic and can cause gastrointestinal distress and other symptoms if eaten. *Jerusalem Cherry (Solanum pseudocapsicum):* This plant produces small, round, red fruits that resemble cranberries. However, the fruits are toxic and can cause symptoms such as vomiting, headache, and, in severe cases, respiratory problems.

Cautions: Caution should be exercised when foraging in areas where pesticides may have been used.

Culinary Uses: Whip up some sauces, relishes, and jams with fresh cranberries to flavor to your dishes. Toss dried cranberries into baked goods, salads, and your trail mix for a sweet and tangy touch. Cranberry juice? It's fantastic on its own, but it also makes a great mixer for cocktails and mocktails. Slather cranberry preserves on your morning toast, or combine them with cheese for an absolutely scrumptious snack. And don't forget to give your meats and sandwiches a tangy twist with cranberry chutney. Trust me, it's a game-changer!

Medicinal Properties: Did you know American cranberries are like little superheroes for your health? Packed with vitamin C, they're fantastic for boosting your immune system. Plus, they come loaded with antioxidants, which are great for helping fend off urinary tract infections. And there's more – cranberry extracts are often used to keep your digestive health on track. Thanks to the tannins in these berries, they've also got some serious anti-inflammatory powers. Oh, and let's not forget, there's some buzz around studies suggesting that cranberries might be a heart's best friend, helping to keep your cardiovascular health in check.

Fun/Historical Fact(s): Native Americans used cranberries as food, medicine, and a natural dye. American sailors ate cranberries to prevent scurvy during long voyages. Cranberry sauce became a staple of Thanksgiving dinner in the United States after early settlers learned to sweeten the tart fruit with maple syrup or honey.

Dog toxicity: American Cranberries are not toxic to dogs. However, consuming large quantities may cause gastrointestinal upset, such as diarrhea or vomiting. It's best to offer cranberries to dogs in moderation as a treat.

American Plum

Prunus americana [Pru-nus uh-mair-i-KAH-nuh]

A part of the Rosaceae (rose) family and goes by names like Wild Plum, August Plum, and Hedge Plum. It produces tart-sweet fruits that are perfect for late summer snacking.

Native Americans knew about these fruits long before settlers arrived, using them for food and medicine. When settlers arrived, they also realized the tree's potential for cultivation.

You can spot these trees in various habitats, like woodland edges and open forest spaces. They like hanging out with other native trees like oaks and maples, and they're often found along hedgerows, fence lines, and field margins, soaking up the sun in well-drained soil. Keep an eye out next time you're out exploring!

Identification:

Growth/Size: It typically grows as a small tree or large shrub, reaching 15 to 25 feet.

Bark/Stem/Root: The bark is reddish-brown and develops fissures as it matures. Its stems are slender and reddish-brown, while the roots are fibrous and spread extensively underground.

Leaf: The leaves are oval-shaped with serrated edges and feature a vibrant green color. They grow alternately along the branches and can reach lengths of 2 to 4 inches.

Flower: It produces beautiful white flowers with five petals arranged in clusters. These blossoms have a pleasant fragrance and bloom in early spring.

Fruit/Seed/Nut: The fruit is a round, reddish-purple drupe, about an inch in diameter. It ripens in late summer and contains a single large seed. When fully ripe, the fruit is soft and juicy, perfect for harvesting.

Non-toxic Look-a-like(s): *Beach Plum (Prunus maritima)* and *Chickasaw Plum (Prunus angustifolia)* resemble American Plum but are non-toxic. They share similar fruits and growth patterns.

Toxic Look-a-like(s): *Buckthorn (Rhamnus cathartica L.)* produces small, dark berries that can be mistaken for plums. Buckthorn berries are toxic to humans, causing nausea, diarrhea, and other digestive issues. *Chokecherry (Prunus virginiana):* Like black cherry, chokecherry is part of the Prunus genus and has edible ripe fruits. However, the seeds, leaves, and bark contain cyanogenic glycosides, posing a risk if consumed in large quantities. Chokecherry fruits are smaller and more astringent.

Cautions: When foraging for American Plum, be cautious of potential pesticide residue if harvesting near agricultural areas. Additionally, avoid consuming fruits that appear moldy or diseased.

Culinary Uses: Plums are like little flavor bombs, perfect for making jams and jellies that'll wow your taste buds. Turn them into pies or cobblers, and you've got a dessert that's hard to beat. Cooking them down into a sauce? It'll elevate any meat dish or dessert. And if you dry them, you get this amazingly sweet, chewy snack. Want to mix things up? Infuse them into liqueurs or vinegar for an unexpected twist of flavor.

Medicinal Properties: American Plum is kind of like nature's tummy soother, known for easing those pesky digestive problems like indigestion and constipation. Plus, it's packed with antioxidants, helping our bodies fight off the wear and tear from oxidative stress. And with a good dose of vitamin C, it's also a buddy to our immune system. But that's not all - rubbing plum extracts on your skin can keep it hydrated and bouncy. And in the world of traditional medicine, it's a go-to for dialing down inflammation and swelling.

Fun/Historical Fact(s): When early European settlers landed in America, they quickly discovered the delights of the American Plum and started mixing it into all sorts of culinary creations, especially jams and preserves. Plus, these trees turned out to be a real boon for wildlife. Birds and small mammals found them to be a great source of food, making these trees not just a human favorite but also a hit with the animal crowd.

Dog Toxicity: American Plum fruits are generally not toxic to dogs. However, consuming large quantities may cause gastrointestinal upset, including vomiting and diarrhea. It's best to monitor your dog's intake of any unfamiliar fruits.

B lack Crowberry
Empetrum nigrum [EM-PET-rum NY-grum]

Black Crowberry belongs to the Ericaceae (heath) family and is also known as Crowberry or Blackberry Heath. In the wild, it thrives in the acidic, nutrient-poor soils of New England's coastal areas, bogs, and subarctic regions. This evergreen shrub boasts small, glossy black berries that are edible and highly prized for their tart flavor, often used in jams, pies, and beverages. Indigenous peoples of the region historically utilized Black Crowberry both for sustenance and medicinal purposes, valuing its high vitamin C content. Today, it continues to play a role in local ecosystems and cultural practices, revered for its hardiness and resilience in harsh environments.

Identification:

GROWTH/SIZE: typically grows low to the ground, forming dense mats. It reaches a height of around 6-12 inches.

BARK/STEM/ROOT: The stems are wiry and woody, with a reddish-brown color. Roots are shallow and spread extensively.

LEAF: The leaves are small, scale-like, and evergreen. They are dark green and arranged in whorls around the stem.

FLOWER: The flowers are tiny, bell-shaped, and reddish-purple. They bloom in late spring to early summer.

FRUIT / SEED / NUT: The fruit is a small, round berry, initially green, turning black when ripe. They are ready to harvest in late summer to early fall.

Non-toxic look-alike(s): *Lingonberry (Vaccinium vitis-idaea)* is similar in appearance and habitat but with larger berries and different flowering patterns. *Lowbush Blueberry (Vaccinium angustifolium)* shares a similar low-growing habit but has distinctive blue-berries. Both are edible.

Toxic look-alike(s): *Bittersweet Nightshade (Solanum dulcamara)* and *Deadly Nightshade (Atropa belladonna)* bear colorful berries that can attract attention, while Empetrum nigrum produces black berries. The berries have a fundamental resemblance, but both nightshade berries contain compounds harmful to humans and many animals if ingested.

Cautions: If you're thinking about tapping into the traditional uses of this plant for health purposes, here's a heads up: just because it's been used in the past doesn't mean it's a substitute for modern medical advice. Plus, if you're dealing with any health issues or taking medications, it's wise to have a chat with your doctor first. You don't want any surprises from unexpected interactions!

For those of you with allergies or sensitive systems, bear in mind that even though it's not notorious for causing reactions, we're all unique. And if you're venturing into the great outdoors to forage or pick these berries yourself, be absolutely sure about what you're picking. Nature is beautiful but tricky, with many plants that look similar but aren't all safe.

Culinary Uses: Have you ever tried black crowberry jam or jelly? It's divine in baked treats like muffins or scones. If you toss some fresh berries into a salad, you get this delightful tart kick. They're also fantastic when simmered into a sauce for drizzling over meats or poultry. For something a bit different, brewing them into tea makes for a refreshingly unique drink.

Medicinal Properties: This little powerhouse is bursting with antioxidants, which are great for your overall health. It's been a go-to remedy for tummy troubles for ages. Plus, it's got antimicrobial properties that could give infections a run for their money. And if you're into herbal teas, this one's a winner—it acts as a diuretic, may help soothe inflammation, and even ease arthritis pain.

Fun/Historical Fact(s): In Norse mythology, these berries were like a shield against evil spirits. People also used them to dye fabrics, creating this stunning deep purple color. If you're going to try using it as a dye, remember the adventure of natural dyeing. Test it on a small fabric piece first to see if it's the color you dream of.

Dog toxicity: Black Crowberry berries are not known to be toxic to dogs. However, if ingested in excess, large quantities may cause gastrointestinal upset, such as vomiting or diarrhea. Monitor your dog's consumption of any wild berries and consult a veterinarian if concerned.

Black Currant

Ribes lacustre [RYE-BEEZ LUH-KUSS-TER]

Black Currant is part of the Grossulariaceae (gooseberry/currant) family and goes by various names, such as Black Swamp Currant, Swamp Black Gooseberry, Prickly Black Gooseberry...well, you get the idea. You can spot it hanging out in moist woodlands, chilling along stream banks, and even sneaking into your backyard garden when you're not looking. Talk about being everywhere at once! And get this: it's a native to places like Massachusetts, Vermont, and New Hampshire.

Identification:

GROWTH/SIZE: a deciduous shrub growing 6 feet tall and 6 feet wide.

BARK/STEM/ROOT: The bark is dark brown and covered with shallow fissures, while the roots are fibrous and spread out shallowly.

LEAF: simple, alternate, and lobed, 1-3 inches long and 1-2 inches wide. The leaf margins are serrated, and the leaf surface is smooth, glossy, and dark green.

FLOWER: small and inconspicuous, 1/8 to 1/4 inch long. They are bell-shaped, with five petals that are pink to red. The flowers bloom in late spring to early summer.

FRUIT/SEED/NUT: small, black berries about a 1/4 inch round. They are covered in fine hair and have a sweet, tart flavor. The seeds are tiny, measuring less than 1/8 inch long.

Non-Toxic Look-a-like(s): *Wild gooseberry* (*Ribes hirtellum*) has lobed leaves and produces small, edible berries. The berries are typically green or yellow rather than black. *Golden currant* (*Ribes aureum*) has a similar growth habit with lobed leaves and small, bell-shaped flowers. However, the flowers are yellow rather than pink or red, and the berries are larger and yellowish-green.

Toxic Look-a-like(s): *Black Nightshade* (*Solanum nigrum*). Its berries resemble those of Black Currant but are poisonous if ingested. It's essential to distinguish between these two plants to avoid accidental poisoning carefully.

Caution: The leaves, stems, and seeds of this plant contain a bit of hydrocyanic acid. Sounds scary, right? But in reality, it's not as bad as it sounds. The amounts are pretty tiny, so they're not really going to cause any trouble. That's why people can eat the seeds along with the fruit and not worry about it.

Culinary Uses: You can pluck them straight off the bush for a quick, fresh treat or toss them into salads, smoothies, or fruit bowls for a little zing. They've got this unique sweet yet tart flavor that just sings alongside other fruits and veggies. And talk about versatile – they're my go-to for jams, jellies, and preserves. Ever drizzled black currant syrup over your pancakes or ice cream? Heaven. They're also perfect for adding a pop of flavor to all sorts of baked goodies. And on those hot summer days, stirring them into water with a bit of sugar and lemon creates the most refreshing drink.

Medicinal Properties: This wonder plant is brimming with health boosters. It's loaded with antioxidants, fighting off inflammation like a hero. Plus, it's packed with antho-cyanins—those are the secret agents that help shield you from infections and even sharpen your vision, especially if you're battling eye conditions like glaucoma. And the fiber? That's your digestive system's best friend, helping everything move along smoothly and warding off constipation.

Fun/Historical Fact(s): This prickly shrub has a bit of a reputation for keeping evil at bay, believed to even discourage snakes. People found its roots pretty handy, using them to craft rope and reef nets. And those sharp thorns? They weren't just defensive. They served as tools for lancing boils, pulling out splinters, and even tattooing.

Dog Toxicity: Black currants are generally considered safe for dogs; however, the leaves and stems contain small amounts of hydrocyanic acid, which can be toxic in large quantities.

Black Huckleberry
Gaylussacia baccata [GAY-LUH-SAY-SHUH BUH-KAY-TUH]

Part of the Ericaceae (heath) family, it goes by some other funky names, too, like "sour-top" or "black whortleberry." But its real claim to fame? A rich history deeply rooted in our region.

Back in the day, indigenous folks and early settlers in places like Maine, New Hampshire, Vermont, Massachusetts, Connecticut, and Rhode Island knew a thing or two about this berry. They didn't just munch on them; they used them for food and even medicine! Pretty neat, huh?

Now, if you're itching to get some of these Black Huckleberries, I've got some insider info for you. You'll want to look near acidic woodlands, pine barrens, and rocky hillsides, where you'll find these little gems. They're like nature's little treasures, waiting for you to discover them in their natural habitat.

So, if you're up for a little adventure and a taste of history, why not go on a hunt for some Black Huckleberries? You might stumble upon a piece of the past while enjoying a sweet, tart snack straight from the land.

Identification:

GROWTH/SIZE: typically grow as small shrubs, reaching about 1 to 4 feet.

BARK/STEM/ROOT: The bark is smooth and brown, while its stems are slender and reddish-brown, often branching out. The roots are fibrous and shallow, spreading out to anchor the plant.

Leaf: The leaves are oval-shaped, glossy green, and alternate along the stem. They have finely-toothed edges and can grow up to 1 inch in length.

Flower: Delicate, bell-shaped flowers bloom in clusters at the tips of branches. They are usually white or pinkish and appear in late spring to early summer.

Fruit/Seed/Nut: The fruit is a small, round berry that is initially green but turns dark blue to black when ripe. It has a sweet and tart flavor and is ready to harvest in late summer to early fall.

Non-toxic Look-a-like(s): Blueberries and bilberries resemble Black Huckleberries due to their appearance and taste.

Toxic Look-a-like(s): Beware of similar-looking plants like Pokeweed and Nightshade, which can be toxic if ingested.

Cautions: When foraging for Black Huckleberries, watch out for poisonous look-alikes and properly identify the plant before consuming it.

Culinary Uses: Snack on them fresh, toss them into pies, cobblers, and jams to elevate the flavor, or blend them into your smoothies for a nutritious boost. You can even make syrup or preserves for drizzling over pancakes or ice cream. And adding them to salads? It adds a delightful, sweet, and tangy twist. It's all so tasty!

Medicinal Properties: These are packed with antioxidants, which basically means they're like superheroes for your health, fighting off all the bad stuff that tries to mess with your body.

They're not just good for you on the inside; they're like natural painkillers, too! Their anti-inflammatory properties can actually help ease those annoying aches and pains, giving you some sweet relief when you need it most.

Fun/Historical Fact(s): They were a favorite snack of famous naturalist Henry David Thoreau during his explorations in New England.

Dog Toxicity: Black Huckleberries are generally safe for dogs in small quantities. However, excessive consumption may cause gastrointestinal upset, including vomiting and diarrhea. It's best to monitor your furry friends and limit their intake.

B unchberry
Cornus canadensis [COR-NUS CA-NA-DEN-SIS]

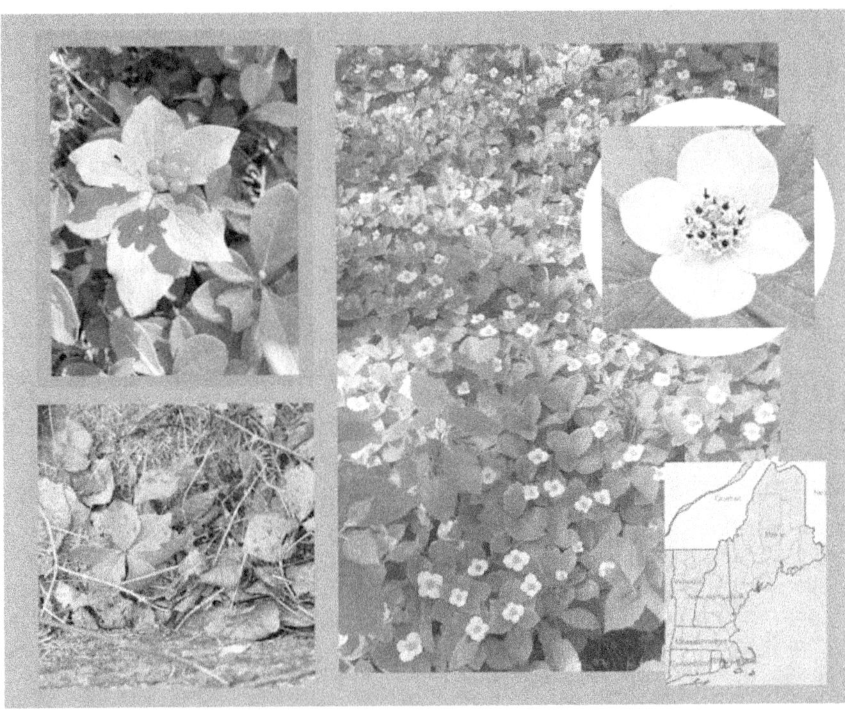

Also known as creeping dogwood or dwarf cornel, it's part of the Cornaceae (dog-wood) family. This plant isn't just pretty; it's packed with history. Indigenous peoples used it for everything from medicine to food. It loves the moist, shady spots in New England's forests, thriving in rich, well-drained soil under the canopy of hardwoods and mixed forests. From Maine to Connecticut, bunchberry is right at home in all the New England states. It's a small plant with a big footprint in the region's natural and cultural landscape.

Identification:

GROWTH/SIZE: typically grows in dense clusters, forming low mats on the forest floor. It reaches a height of only 4 to 8 inches.

BARK/STEM/ROOT: The stems are smooth and erect, bearing distinctive bright red nodes. The roots are shallow and fibrous, spreading horizontally underground.

LEAF: The leaves are opposite, ovate, and glossy green, with prominent parallel veins. They grow in whorls of six around the stem and turn vibrant red in the fall.

FLOWER: produces small, star-shaped flowers with four white or cream-colored petals. These flowers bloom in late spring to early summer and are nestled in a cluster surrounded by four large, petal-like bracts.

FRUIT / SEED / NUT: The fruit is a cluster of bright red berries and is edible when ripe in late summer. Each berry contains several small seeds.

Non-toxic Look-a-like(s): *Canada Mayflower (Maianthemum canadense)* is similar in appearance with glossy green leaves but lacks the red bracts of bunchberry. *Starflower (Trientalis borealis)* - Resembles bunchberry in growth pattern but has white, star-shaped flowers.

Toxic Look-a-likes: *Dwarf Dogwood (Cornus suecica)* - Looks similar to bunchberry but lacks the bright red nodes on the stems. *False Solomon's Seal (Maianthemum racemosum)* - It resembles bunchberry but has a different leaf arrangement and lacks distinctive red bracts.

Cautions: While bunchberry is generally safe, proper identification is essential to avoid confusion with toxic look-a-likes.

Culinary Uses: You can munch on the berries straight off the bush or turn them into jams, jellies, and sauces. Ever tried brewing the leaves into tea? It's got a gentle flavor and might just be the health kick you're looking for. And don't get me started on dried berries in baked treats – think muffins and pancakes turned up a notch. Wrap bunchberry leaves around fish or chicken for a tasty twist, and toss fresh berries into salads. That's a game-changer for both color and flavor.

Medicinal Properties: Bunchberry tea is believed to have anti-inflammatory properties and may aid in digestion. A poultice made from crushed leaves can help relieve minor skin irritations and insect bites. The berries are rich in antioxidants and vitamin C, promoting overall health and immunity. Bunchberry leaf infusions have traditionally been used to alleviate sore throats and coughs. Some indigenous cultures used bunchberry preparations to treat stomach ailments and fevers.

Fun/Historical Fact(s): Indigenous peoples of North America traditionally used bunchberry for various medicinal purposes, including treating wounds and stomach issues. Bunchberry is often considered a symbol of the boreal forest and is celebrated for its resilience and adaptability. In some regions, bunchberry berries were used to make red dye for textiles and baskets.

Dog toxicity: Bunchberry berries are generally considered non-toxic to dogs in small quantities. However, consuming large amounts may lead to gastrointestinal upset, including vomiting and diarrhea. It's advisable to monitor your dog's consumption of bunchberry berries and consult a veterinarian if any adverse symptoms occur.

Cloudberry
Rubus chamaemorus [ROO-BUS KAH-MEE-MOH-RUHS]

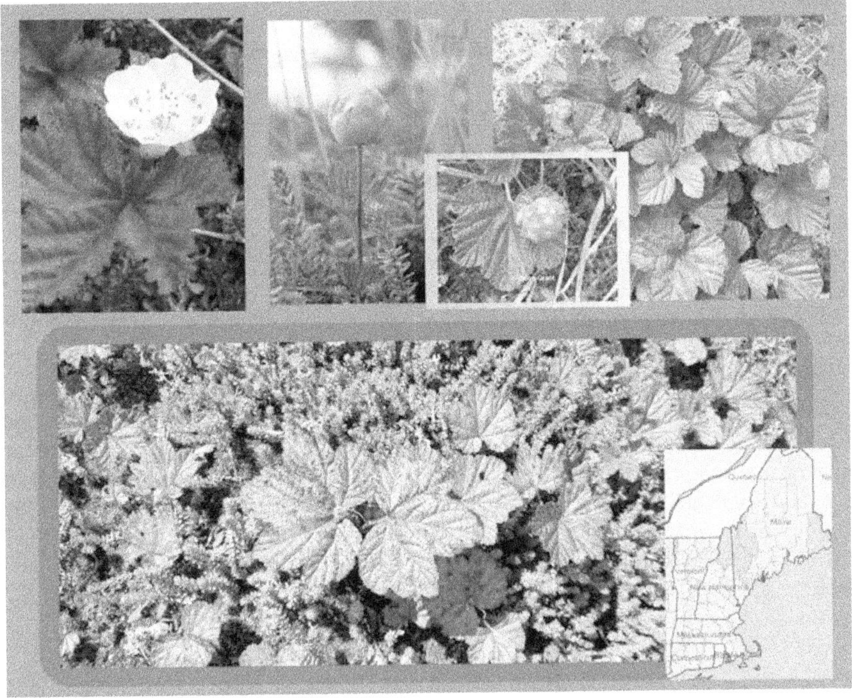

Cloudberry is a fascinating plant native to New England. It belongs to the Rosaceae (rose) family and is cherished for its unique appearance and delicious berries. You can find and forage for cloudberry in specific boggy areas and wetlands across New England, particularly in Maine and parts of Vermont and New Hampshire. It's considered native to these states in the region.

Identification:

GROWTH / SIZE: typically grows low to the ground in a creeping manner, forming dense mats. It's relatively small, with 10-25 centimeters-long stems.

BARK / STEM / ROOT: The stems are slender and greenish, often tinged with reddish hues. The bark is smooth and can be easily peeled off. The roots are shallow and fibrous, spreading horizontally to anchor the plant.

LEAF: The leaves are roundish with three to five lobes, similar in appearance to maple leaves. They're green on top and whitish underneath, with fine hairs. Leaves grow in clusters along the stems.

FLOWER: The flower is white and has five petals, forming a cup-like shape. Flowers bloom in late spring to early summer, attracting pollinators like bees and butterflies.

FRUIT / SEED / NUT: The fruit is a soft, juicy berry that ripens from green to golden-orange. Each berry is made up of numerous small drupelets. It's ready to harvest in mid to late summer and offers a sweet-tart flavor.

Non-toxic Look-a-like(s): Salmonberry and Thimbleberry resemble cloudberry in appearance, with similar-looking berries and leaves.

Toxic Look-a-like(s): Beware of plants like bittersweet nightshade and white baneberry, which have berries that may look similar to cloudberry but are toxic if ingested.

Cautions: Be cautious of potentially hazardous terrain when foraging for cloudberry in boggy areas. Avoid areas with standing water or soft, unstable ground.

Culinary Uses: Snack on fresh cloudberry right off the bush, or whip up some cloudberry jam or jelly to slather on your morning toast. For a twist on dessert, try baking cloudberry into pies or tarts. If you want to mix things up in your smoothies or yogurt, toss in some cloudberry for that extra flavor. And don't forget, cloudberry can add a unique touch to sauces, making it a perfect companion for savory dishes like chicken or pork.

Medicinal Properties: Packed with antioxidants, it's got your back when boosting your immune system. And if you've ever had joint pain, you'll be happy to know Cloudberry might be the soothing friend you need, thanks to its anti-inflammatory powers. This fruit is practically a spa treatment for your skin, aiding in keeping it healthy and even helping wounds heal faster. Cloudberry is just as amazing on the inside, helping your digestion run smoothly and easing those not-so-fun gastrointestinal issues. And for anyone keeping an eye on their blood sugar levels, cloudberry could be a game-changer in keeping things balanced. It's quite the versatile little berry!

Fun/Historical Fact(s): Cloudberry is sometimes called the "Arctic raspberry" due to its prevalence in cold northern regions. In Scandinavian folklore, cloudberry is associated with good luck and fertility. The word "chamaemorus" in its scientific name means "ground apple," referencing its low-growing habit and apple-like flavor.

Dog Toxicity: Cloudberry is non-toxic to dogs and generally safe to consume in moderation.

Cowberry
Vaccinium vitis-idaea [VAK-SIN-ee-um vee-tis ih-DEE-uh]

The Cowberry, known as lingonberry or by a host of other names like foxberry or redberry, is part of the Ericaceae (heath) family. This little plant is quite the survivor, often found in New England's dry woodlands, heathlands, and rocky slopes. It's a favorite because it can thrive in tough places like pine barrens and sandy plains, even where the soil lacks nutrients. Indigenous peoples and early settlers valued the cowberry for its medicinal benefits and as a tasty addition to their meals.

Identification

GROWTH / SIZE: typically grows low to the ground, forming dense mats. It reaches a height of around 6 to 8 inches, with a spread of up to 12 inches.

BARK / STEM / ROOT: The bark of this plant starts out a reddish-brown to grayish-brown and is thin and smooth when the plant is young. As it ages, it may develop shallow furrows and fissures. The stems, which match the bark in color, are slender and wiry. They vary in length, ranging from a few inches to several feet, and tend to grow close to the ground in dense mats. These stems are also covered in fine hairs, giving them a soft, fuzzy appearance. As for the roots, they're pretty shallow, only extending a few inches to about a foot below the surface. They're fibrous and branching, which helps to anchor the plant securely in the ground.

LEAF. The bunchberry sports small, leathery, dark green leaves that keep it green all year, even through droughts and harsh winds. These leaves are tiny, just about half an inch to an inch long. They're slender, oval-shaped, and arranged one by one along the stem with smooth edges and pointed tips. A slight curl at the edges and prominent veins give them a distinct, textured look.

FLOWER: The flowers are either a delicate pink or a soft pinkish-white. They're tiny, just about a quarter inch across, shaped like a bell or an urn. The petals come together into a thin tube that opens into a corolla with five lobes. Inside, five rounded petals spread out. These flowers usually group together in clusters at the ends of slender, upright stems, which makes the plant look even more striking when it's in full bloom.

FRUIT / SEED / NUT: These fruits are about the size of a small pea or blueberry, ranging from 6-10 millimeters. They're round to slightly flattened, with smooth, shiny skins that shift from bright red to deep crimson as they ripen. They tend to stick around on the plant through the winter, standing out brightly against the snow. Inside, you'll find a bunch of tiny, brownish seeds with a slight crunch. The flesh is juicy and tangy, kind of like cranberries but milder. They're best picked late in the summer when plump and fully red.

Non-toxic Look-a-like(s): Partridgeberry and Lingonberry resemble Cowberry in appearance but are non-toxic and safe to consume.

Toxic Look-a-like(s): *Wintergreen (Gaultheria procumbens)* and *Pipsissewa (Chimaphila umbellata)* share several similarities with Cowberry. They thrive in forested, acidic soils and prefer the partial shade of the understory in coniferous and mixed forests. These low-growing, evergreen shrubs have small, glossy, and leathery leaves, enhancing their water conservation in dry, shady habitats. Both their small, bell-shaped flowers and the fruits they produce contribute to their visual similarity—Cowberry and Wintergreen with their white to pinkish pendulous flowers and red berries, and Pipsissewa with a similar floral structure but less colorful fruits.

Cautions: When foraging, avoid mistaking it for similar-looking toxic plants, especially Wintergreen and Pipsissewa.

Culinary Uses: You can toss them fresh into salads for a tangy kick. They also make great jams, jellies, and syrups. Drying the leaves adds a nice flavor to teas and can even spice up your meats and fish. And don't forget desserts—throw some berries into pies and cobblers for something different.

Medicinal Properties: Cowberry leaves are quite the all-rounder. They contain methyl salicylate, which is great for easing pain in sore muscles and joints. If you brew some tea from the leaves can help settle your stomach and reduce bloating. Chewing the leaves is a quick way to freshen your breath and keep your mouth healthy. You can also make poultices from them to calm inflamed skin and soothe irritations. Plus, the berries are packed with antioxidants, boosting your immune system.

Fun/Historical Fact(s): Indigenous peoples in North America once used the leaves of local plants to treat headaches and fevers naturally. Similarly, early European settlers, during times when imported tea was scarce, would brew tea from these leaves as a substitute.

Dog Toxicity: Cowberries are safe for dogs to eat and usually don't cause any harm. But, just like anything else, eating too much can upset their stomach. So, it's a good idea to keep an eye on how much your pet is munching on.

D ewberry
Rubus flagellaris [ROO-bus flaj-uh-LAIR-iss]

Dewberry, a native North American plant, has long been a go-to for erosion control and wildlife habitat restoration. Part of the Rosaceae (rose) family, this perennial shrub doesn't just hold the soil together—it also supports local wildlife, providing both sustenance and shelter. Known by several names like Northern Dewberry, American Dewberry, Running Blackberry, and Trailing Blackberry, it thrives in the open woods, meadows, and along the edges of forests. It's particularly fond of moist, well-drained soils. More than just a practical plant, dewberry is a crucial part of its ecosystem, blending utility with natural beauty.

Identification:

GROWTH/SIZE: a deciduous shrub that grows up to 3 feet tall and 6 feet wide.

BARK/STEM/ROOT: The stems are thorny and green when young turning reddish brown as they mature. They are slender and flexible. The roots are fibrous and shallow, spreading horizontally beneath the soil's surface.

LEAF: The leaves are palmately compound, with three to five leaflets that are oval or oblong in shape and measure 1 to 3 inches long and 1/2 to 1 inch wide. The leaflets are dark green and shiny on top and pale and fuzzy underneath. They are arranged alternately along the stem.

FLOWER: The flowers are white or pink, with five petals that measure 1/2 to 3/4 inches across. They appear in early summer, from May to June, and are borne singly or in small clusters on the ends of the branches.

Fruit/seed/nut: The fruit is a juicy, edible berry that is dark red to black and measures 1/2 to 3/4 inches across. The berry comprises many small, fleshy drupelets containing a single, hard seed. The fruit ripens in mid-summer, from July to August, and is sweet and flavorful.

Non-toxic Look-a-like(s): *Allegheny blackberry* (*Rubus allegheniensis*), *Pennsylvania blackberry* (*Rubus pensilvanicus*), and *Black raspberry* (*Rubus occidentalis*) are all edible and can be confused with dewberry. As a part of the Rubus genus, all four plants have telltale thorns.

Toxic Look-a-like(s): none to speak of.

Caution: The flowers, with their fragrant nectar, attract many native bees. They also provide nesting materials and structures for the native bees. It frequently shares a habitat with poison ivy.

Culinary Preparation: Northern dewberries are quite a versatile treat. You can enjoy them fresh or whip them up into all sorts of delicious recipes, like jams, jellies, pies, and syrups. Beyond their fresh use, these berries can also be transformed into a delightful syrup or frozen to savor later. And don't overlook the leaves—dried, they make a fantastic tea.

Medicinal Properties: The root of this plant is quite the powerhouse—it acts as an astringent, stimulant, and tonic. People historically used the leaves and roots to brew a tea that worked wonders internally, helping reduce inflammation and swelling, and even easing digestion and stomach cramps. They also made poultices from these same parts to speed up the healing of superficial wounds and sores, while warding off infection. Plus, it was commonly used to boost urine production and facilitate the removal of toxins from the body. A real multitasker, this plant has been a go-to for natural healing.

Fun Fact: The fruit is an essential summer food source to many upland gamebirds, songbirds, and mammals, while rabbits and deer browse on the leaves and stems.

Dog Toxicity: These berries are not toxic to your pet.

Eastern Teaberry

Gaultheria procumbens [GAWL-*THEER*-EE-*UH PROH*-KUM-BENZ]

Let's talk about a cool little plant that you might stumble upon in New England's forests. Part of the Ericaceae (heath) family, it goes by more familiar names like wintergreen or teaberry. This plant loves the shady, damp spots of the forest, making it a common sight in areas across New England. So next time you're out in those lush, green woods, keep an eye out for teaberry—it's a small piece of the region's rich botanical tapestry.

Identification:

GROWTH / SIZE: a low-growing shrub, usually around 6-8 inches in height.

BARK / STEM / ROOT: The stems are slender, reddish-brown, and woody, while the roots delve into the forest floor, anchoring the plant securely. The bark is smooth and can sometimes peel in strips.

LEAF: The leaves are glossy, dark green, and leathery with a distinctive oval shape. They grow alternately along the stem and are about 1-2 inches long.

FLOWER: In late spring to early summer, you might catch a glimpse of the small, white, bell-shaped flowers hanging delicately from the stems.

FRUIT / SEED / NUT: As summer fades into fall, the plant produces bright red berries that are round and about the size of a pea. These berries are ready to harvest when they're fully ripe and juicy.

Non-toxic Look-a-like(s): *Partridgeberry (Mitchella repens)* also has glossy green leaves and red berries. Another is the *Creeping Snowberry (Gaultheria hispidula),* which has similar growth habits and berries but is not as aromatic.

Toxic Look-a-like(s): *Winterberry (Ilex verticillata)* is a bit of a double-edged sword. While those bright red berries might catch your eye, they belong to a completely different plant family and pack a punch with minor toxicity. Eating them could lead to some unpleasant symptoms like vomiting or diarrhea because they contain saponins in both the fruits and leaves. So, as much as they stand out in the landscape, it's best to admire them from a distance.

Cautions: While it's generally safe when consumed in moderation, excessive consumption can lead to stomach upset due to its methyl salicylate content. Always be sure of proper identification before foraging any plant.

Culinary Uses: Steep the leaves in hot water to brew a refreshing tea. Add chopped leaves to salads for a minty flavor. Infuse oil with wintergreen leaves for a unique salad dressing. Use the berries to make jams, jellies, or sauces. Incorporate dried leaves into homemade candies or desserts for a hint of wintergreen flavor.

Medicinal Properties: A poultice made from crushed leaves can relieve minor aches and pains. Soothe sore muscles by adding wintergreen oil to a warm bath. Steam inhalation using wintergreen leaves can alleviate respiratory congestion. Applying a diluted wintergreen oil solution can treat minor skin irritations. Wintergreen tea can also be used as a mild diuretic to help flush toxins from the body.

Fun/Historical Fact(s): Native American tribes used Gaultheria procumbens for its medicinal properties, including treating headaches and fevers. Early American colonists brewed wintergreen tea as a caffeine-free alternative to traditional tea. The leaves of Gaultheria procumbens were once used as a flavoring agent in chewing gum and candies.

Dog toxicity: While it's not considered highly toxic to dogs, ingestion of large quantities can lead to gastrointestinal upset, vomiting, and diarrhea. To avoid any potential discomfort, it's best to keep curious pups away from this plant.

Nantucket Shadbush

Amelanchier nantucketensis [AM-UH-LAN-KEE-ER NAN-TUH-KET-EN-SIS]

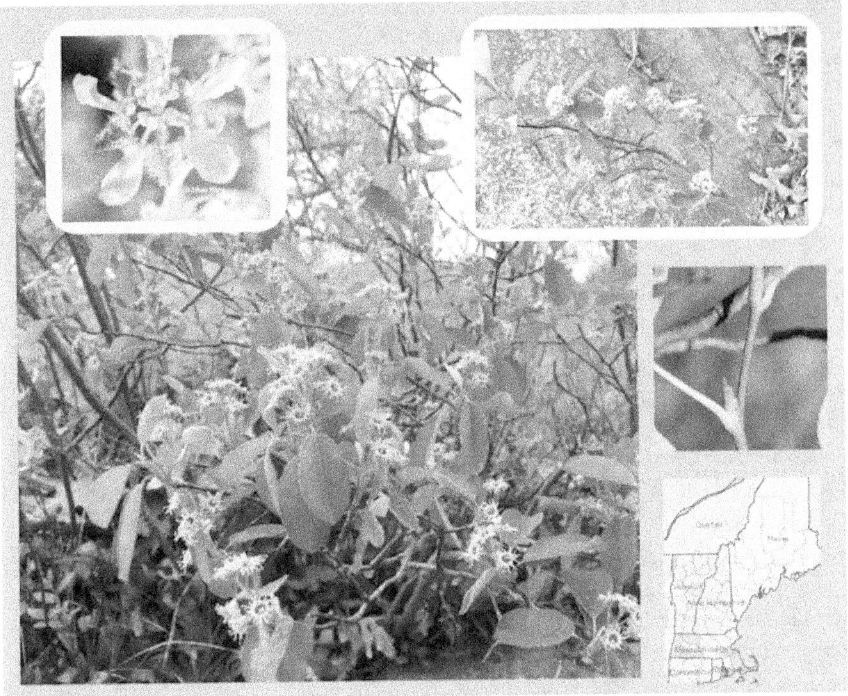

Nantucket serviceberry belongs to the Rosaceae (rose) family. Its common names include the Nantucket serviceberry or simply serviceberry. It's commonly found in forests, woodlands, and edges of fields.

Identification:

GROWTH / SIZE: Amelanchier nantucketensis typically grows as a small tree or large shrub, reaching heights of up to 20 feet.

BARK / STEM / ROOT: The bark is smooth and gray, the stems slender and reddish-brown, and the roots shallow and fibrous.

LEAF: The leaves are oval-shaped with finely toothed edges, green in color, and arranged alternately on the branches. In the fall, they turn vibrant shades of red and orange.

FLOWER: The flowers are white, delicate, and star-shaped, growing in clusters at the ends of branches in early spring.

FRUIT / SEED / NUT: The fruit is a small round berry, initially green, turning red, then purplish-black when ripe. The seeds are small and numerous within the fruit. They are ready to harvest in late spring to early summer.

Non-toxic Look-a-like(s): Similar non-toxic plants include other species of Amelanchier (serviceberries) and some varieties of Viburnum.

Toxic Look-a-like(s): *Holly (Ilex spp.)* can have a similar stature and berry-like appearance to its red fruits. However, the berries are toxic to humans and can cause vomiting, diarrhea, and abdominal pain if ingested. *Yew (Taxus spp.)* produces red berries that could be confused with those of serviceberry plants. All parts of the yew plant, especially the seeds inside the berries, are highly toxic and can cause severe poisoning or even death.

Cautions: While Amelanchier nantucketensis is generally safe to forage, be cautious of potential pesticide use in urban or agricultural areas.

Culinary Uses: You can enjoy the freshness right off the bush or get creative in the kitchen. Imagine making your own jams and jellies or baking them into mouth-watering pies, muffins, or crumbles. If you're into beverages, you might try brewing them into a soothing tea or blending them into vibrant smoothies. And for an extra touch of sweetness, how about infusing them into syrups or sauces that can elevate any dessert? There's just so much you can do!

Medicinal Properties: Rich in antioxidants and vitamins, it bolsters overall health. There's talk that it can also help reduce inflammation and boost digestion. Traditionally, people have turned to it to treat colds and fevers. Its bark and roots are also valued in herbal medicine for their astringent properties, which can tighten and tone tissues. And if that wasn't enough, it's also consumed for potential cardiovascular benefits.

Fun/Historical Fact(s): The name "serviceberry" is believed to originate from its flowering, which coincided with the time when funeral services could be held in areas with harsh winters. Some birds, such as robins and cedar waxwings, are particularly fond of the berries and play a role in seed dispersal.

Dog Toxicity: Amelanchier nantucketensis berries are not toxic to dogs. However, consuming large quantities may cause gastrointestinal upset, such as vomiting or diarrhea. It's advisable to monitor your pet's consumption of any unfamiliar plants.

S ea Buckthorn

Hippophae rhamnoides [Hip-oh-fay RAM-noy-deez]

Sea Buckthorn, or as some might call it, Sandthorn or Seaberry, truly has a fascinating tale. It belongs to the botanical family Elaeagnaceae and has made quite a home for itself in New England. You'll find it thriving along the coast, dotting sandy dunes, and even clinging to rocky terrains. Native to states like Maine, New Hampshire, and Massachusetts, this remarkable plant is as hardy as it is versatile, making it a standout in the region's diverse landscapes.

Identification:

GROWTH/SIZE: this deciduous shrub typically grows up to 2-4 meters tall. It has a sprawling growth pattern with long, arching branches.

BARK/STEM/ROOT: The bark is grayish-brown with small scales. Its stems are thorny and densely covered with silvery-green leaves. The roots are shallow and fibrous, helping the plant anchor in sandy soils.

LEAF: The leaves are lanceolate and silvery-green in color with a silvery underside. They grow alternately along the stems and can reach about 5-8 centimeters in length.

FLOWER: The flowers are small and yellowish-orange and appear in clusters along the branches. They bloom in late spring to early summer, adding a vibrant touch to the landscape.

FRUIT/SEED/NUT: The fruits are small, round berries that are bright orange in color when ripe. They grow densely along the branches and are ready for harvest in late summer to early autumn. Each berry contains a small seed surrounded by juicy pulp.

Non-toxic Look-a-like(s): *Silver Buffaloberry (Shepherdia argentea)* has silver-green leaves and orange berries. *Common Buckthorn (Rhamnus cathartica)* shares a similar leaf shape but lacks the silvery underside.

Toxic Look-a-like(s): *Poison Ivy (Toxicodendron radicans)* Both have clusters of berries, but Poison Ivy has three leaflets and causes skin irritation. *Deadly Nightshade (Atropa belladonna)* Berries are similar in color but extremely toxic if ingested.

Cautions: While Sea Buckthorn is generally safe, be cautious of its thorny stems while foraging. Also, ensure proper identification to avoid confusion with toxic look-alikes.

Culinary Uses: Make delicious jams and jellies from the tart berries. Brew refreshing teas or infusions with dried leaves and berries. Use the oil extracted from the berries in salad dressings or marinades. Incorporate the berries into smoothies or desserts for a nutritious boost. Experiment with Sea Buckthorn syrup for pancakes or waffles.

Medicinal Properties: Rich in vitamins C and E, Sea Buckthorn boosts immunity and promotes healthy skin. The oil is used topically to treat burns, wounds, and eczema. Consuming Sea Buckthorn may aid in digestion and relieve symptoms of gastric ulcers. It's believed to have anti-inflammatory properties, beneficial for arthritis and joint pain. Sea Buckthorn supplements are used to support cardiovascular health and cholesterol management.

Fun/Historical Fact(s): Sea Buckthorn has a storied past, woven deeply into the fabric of traditional Chinese medicine thanks to its remarkable healing properties. In ancient Greece, they even used it to treat horses after grueling battles, which is how it got its name. And its legacy didn't stop there. During World War II, Soviet soldiers turned to Sea Buckthorn berries to treat radiation burns. This plant has been a trusty ally in healing across cultures for centuries.

Dog Toxicity: Sea Buckthorn berries are not toxic to dogs. However, excessive consumption may cause mild gastrointestinal upset, such as vomiting or diarrhea. Monitor your furry friend's intake and consult a veterinarian if any adverse symptoms occur.

Swamp Red Currant
Ribes triste [RY-BEEZ TRIS-TAY]

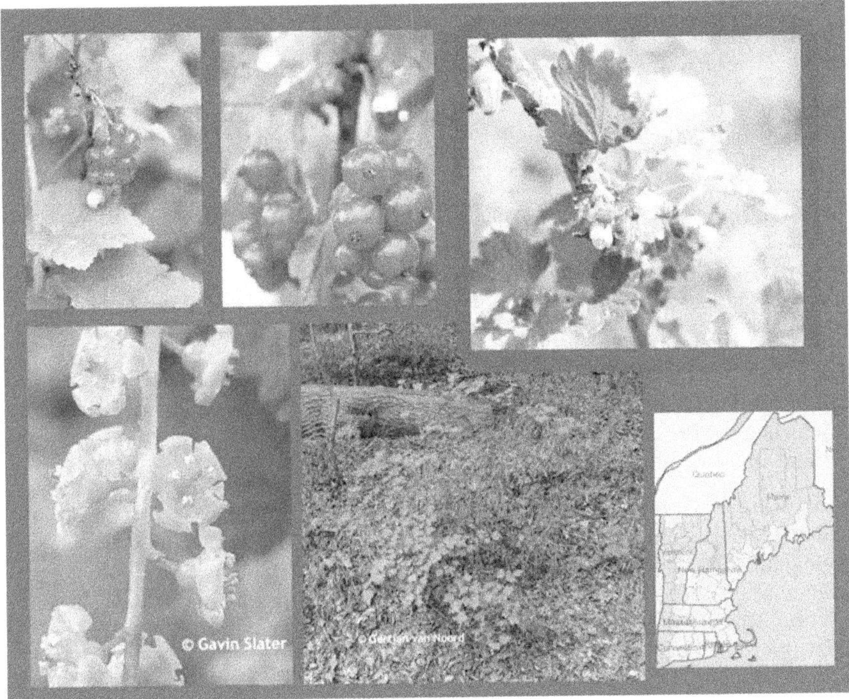

Swamp Red Currant belongs to the Grossulariaceae (gooseberry/currant) family. Its common names include Wild Red Currant and Swamp Gooseberry. This resilient plant has been a part of the New England landscape for centuries, cherished for its ornamental beauty and culinary and medicinal uses. Swamp Red Currant thrives in damp, wooded areas, often near streams or wetlands.

Identification:

GROWTH/SIZE: typically grows as a shrub, reaching about 2 to 4 feet.

BARK/STEM/ROOT: The bark is smooth and reddish-brown, while its stems are slender and woody. The roots extend shallowly, spreading outwards from the base of the plant.

LEAF: The leaves are green, lobed, and palmately veined, resembling the shape of a maple leaf. They grow alternately along the stems, typically around 2 to 4 inches long.

FLOWER: The flowers are small and bell-shaped, hanging delicately from the branches in clusters. They are reddish-pink in color and bloom in late spring to early summer.

FRUIT/SEED/NUT: The fruit is a round, translucent berry, initially green but ripening to a bright red color. They grow in clusters and are ready to harvest in late summer to early fall.

Non-Toxic Look-a-like(s): *Wild Strawberry (Fragaria vesca)* - Similar in fruit size and color, but with distinctively different leaves. *Red Raspberry (Rubus idaeus)* - Shares a similar growth habit but has larger aggregate fruit.

Toxic Look-a-like(s): *Bittersweet Nightshade (Solanum dulcamara)* - Similar vine-like growth, but with purple flowers and toxic red berries. *Poison Ivy (Toxicodendron radicans)* - Shares a woody stem and leaf shape but causes skin irritation upon contact.

Cautions: While Swamp Red Currant is generally safe for consumption, be cautious of potential look-alike plants, especially toxic ones like Bittersweet Nightshade and Poison Ivy.

Culinary Uses: Enjoy the tart berries straight from the bush. Jams and jellies: Make delicious spreads with the harvested berries. Create flavorful syrups for cocktails or desserts. Add the berries to pies, muffins, or scones. Make tangy sauces to accompany savory dishes.

Medicinal Properties: The leaves can be brewed into a tea to alleviate inflammation. The berries are rich in antioxidants, promoting overall health. Consuming the berries can aid digestion and relieve gastrointestinal discomfort. Berries boost Vitamin C, supporting the immune system. C The plant can act as a mild diuretic, aiding urinary tract health.

Fun/Historical Fact(s): Native American tribes used the Swamp Red Currant for food and medicine, appreciating its versatile properties. Early European settlers in the region also embraced the Swamp Red Currant, incorporating it into their culinary and medicinal practices. The plant's name, "triste," comes from Latin, meaning "sad" or "gloomy," likely referring to its preference for damp habitats.

Dog Toxicity: Swamp Red Currant berries are not known to be toxic to dogs. However, moderation is key, as excessive consumption may cause gastrointestinal upset.

Thimbleberry

Rubus parviflorus [ROO-BUHS PAR-VI-FLOR-US]

Thimbleberry is a member of the Rosaceae (rose) family. This plant is cherished for its lovely flowers, attractive foliage, and edible berries. Thimbleberry is also known by other common names, such as Western Thimbleberry and Salmonberry, although it should not be confused with Rubus spectabilis, also known as Salmonberry. Thimbleberry is native to western North America, from Alaska to northern Mexico, with a particular prevalence in the Pacific Northwest and the Rocky Mountain regions. It thrives in various habitats, including moist woodlands, forest edges, and meadows. Thimbleberry prefers well-drained soils and can be found in full sun to partial shade.

Identification:

GROWTH/SIZE: It's a relatively small shrub growing 3-6 feet tall. Its growth habit is erect and spreading, with a tendency to form dense thickets.

BARK/STEM/ROOT: The bark is smooth, reddish-brown, and peels away in thin strips as it ages. The stems are slender and unarmed, lacking thorns, distinguishing them from many other Rubus species.

LEAF: It has large, maple-like leaves that are simple, alternate, and lobed. The leaves have serrated edges and are bright green on the upper surface, with a lighter green and somewhat hairy lower surface.

FLOWER: It produces large, white, five-petaled flowers in late spring to early summer. The flowers are about 2 inches wide and are pollinated by various insects.

FRUIT/SEED/NUT: Its fruit is a red, raspberry-like drupelet aggregate that matures mid to late summer. The berries are soft, juicy, and easily detach from the receptacle, giving them a thimble-like appearance.

Non-Toxic Look-a-like(s): *Salmonberry (Rubus spectabilis)* has similar leaves and growth habits, but its berries are orange to red, and the stems have small prickles.

Cautions: none known

Culinary Preparation: Thimbleberries are prized for their sweet, tangy, and mildly tart flavor. They can be eaten fresh, used in jams, jellies, and pies, or added to yogurt and smoothies. Due to their delicate nature, They are not commonly found in commercial markets, making them a special treat for those who forage.

Medicinal Properties: Native Americans utilized Thimbleberry for various medicinal purposes, including treating wounds, burns, and digestive issues. Some modern herbalists use Thimbleberry leaves to make a poultice for skin ailments.

Fun/Historical Fact(s): Thimbleberry leaves were used by Native Americans and early settlers as a natural toilet paper due to their large size, soft texture, and availability in the wilderness.

Dog Toxicity: Thimbleberry is not considered toxic to dogs. If your dog consumes Thimbleberry and exhibits symptoms such as vomiting, diarrhea, or lethargy, consult your veterinarian for guidance.

PART FOUR
HERBS AND GRASSES

B lue Vervain

Verbena hastata [VER-BEE-NUH HA-STAY-TUH]

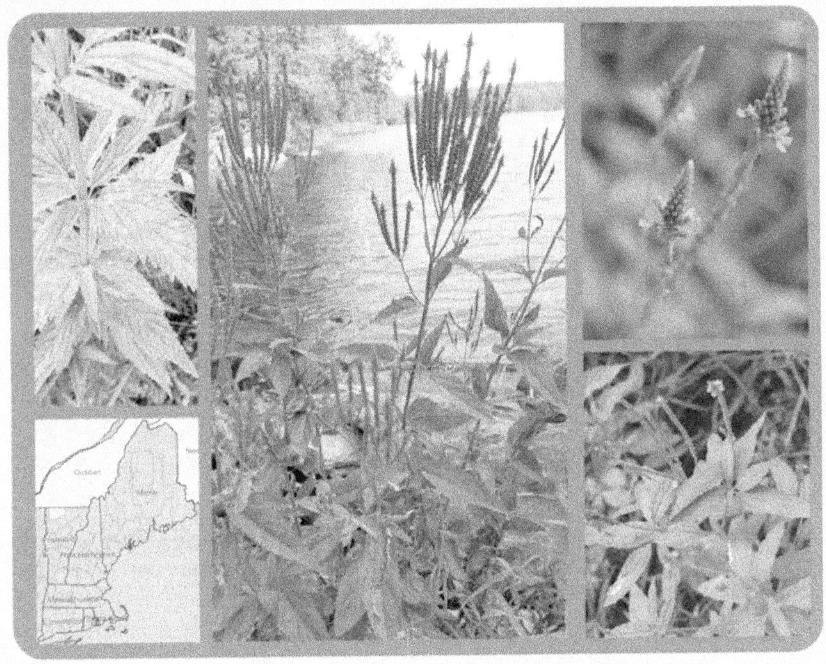

Blue Vervain is a fascinating herb belonging to the Verbenaceae (verbena) family. Historically, it has been highly regarded for its medicinal properties and has been used across different cultures. The plant goes by other common names, such as Swamp Verbena, Wild Hyssop, and American Vervain. Native to North America, it can be found in various parts of the United States. This adaptable plant is typically found in moist environments such as meadows, wetlands, and along the edges of streams and rivers.

Identification:

GROWTH / SIZE: Blue Vervain can grow up to 6 feet tall, making it a prominent feature in the landscapes where it's found.

BARK / STEM / ROOT: The plant has a square, slender, and branched stem with small hairs. The fibrous root system helps the plant anchor itself in its wet environment.

LEAF: The leaves are opposite, lance-shaped, and serrated, measuring 2 to 6 inches long. The leaves are attached to the stem by short petioles.

FLOWER: The showy blue to-violet flowers bloom from June to September, forming slender spikes reaching up to 8 inches. Each flower measures about 1/8 inch across.

FRUIT / SEED / NUT: produces small, dry, nut-like fruits containing several seeds after flowering.

Non-Toxic Look-A-Like(s): *White Vervain (Verbena urticifolia)* the primary difference is the color of the flowers, which are white or greenish-white.

Toxic Look-a-like(s): *Foxglove (Digitalis purpurea)*: This plant has tall, spike-like clusters of flowers similar to those of Blue Vervain. However, the bell-shaped flowers range from purple to pink or white. All parts of the Foxglove plant are toxic and can affect the heart. *Larkspur (Delphinium spp.)* features tall spikes of flowers and can be mistaken for Blue Vervain at a glance. It is usually more intricately shaped and comes in various colors, including blue, purple, and white. They contain alkaloids that are highly toxic to humans and livestock.

Cautions: Blue Vervain is generally considered safe.

Culinary Uses: Blue Vervain is not typically used in culinary preparations; it tastes somewhat bitter. However, the leaves can be brewed into tea for those who enjoy its flavor and potential health benefits.

Medicinal Uses: Traditionally, Blue Vervain has been used as a natural remedy for a variety of ailments, including anxiety, insomnia, and digestive issues. It has also been used as an expectorant, diuretic, and anti-inflammatory agent.

Fun/Historical Fact(s): In ancient Roman and Greek mythology, Blue Vervain was considered a sacred herb associated with the divine and often used in purification rituals.

Dog Toxicity: Blue Vervain is not considered toxic to dogs. If your dog shows signs of distress, such as vomiting, diarrhea, or lethargy, after consuming any part of the plant, consult your veterinarian.

Boneset
Eupatorium perfoliatum [YOO-PUH-*TOR*-EE-UM PUR-FOH-LEE-*AH*-TUM]

This plant belongs to the Asteraceae (aster/daisy) family. But don't worry about remembering that scientific name—most folks call it Boneset! Its name comes from its historical use in treating breakbone fever, a disease that causes intense bone pain. You can find bonesets growing in the lush woodlands and meadows of the New England region. It's native to states like Massachusetts, Connecticut, Vermont, New Hampshire, Maine, and Rhode Island. Look for it along stream banks, damp soils, or marshy areas.

Identification:

GROWTH/SIZE: typically grows to be about 2 to 4 feet tall and has a clumping growth pattern.

BARK/STEM/ROOT: Its stems are sturdy and hairy and can range from green to purplish-brown in color. The roots are fibrous and shallow.

LEAF: The leaves are lance-shaped, grow opposite each other on the stem, and can reach up to 6 inches in length. They have a dark green color and are slightly serrated along the edges.

FLOWER: Boneset produces clusters of small, white flowers that resemble miniature daisies. These flowers bloom from mid-summer to early fall.

Fruit / Seed / Nut: After flowering, it develops small, dry seeds dispersed by the wind. Once the flower heads turn brown, the seeds are ready to harvest.

Non-toxic Look-a-likes: Joe-Pye Weed shares similar clusters of small white flowers.

Toxic Look-a-likes: Water and poison hemlock have clusters of small white flowers but are highly toxic if ingested.

Cautions: When foraging for boneset, always be cautious not to confuse it with toxic look-alike plants. Properly identifying boneset is essential before using it for any purpose.

Culinary Uses: Brew boneset tea by steeping the dried leaves and flowers in hot water for a soothing herbal drink. Infuse honey with boneset flowers for a natural sweetener with medicinal properties. Add fresh leaves to salads for a nutritious boost. Use boneset leaves and flowers as a flavorful garnish for soups and stews. Create a tincture by steeping it in alcohol for a concentrated herbal extract.

Medicinal Properties: Boneset tea is traditionally used to relieve common cold and flu symptoms, such as fever and body aches. It has anti-inflammatory properties that may help alleviate joint pain and arthritis. Boneset is believed to stimulate the immune system, promoting overall wellness. Infusions of boneset can be used as a natural diaphoretic to induce sweating and reduce fevers. It may also have mild diuretic effects, aiding in eliminating toxins from the body.

Fun/Historical Fact(s): During the American Civil War, Boneset gained popularity as a medicinal herb used to treat soldiers suffering from fever and infections. Native American tribes, such as the Cherokee and Iroquois, have a long history of using Boneset for its medicinal properties. The name "Boneset" also comes from its historical use in traditional folk medicine to help set broken bones.

Dog Toxicity: Boneset is mildly toxic to dogs if ingested. Symptoms may include gastrointestinal upset, vomiting, diarrhea, and lethargy. If you suspect your dog has consumed boneset, contact your veterinarian immediately for guidance and treatment.

Canadian Goldenrod

Solidago canadensis [SO-LI-DA-GO KA-NA-DEN-SIS]

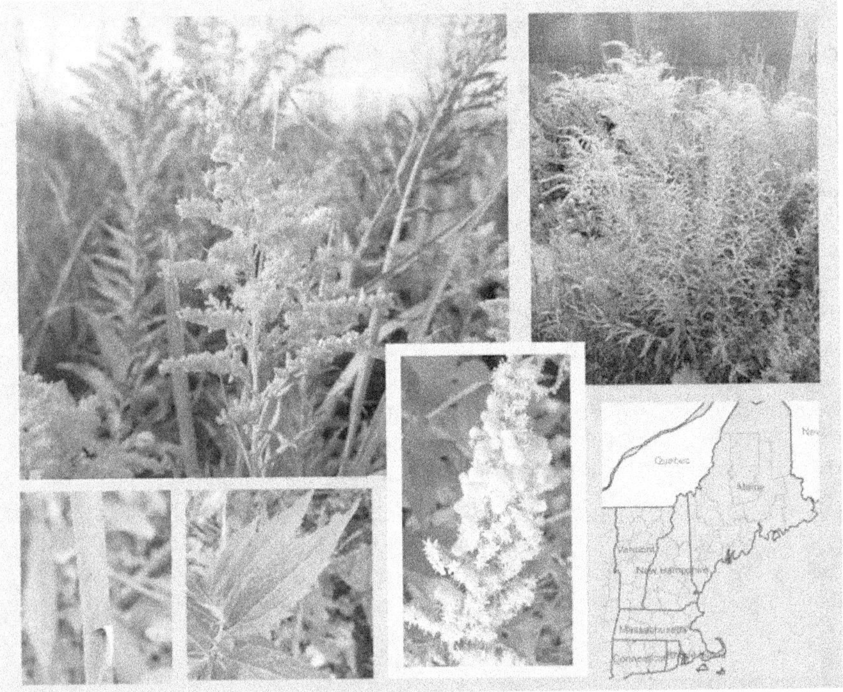

Goldenrod belongs to the Asteraceae (aster/daisy) family and goes by several common names, including Solidago canadensis and Canadian goldenrod. You can find it in abundance throughout the New England region, especially in fields, meadows, and along roadsides. States such as Massachusetts, Vermont, and Maine consider it native to their lands. It thrives in sunny locations with well-drained soil.

Identification:

GROWTH/SIZE: typically grows in clumps and can reach heights of 3 to 6 feet.

BARK/STEM/ROOT: The stems are erect and cylindrical, with smooth greenish-brown bark. Its roots are fibrous and shallow, spreading horizontally.

LEAF: The leaves are lance-shaped, alternate along the stem, and have serrated edges. They are dark green in color, grow in a spiral pattern around the stem, and can grow up to 6 inches long.

FLOWER: The bright yellow flowers form dense, plume-like clusters at the top of the stem. They bloom from late summer to early fall and attract pollinators such as bees and butterflies.

FRUIT/SEED/NUT: After flowering, it produces small, dry seeds with fluffy white hairs attached. The wind disperses these seeds, which are ready to harvest in late autumn.

Non-toxic look-a-like(s): Sunflowers and daisies share similar bright yellow flowers.

Toxic look-alike(s): Ragweed and horseweed have similar leaf shapes but lack vibrant yellow flowers.

Cautions: While Canadian Goldenrod is generally safe for foraging, potential allergies, especially for individuals sensitive to pollen, should be considered.

Culinary Uses: The leaves can be used fresh in salads or cooked like spinach. For a flavorful twist, infuse the flowers in vinegar or honey. Dry the flowers and leaves to make herbal tea. Add chopped leaves to soups or stews for added flavor. Use the dried flowers to make a goldenrod-infused oil for culinary purposes.

Medicinal Properties: It has diuretic properties and can help with urinary tract infections. It is also used to alleviate symptoms of allergies and hay fever. The plant's anti-inflammatory properties make it useful for treating arthritis and joint pain. Canadian Goldenrod tea can soothe sore throats and coughs. It is believed to have antiseptic qualities and can be used topically to clean wounds.

Fun/Historical Fact(s): Native American tribes used it for various medicinal purposes, including treating wounds and fevers. Thomas Edison experimented with Canadian Goldenrod to find a domestic source of rubber. The plant's name, Solidago, comes from the Latin words "solidus," meaning "whole," and ago, meaning "to make," referring to its traditional use in herbal medicine.

Dog Toxicity: Canadian Goldenrod is not considered toxic to dogs. However, excessive consumption may cause mild gastrointestinal upset, such as vomiting or diarrhea. Always monitor your pet's intake of unfamiliar plants and consult a veterinarian if any concerning symptoms arise.

Canadian Wild Ginger

Asarum canadense [UH-SAIR-UM KUH-NAY-DEN-SEE]

Canadian Wild Ginger belongs to the Aristolochiaceae (birthwort) family. In the New England region, it goes by several common names, including "snakeroot" and "heart snakeroot." Indigenous peoples and early settlers used it for medicinal purposes due to its unique properties. You can find it nestled in the shaded, moist forests of the New England region. States like Massachusetts, Connecticut, and Vermont consider it native, where foragers can discover it flourishing in the undergrowth.

Identification:

GROWTH/SIZE: This plant spreads slowly, forming dense patches in woodland areas. It typically reaches about 6-8 inches in height.

BARK/STEM/ROOT: The underground rhizomes produce knobby, branching stems with dark brown to purplish coloration. The roots are fibrous and possess a spicy aroma when crushed.

LEAF: The heart-shaped leaves emerge from the rhizomes. They feature deep green hues with prominent veining. They grow in pairs and can reach up to 6 inches in width.

FLOWER: The inconspicuous maroon to brownish-purple flowers bloom close to the ground in early spring. Their shape resembles a pipe, and they often hide beneath the foliage.

FRUIT/SEED/NUT: After flowering, the plant produces small, fleshy fruits resembling berries. Inside, you'll find seeds that ants disperse. The fruits ripen in late spring to early summer.

Non-toxic Look-a-like(s): *Ginger (Zingiber officinale)* and *Ground Ivy (Glechoma hederacea)* due to their similar leaf shapes and ground-hugging growth habits.

Toxic Look-a-like(s): It's important to differentiate between Canadian Wild Ginger and Birthwort (Aristolochia species) and Dutchman's Breeches (Dicentra cucullaria), which can be toxic if ingested.

Cautions: While Canadian Wild Ginger is not known to be toxic to humans, practicing caution when foraging is essential. Always ensure proper identification and avoid consuming any plant material if you're unsure.

Culinary Uses: Infuse fresh or dried leaves in hot water for a soothing tea. Use the rhizomes as a flavoring agent in soups or stews. Incorporate chopped leaves into salads or herbal butter. Brew a tincture by steeping the roots in alcohol for a home-made herbal remedy. Experiment with pickling the rhizomes for a zesty addition to dishes.

Medicinal Properties: Digestive Aid: Canadian Wild Ginger can help alleviate digestive discomfort and improve appetite. **Anti-inflammatory:** It possesses anti-inflammatory properties, making it useful for soothing sore muscles and joints. **Antimicrobial:** The plant's constituents exhibit antimicrobial activity, aiding in fighting off infections. **Menstrual Support:** It has been traditionally used to regulate menstrual cycles and ease menstrual cramps. **Respiratory Health:** Canadian Wild Ginger may help relieve symptoms of respiratory ailments like coughs and congestion.

Fun/Historical Fact(s): Indigenous peoples of North America used Canadian Wild Ginger medicinally for various ailments, including headaches and sore throats. Early European settlers in the New England region adopted its use, incorporating it into their herbal remedies and tonics. The plant gets its name "Wild Ginger" due to its rhizomes' spicy aroma, reminiscent of true ginger.

Dog Toxicity: Canadian Wild Ginger is not considered toxic to dogs. However, it's always best to prevent pets from consuming large quantities of any plant material, as it may cause gastrointestinal upset.

C atnip
Nepeta cataria [NUH-PEE-TUH KUH-TAIR-EE-UH]

Catnip belongs to the Lamiaceae (mint) family. Commonly referred to as catnip, catwort, or catmint, this plant has been cherished for centuries for its aromatic properties. It's believed to have originated in Europe and Asia but found its way to North America during early colonization. Catnip grows abundantly in various areas across the New England region. It's commonly foraged in meadows, roadsides, and disturbed areas. States like Massachusetts, Vermont, and Maine boast catnip as a native plant, where it thrives in the region's temperate climate.

Identification:

GROWTH / SIZE: typically grows bushy and reaches 2 to 3 feet.

BARK / STEM / ROOT: the stems are square-shaped and greenish in hue. The fibrous roots tend to spread horizontally underground. The bark is smooth and can range from green to brown.

LEAF: the leaves are triangular or heart-shaped, with serrated edges. They grow opposite each other on the stem and are typically vibrant green. When crushed, the leaves emit a distinct minty fragrance.

FLOWER: it produces small, tubular-shaped flowers that are usually white with purple spots or stripes. They grow in clusters at the top of the stems and bloom from late spring to early fall.

Fruit/Seed/Nut: After flowering, it forms small, brown nutlets that contain the plant's seeds. These nutlets are ready to harvest in late summer or early fall.

Non-toxic Look-a-like(s): Lemon balm and peppermint share similar growth habits and leaf shapes to catnip.

Toxic Look-a-like(s): Ground ivy and spotted spurge resemble catnip in appearance but are toxic if ingested.

Cautions: Avoid contamination from nearby pollutants or pesticides when foraging for catnip. Additionally, ensure proper identification to avoid harvesting toxic look-a-likes.

Culinary Uses: The leaves can be used fresh or dried to make herbal teas. Add chopped leaves to salads for a hint of minty flavor. Infuse it into vinegar or oil for a unique culinary twist. Use catnip as a seasoning in meat or vegetable dishes. Incorporate dried catnip into baked goods like cookies or muffins.

Medicinal Properties: Catnip tea is known for its calming effects and can help alleviate stress and anxiety. It may aid in digestion and relieve symptoms of indigestion or bloating. Catnip poultices can be applied topically to reduce swelling and inflammation. It's believed to have mild sedative properties, promoting relaxation and sleep. Catnip tinctures or extracts are sometimes used to relieve menstrual cramps.

Fun/Historical Fact(s): Ancient Egyptians revered catnip for its medicinal properties and used it to treat various ailments. Catnip has a euphoric effect on many cats due to a compound called nepetalactone found in its leaves and stems. In the Middle Ages, humans consumed catnip tea for its supposed ability to induce visions and enhance psychic abilities.

Dog toxicity: Catnip is not toxic to dogs. Although they may show mild interest in the plant, it won't harm them if ingested.

Comfrey

Symphytum officinale [SIM-FI-TUM UH-FIS-I-NAY-LEE]

A fascinating plant with a rich history in the New England region! Comfrey, scientifically known as *Symphytum officinale*, belongs to the Boraginaceae (dogbane) family. But around these parts, it goes by many names like "knitbone," "bruise wort," or simply "comfrey." You can find comfrey growing in damp, fertile areas near streams, rivers, and ponds. In New England, states like Maine, Vermont, New Hampshire, Massachusetts, Connecticut, and Rhode Island boast comfrey as a native plant. Keep your eyes peeled in moist woodlands, meadows, and even in your own backyard!

Identification:

GROWTH / SIZE: Comfrey is a robust perennial herb, growing up to 3-4 feet tall. It spreads through thick, fleshy roots, forming dense clumps.

BARK / STEM / ROOT: The stems are hairy, sturdy, and hollow, with a reddish tint. The roots are deep, black, and knobby, packed with nutrients.

LEAF: The leaves are large, lance-shaped, hairy, and rough in texture. They grow in a spiral pattern around the stem and reach a foot long.

FLOWER: the bell-shaped flowers, which range from pink to purple or white, bloom in early summer. They cluster at the end of the stems, attracting bees and other pollinators.

Fruit/Seed/Nut: After flowering, it produces small, nut-like seeds within prickly pods. The seeds are ready to harvest when the pods turn brown and dry out.

Non-toxic Look-a-like(s): *Borage (Borago officinalis)* has rough, hairy leaves and star-shaped flowers that are typically bright blue and grow singly on stems. These are also edible.

Toxic Look-a-like(s): *Green Hellebore (Helleborus viridis)* and *Stinking Hellebore (Helleborus foetidus)* have flowers that are more diverse in color (ranging from green to white, pink, purple, and even black) and shape, but they typically have a more cupped or saucer-shaped appearance and are often nodding.

Cautions: While comfrey has many beneficial uses, it contains alkaloids that can be harmful if ingested in large quantities. It's best to avoid internal use and consult with a healthcare professional before using it medicinally.

Culinary Uses: Comfrey leaves can be chopped and added to salads for a nutritious boost. Create a healing poultice by crushing fresh comfrey leaves and applying them to bruises or sprains. Make a soothing comfrey tea by steeping dried leaves in hot water for a few minutes. Infuse oil with comfrey leaves to make a healing salve for minor cuts and burns. Use comfrey root to make a decoction to relieve joint pain and inflammation.

Medicinal Properties: Comfrey is renowned for its ability to speed up healing wounds and fractures. It possesses anti-inflammatory properties, making it useful for treating arthritis and muscle pain. Comfrey's astringent qualities make it effective in treating minor cuts, scrapes, and insect bites. It can be used as a poultice to alleviate the pain and swelling associated with sprains and strains. Comfrey contains compounds that promote cell regeneration, aiding in the repair of damaged tissue.

Fun/Historical Fact(s): Comfrey has been used for centuries in traditional herbal medicine for its wound-healing properties. Its name, "knitbone," stems from its historical use in helping heal broken bones and fractures. Comfrey has been cultivated in gardens since ancient times for its medicinal and soil-enhancing properties.

Dog Toxicity: Comfrey can be toxic to dogs if ingested in large amounts. Symptoms of comfrey toxicity in dogs may include vomiting, diarrhea, and liver damage. It's best to keep comfrey out of reach of curious pets and seek veterinary attention if ingestion occurs.

Deer Tongue Grass

Panicum clandestinum [PAN-ih-kum klan-DES-tin-um]

Deer Tongue Grass belongs to the Poaceae (grass) family and is known by common names such as Velvet Grass, Fowl Meadow Grass, and Tussock Grass. It has been a part of New England's landscape for centuries, quietly adding beauty to its surroundings. It can be found in meadows, fields, and open woodlands, where it thrives in the cool climate and fertile soil.

Identification:

Growth / Size: typically grows in tufts or clumps, reaching 1 to 2 feet tall.

Bark / Stem / Root: The stems are slender and cylindrical, often tinged with red or purple at the base. The roots are fibrous and shallow, spreading horizontally to anchor the plant firmly in the ground.

Leaf: The leaves are narrow and elongated, resembling the shape of a deer's tongue (hence the name). They are usually green in color, with a slightly glossy appearance, and grow in a dense, upright fashion.

Flower: In late spring to early summer, it produces delicate, feathery flowers in shades of green, tinged with hints of purple or pink. These flowers form on long, slender stalks and sway gracefully in the breeze.

Fruit / Seed / Nut: develops small, inconspicuous seeds dispersed by the wind after flowering. The tiny, light brown seeds are ready for harvest in late summer to early fall.

Non-toxic Look-a-like(s): *Lemongrass (Cymbopogon citratus)* is a tall, stalky plant with a fresh, lemony scent and a citrus flavor. The leaves are similar in shape, being long and blade-like. *Sweetgrass (Hierochloe odorata)* is another grass-like plant with long, fragrant leaves. It is known for its sweet vanilla-like scent, especially when dried.

Toxic Look-a-like(s): *Fall Panicum (Panicum dichotomiflorum)* has a similar growth habit and leaf structure. It also produces a panicle of spikelets.

Cautions: While Deer Tongue Grass itself is not toxic, it's essential to be cautious when foraging, as there may be look-alike plants in the vicinity that could be harmful if ingested.

Culinary Uses: Add young leaves to salads for a fresh, slightly nutty flavor. Brew dried leaves into a soothing herbal tea. Use the feathery flowers as a decorative garnish for desserts or cocktails. Cook tender stems and leaves in stir-fries for a nutritious addition. Simmer the grass blades with other vegetables to create a flavorful broth for soups.

Medicinal Properties: Deer Tongue Grass has been used traditionally to soothe digestive discomforts like indigestion and bloating. Infusions may help reduce inflammation and alleviate mild pain. A tea made from the blades may promote healthy kidney function and help reduce water retention. Gargling with the tea may help freshen your breath and soothe minor oral irritations. Applying poultices made from mashed leaves may help relieve minor skin irritations and insect bites.

Fun/Historical Fact(s): Native Americans used Deer Tongue Grass for its medicinal properties, often incorporating it into herbal remedies for various ailments. Early European settlers in New England admired the resilience and beauty of Deer Tongue Grass, often incorporating it into their landscaping designs. Its graceful appearance has inspired poets and writers, symbolizing resilience and adaptability in the face of adversity.

Dog toxicity: Deer Tongue Grass is not known to be toxic to dogs. However, ingestion of large quantities may still cause mild gastrointestinal upset, so it's best to monitor your furry friends when they're exploring outdoors. If you notice any unusual symptoms, consult your veterinarian promptly.

J ewelweed

Impatiens capensis [IM-*PAY*-SHENZ KUH-*PEN*-SIS]

Jewelweed belongs to the Balsaminaceae (balsam) family and has several other common names, including touch-me-not, spotted touch-me-not, orange balsam, and spotted jewelweed. It's often found along the edges of streams and in shady woodland spots. People in this region have known about it for generations. Indigenous communities revered it for its healing powers, using its juice to soothe skin irritations from encounters with poison ivy and pesky insect bites. They affectionately called it "touch-me-not." Even today, we cherish Jewelweed for its natural remedies, often finding it in herbal potions and skin care products that seek to harness its calming properties.

Identification:

GROWTH/SIZE: typically grows between 3 to 5 feet tall, forming dense patches in moist soil.

BARK/STEM/ROOT: The stems are succulent, translucent, and hollow, with reddish coloring. The roots are shallow and fibrous, spreading out widely underground.

LEAF: Its oval leaves have toothed edges, resembling a tiny canoe. They're bright green and shimmer distinctively silver-white when held in sunlight.

FLOWER: The flowers are pendulous, trumpet-shaped, and dangle delicately from the stems. They come in shades of orange or yellow and bloom from late spring to early fall.

Fʀᴜɪᴛ/Sᴇᴇᴅ/Nᴜᴛ: The fruits are small, elongated capsules that explode upon touch, dispersing seeds in all directions. They're green when immature and turn brown when ripe, ready for harvest in late summer.

Non-toxic Look-a-like(s): *Wood Nettle (Laportea canadensis)* is found in similar shaded, moist environments, often near streams or in woodland areas. Its leaves are toothed and arranged in an opposite pattern, similar to Jewelweed. However, Wood Nettle leaves have a rougher texture and are covered in stinging hairs that can cause irritation upon contact, unlike Jewelweed's smooth, succulent leaves. Despite its stinging hairs, Wood Nettle is edible when cooked, with a flavor akin to spinach. *Clearweed (Pilea pumila)* shares the translucent appearance of Jewelweed's stems but lacks the vibrant, trumpet-shaped flowers. Its leaves are similarly arranged in an opposite pattern, but they are smoother and lack the serrated edges of Jewelweed. While not as well-known for its edibility, Clearweed is non-toxic and has been used in traditional herbal medicine for its potential medicinal properties.

Toxic Look-a-like(s): *Pale Jewelweed (Impatiens pallida)* lacks the same medicinal properties and, more importantly, contains potentially harmful compounds. *Spotted Touch-Me-Not (Impatiens capensis)* has showy orange flowers and toothed leaves, but its toxic sap can cause skin irritation in sensitive individuals. Both Pale Jewelweed and Spotted Touch-Me-Not contain chemical compounds such as alkaloids and glycosides, which can cause adverse reactions ranging from skin irritation to gastrointestinal distress if ingested.

Cautions: While jewelweed is generally safe, always be cautious when foraging in the wild. Avoid areas with heavy pollution or contamination, as the plant may absorb harmful substances from the soil and water.

Culinary Uses: Steep the leaves in hot water to make jewelweed tea, a refreshing beverage. Add chopped jewelweed leaves to salads for a nutritious crunch. Use jewelweed stems as a substitute for celery in soups and stews. Blend jewelweed with fruits to make a tangy smoothie. Infuse jewelweed flowers in vinegar for a unique salad dressing.

Medicinal Properties: Jewelweed sap can soothe skin irritations, such as poison ivy rashes and insect bites. Brew jewelweed tea to alleviate symptoms of minor digestive issues. Apply crushed jewelweed leaves to minor burns and sunburns for relief. Make a poultice from jewelweed to reduce swelling and inflammation. Gargle with jewelweed infusion to ease sore throats and mouth ulcers.

Fun/Historical Fact(s): Native Americans used jewelweed as a natural remedy for various ailments, earning it the nickname "nature's medicine cabinet." Early European settlers believed that carrying a sprig of jewelweed would protect them from evil spirits and bad luck. In folklore, jewelweed flowers are said to glow with an otherworldly light on moonlit nights, guiding lost travelers through the forest.

Dog toxicity: Jewelweed is generally safe for dogs. However, consuming large quantities may cause gastrointestinal upset, including vomiting and diarrhea. Keep an eye on your furry friends and contact a veterinarian if they show any unusual symptoms after ingesting jewelweed.

L emon Balm

Melissa officinalis [MEH-LISS-UH OH-FISH-IH-NAH-LIS]

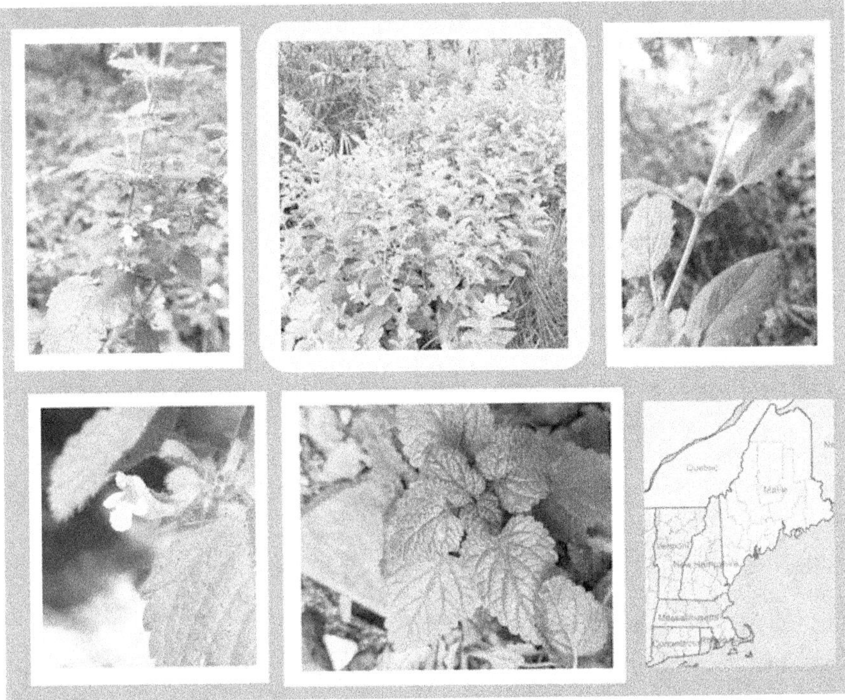

Lemon Balm belongs to the Lamiaceae (mint) family and is known as balm, common balm, bee balm, garden balm, sweet balm, and honey plant. This aromatic herb can often flourish in sunny woodland edges, stream banks, and disturbed habitats such as roadsides and abandoned fields. Its native range spans Europe, North Africa, and Western Asia, but it has been naturalized in various parts of North America, including New England. Lemon Balm has a rich history dating back to ancient times, and it is prized for its culinary, medicinal, and aromatic properties. Renowned for its lemony scent and mild flavor, it has been traditionally used in teas, culinary dishes, and herbal remedies for its calming and soothing effects on the mind and body.

Identification:

GROWTH / SIZE: typically grows bushy, reaching heights of about 1 to 2 feet.

BARK / STEM / ROOT: The stems are square-shaped and light green, with a slightly fuzzy texture. The roots are shallow and fibrous, spreading out near the surface.

LEAF: The heart-shaped leaves are bright green and have serrated edges. When crushed, they grow opposite each other on the stem and emit a strong lemon fragrance.

FLOWER: produces small white or pale yellow flowers in clusters along the stem. It blooms from late spring to early summer, attracting bees and other pollinators.

Fruit/Seed/Nut: produces small brown seeds enclosed in tiny nutlets. It is ready to harvest in late summer to early fall.

Non-toxic Look-a-like(s): Bee Balm (Monarda didyma) has square stems and opposite leaves. However, Bee Balm typically has scarlet, pink, or lavender flowers clustered at the top of the stem. Both plants belong to the same family and share a refreshing, citrusy scent when their leaves are crushed. *Mint (Mentha spp.)* can be easily mistaken for Lemon Balm due to its similar leaf shape and growth habit. However, Mint leaves tend to be darker green and have a stronger, distinctly minty aroma compared to Lemon Balm's lemony fragrance.

Toxic Look-a-like(s): *White Deadnettle (Lamium album)* has heart-shaped leaves with toothed margins. *Henbit Deadnettle (Lamium amplexicaule)*as rounded, deeply lobed leaves. They both have square stems like Lemon Balm, and both have small, tubular, pinkish-purple flowers similar to Lemon Balm, but they grow in clusters along the stem, whereas Lemon Balm typically has larger, white or pale pink flowers that grow in terminal spikes. The toxic component in both is not well documented, but ingesting large quantities of their leaves can cause digestive upset in humans and animals.

Cautions: While Lemon Balm is generally safe for consumption, it's essential to be cautious when foraging. Always positively identify the plant and avoid harvesting from areas that may have been sprayed with pesticides or other chemicals.

Culinary Uses: Make refreshing lemon balm tea by steeping fresh leaves in hot water. Add chopped leaves to salads or fruit salads for a burst of flavor. Infuse vinegar with Lemon Balm for salad dressings or marinades. Use it as a garnish for desserts like ice cream or lemon bars. Incorporate it into homemade pesto for a unique twist.

Medicinal Properties: When brewed into a calming tea, it relieves stress and anxiety. It also aids in digestion and soothes upset stomachs. When consumed before bedtime, it helps promote restful sleep. It can also be used topically to alleviate insect bites and minor skin irritations. Its antioxidant properties support overall immune health.

Fun/Historical Fact(s): Lemon Balm was believed to have been introduced to England by the Romans over 2,000 years ago. In the Middle Ages, Lemon Balm attracted bees to hives and kept them content. Thomas Jefferson, the third President of the United States, cultivated Lemon Balm in his garden at Monticello.

Dog Toxicity: Lemon Balm is generally considered safe for dogs in small quantities. However, consuming large amounts may cause mild gastrointestinal upset, such as vomiting or diarrhea.

Poverty Oatgrass

Danthonia spicata [DAN-THOH-NEE-UH SPY-KAH-TUH]

Poverty Oatgrass is a Poaceae (grass) family member and is known by several other common names, including poverty grass, poverty oat, poverty bentgrass, and poverty fescue. It thrives in the wild expanses of the New England region, particularly in open woodlands, meadows, and rocky slopes. This hardy perennial grass plays a vital ecological role in stabilizing soil and providing habitat for various wildlife species. Today, while often overlooked, Poverty Oatgrass remains an essential component of New England's diverse ecosystems, symbolizing the enduring relationship between humans and the natural world.

Identification:

GROWTH/SIZE: typically forms dense tufts or clumps, reaching heights of 1-2 feet.

BARK/STEM/ROOT: The stems are slender and wiry, often reddish-brown in color, and can grow up to 2 feet tall. The roots are fibrous and shallow, helping the plant withstand harsh conditions.

LEAF: Its narrow leaves are green or bluish-green, growing in a basal rosette. They are about 3-6 inches long and have a folded or rolled appearance.

FLOWER: The flowers are small and inconspicuous, forming dense, spike-like clusters at the top of the stems. They are typically pale yellow or reddish-brown and bloom from late spring to early summer.

FRUIT/SEED/NUT: The plant produces small seeds in tiny capsules. These seeds are ready for harvest in late summer or early fall and often appear brownish.

Non-toxic Look-a-like(s): *Blue Wild Indigo (Baptisia australis)* can be easily distinguished by its distinctive blue-green foliage and tall spikes of blue flowers. Additionally, its flowers bloom in a different season, typically in late spring to early summer. *Canada Bluegrass (Poa compressa)* has flattened stems and blue-green leaves. It forms dense clumps, while Poverty Oatgrass grows in looser tufts.

Toxic Look-a-like(s): *Darnel (Lolium temulentum)* has slender green stems and spike-like seed heads. However, its seeds have a slightly different shape. The seeds are longer and have a characteristic black coloration. It contains toxic compounds called ergot alkaloids, which can cause symptoms of poisoning if ingested in large quantities. These alkaloids affect the nervous system and can lead to dizziness, vomiting, and even hallucinations. *Ryegrass (Lolium perenne)* has slender blades and dense spike-like seed heads. Compared to poverty oatgrass, the seed heads of ryegrass are typically denser and more compact. Additionally, Ryegrass seeds are larger and shiny. It can contain toxic alkaloids known as lolines, particularly when infected by fungal endophytes. Ingestion of these alkaloids can lead to neurological symptoms in livestock, such as tremors and convulsions.

Cautions: While Poverty Oatgrass is generally safe for foraging, be cautious when harvesting in areas that may have been treated with pesticides or herbicides.

Culinary Uses: Add young leaves to salads for a nutritious boost. Steep dried leaves in hot water for a soothing herbal tea. Use chopped leaves as a thickening agent in soups and stews. Ground seeds can be used as a gluten-free flour alternative. Crushed seeds can add a nutty flavor to dishes like rice or quinoa.

Medicinal Properties: Poverty Oatgrass tea may help alleviate digestive discomfort. Applied topically, a poultice made from mashed leaves may reduce inflammation. Infusions made from the plant may support kidney health and encourage urination. Consumption of Poverty Oatgrass may provide antioxidant benefits. Applied to cuts or abrasions, the plant may help promote healing.

Fun/Historical Fact(s): During the Great Depression, Poverty Oatgrass gained popularity as a forage crop due to its resilience and nutritional value. Its historical significance traces back to indigenous communities who recognized its utility for weaving baskets and crafting mats, utilizing its fibrous stems. European settlers later utilized it as forage for livestock due to its resilience and palatability. Early European settlers often referred to Poverty Oatgrass as "bentgrass" due to its tendency to bend in the wind.

Dog toxicity: Poverty Oatgrass is not known to be toxic to dogs. However, consumption in large quantities may cause mild gastrointestinal upset, such as vomiting or diarrhea. If your dog ingests large amounts of any unfamiliar plant, it's best to contact a veterinarian for advice.

R ed Clover
Trifolium pratense [TRY-*FOH*-LEE-UM PRUH-*TEN*-SEE]

Red Clover is a Fabaceae (legume) family member and is also known by several other common names, including wild clover, meadow clover, cow clover, and purple clover. It's renowned for its vibrant crimson-hued flowers and trifoliate leaves. In the wilds of the New England region, one can often spot Red Clover flourishing in meadows, fields, and along roadsides, its cheerful blooms adding a splash of color to the landscape. Historically, Red Clover has been valued for its medicinal properties, and Native American tribes use it to treat various ailments. Later, European settlers brought it to the Americas, where it became naturalized and continues to be cherished for its ornamental beauty and its role in sustainable agriculture, as it enriches the soil through nitrogen fixation.

Identification:

GROWTH / SIZE: typically grows in clusters, reaching heights of 1 to 2 feet. Its growth pattern is low to the ground, with sprawling stems that spread outwards.

BARK / STEM / ROOT: The stems are slender and slightly hairy, featuring a reddish hue. The roots are fibrous and shallow, anchoring the plant firmly in the soil. The bark is not prominent due to the herbaceous nature of the plant.

LEAF: The leaves are trifoliate, consisting of three leaflets arranged in a clover-like pattern. They are green with a distinctive white V-shaped mark, and each leaflet is oval-shaped with serrated edges.

FLOWER: The flower is a beautiful globe-shaped cluster of tiny, magenta-colored florets. It blooms from late spring to early fall, attracting bees and other pollinators with its sweet nectar.

FRUIT/SEED/NUT: produces small, round seed pods that contain several seeds. The pods are green and turn brown as they mature. The seeds are ready to harvest when the pods have dried and turned brown.

Non-toxic Look-a-like(s): *White Clover (Trifolium repens)* has white flowers. *Crimson Clover (Trifolium incarnatum)* has deeper red flowers.

Toxic Look-a-like(s): *Black Medic (Medicago lupulina)* has yellow flowers and trifoliate leaves, but it's toxic if consumed in large quantities. *Crown Vetch (Securigera varia)* features pinkish-purple flowers in dense clusters, but it's considered toxic to livestock.

Cautions: While Red Clover is generally safe for foraging, avoiding areas that may have been treated with pesticides or herbicides is essential. Additionally, individuals with certain medical conditions should consult a healthcare professional before using Red Clover medicinally.

Culinary Uses: Red Clover flowers can be added to salads for a pop of color and a mild, sweet flavor. The leaves can be dried and brewed into a tea, offering a refreshing herbal drink. Infuse olive oil with Red Clover blossoms to create a flavorful dressing for salads or roasted vegetables. Dried red clover as a garnish or in soups or stews to add a subtle herbal taste. Make Red Clover jelly by steeping the flowers in water and combining them with sugar and pectin.

Medicinal Properties: Red Clover is known for its traditional use in easing menopausal symptoms due to its phytoestrogen content. It's believed to support skin health and may be used topically to soothe irritations or minor wounds. Red Clover tea is often consumed to promote detoxification and support liver health. Some herbalists recommend Red Clover as a mild expectorant to relieve coughs and respiratory congestion. It's also used in folk medicine to help lower cholesterol levels and promote heart health.

Fun/Historical Fact(s): Red Clover has been cultivated for centuries and was historically prized for its fertility-enhancing properties in agriculture. It's a popular choice for cover cropping due to its ability to fix nitrogen in the soil, enriching it for other plants. In Celtic folklore, Red Clover was considered a symbol of good luck and was believed to ward off evil spirits.

Dog Toxicity: Red Clover is generally considered safe for dogs in small quantities and is not known to be toxic. However, as with any plant, ingesting large amounts may cause gastrointestinal upset such as vomiting or diarrhea.

Softstem Bulrush

Schoenoplectus tabernaemontani [SHOO-NUH-PLEK-TUS TAB-ER-NEE-MON-TAH-NEE]

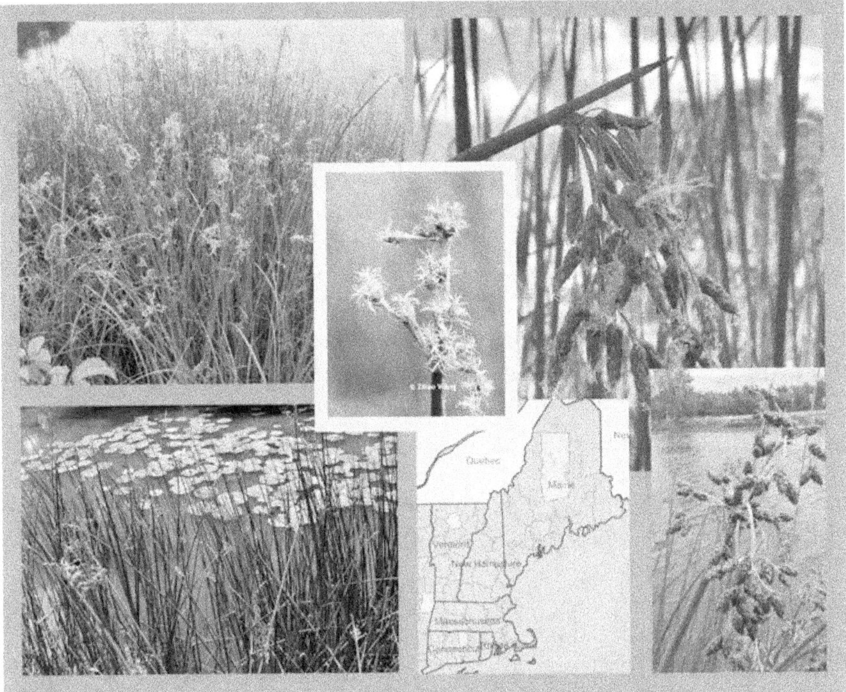

Softstem bulrush is a perennial aquatic plant belonging to the Cyperaceae (sedge) family. Also referred to as Softstem Club-Rush or Gray Club-Rush, this plant thrives in wetland habitats, particularly in marshes, swamps, and along the edges of ponds and streams. You can find it flourishing in areas with consistent moisture such as the margins of lakeshores and wet meadows. Its fibrous stems were used in weaving mats, baskets, and even as thatching material for shelters. Today, softstem bulrush plays a crucial ecological role in wetland ecosystems while also being cultivated for ornamental and erosion control purposes.

Identification:

GROWTH / SIZE: typically grows in clumps and can reach heights of 3 to 6 feet.

BARK / STEM / ROOT: The stems are round and smooth, often greenish-brown in color, and can grow quite tall. The roots are fibrous and spread out underground.

LEAF: The leaves are long and slender, with a green color and a tapering shape. They grow in a tuft at the base of the stem.

FLOWER: The flowers are small and brownish in color. They form clusters at the tips of the stems and bloom from late spring to early summer.

Fʀᴜɪᴛ / Sᴇᴇᴅ / Nᴜᴛ: The fruits are small nutlets enclosed in bracts. They turn brown as they mature and are ready to harvest in late summer.

Non-toxic Look-a-like(s): *Common cattail (Typha latifolia)* is a non-toxic plant that resembles softstem bulrush in wetland habitats.

Toxic Look-a-like(s): Poison and water hemlock are toxic plants that may resemble softstem bulrush, especially in their stem and leaf structures.

Cautions: When foraging softstem bulrush, be cautious of potential contamination from polluted water sources and be mindful of wetland preservation regulations.

Culinary Uses: The young shoots can be harvested and added to salads for a crunchy texture. The roots can be boiled and eaten like potatoes. The seeds can be ground into flour for baking. The stems can be pickled for a tangy snack. The leaves can be used to wrap food for steaming or grilling.

Medicinal Properties: The roots can be brewed into a tea to treat digestive issues. The leaves can be poulticed onto wounds to promote healing. The seeds can be used to make a soothing poultice for skin irritations. The stems can be chewed to relieve toothaches. A decoction made from the whole plant can be used as a diuretic.

Fun/Historical Fact(s): Softstem bulrush has been used by Indigenous peoples for centuries for making baskets, mats, and other woven goods. In ancient times, the fluffy seed heads of bulrushes were used as tinder for starting fires. Softstem bulrush plays a vital role in wetland ecosystems by providing habitat for various wildlife species.

Dog toxicity: Softstem bulrush is not known to be toxic to dogs. However, ingestion of large quantities may cause mild gastrointestinal upset, such as vomiting or diarrhea. Monitor your pet if they consume large amounts of the plant and consult a veterinarian if any symptoms persist.

S tinging Nettle

Urtica dioica [YOOR-TIH-KUH DEE-OH-IH-KUH]

Stinging Nettle belongs to the Urticaceae (nettle) family and is renowned for its stinging hairs that cause irritation upon contact. Often dubbed "common nettle" or simply "nettle," this perennial herbaceous plant thrives in temperate regions worldwide, including the woodlands, meadows, and disturbed habitats of New England. Despite its notorious sting, it holds a storied history of culinary, medicinal, and textile use dating back centuries. Ancient civilizations utilized its fibers for textiles, while herbalists praised its medicinal properties, from treating arthritis to relieving allergies. Today, it remains a valuable resource in herbal medicine and cuisine, appreciated for its nutritional content and diverse applications.

Identification:

GROWTH/SIZE: It typically grows in dense clusters and can reach heights of up to 3 to 7 feet.

BARK/STEM/ROOT: The stems are covered in tiny, stinging hairs that can cause irritation upon contact. They are green in color and have a ridged texture. The roots are fibrous and spread out extensively underground.

LEAF: The leaves are oval-shaped with serrated edges. They have a deep green color and grow opposite each other along the stem. Nettle leaves can grow to be several inches long.

Flower: it produces small, greenish-white flowers arranged in clusters along the stem. They bloom from late spring to early autumn.

Fruit/Seed/Nut: After flowering, it produces small, round seeds contained within a greenish-brown casing. These seeds are ready to harvest in late summer to early autumn.

Look-a-like(s): *Wood nettle (Laportea canadensis)* has a moderate toxicity rating and causes minor skin irritation lasting only a few minutes. It is also edible but must be handled with care. It typically has more deeply serrated leaves, and its stems are often reddish in color. It also tends to prefer shadier habitats. *Bull nettle (Cnidoscolus stimulosus)* has a low toxicity rating and can cause severe stinging of the skin lasting no longer than one hour. It can cause more serious reactions in some people.

Cautions: When foraging for stinging nettles, it's essential to wear protective clothing to prevent skin irritation from the stinging hairs on the stems and leaves.

Culinary Uses: Boil nettles with potatoes, onions, and broth for a hearty soup. Blend blanched nettles with garlic, pine nuts, olive oil, and Parmesan cheese for a flavorful pesto. Steep dried nettle leaves in hot water for a nutritious herbal tea. Add cooked nettles to a quiche filling for a nutritious and savory dish. Sauté nettles with garlic, ginger, and soy sauce for a nutritious and flavorful side dish.

Medicinal Properties: Nettle has been used to reduce inflammation associated with conditions like arthritis. Nettle tea may help promote urine production and relieve symptoms of bloating. Some people use nettle supplements to alleviate symptoms of seasonal allergies. Nettle is packed with vitamins and minerals, including iron and vitamin C. Poultices made from nettle leaves have been applied to wounds to aid in healing.

Fun/Historical Fact(s): In medieval Europe, stinging nettles were used to make fiber for textiles, including clothing and bed linens. Ancient Romans believed that flogging oneself with nettle leaves could alleviate rheumatic pains. During World War II, stinging nettle was cultivated in the UK as a source of fiber for making uniforms and other wartime necessities.

Dog Toxicity: Stinging nettle is generally not toxic to dogs. However, ingestion may cause mild gastrointestinal upset, so it's best to monitor your pet if they consume any.

Valerian
Valeriana officinalis [VAH-LUH-REE-AH-NUH OH-FIH-SUH-NAH-LIS]

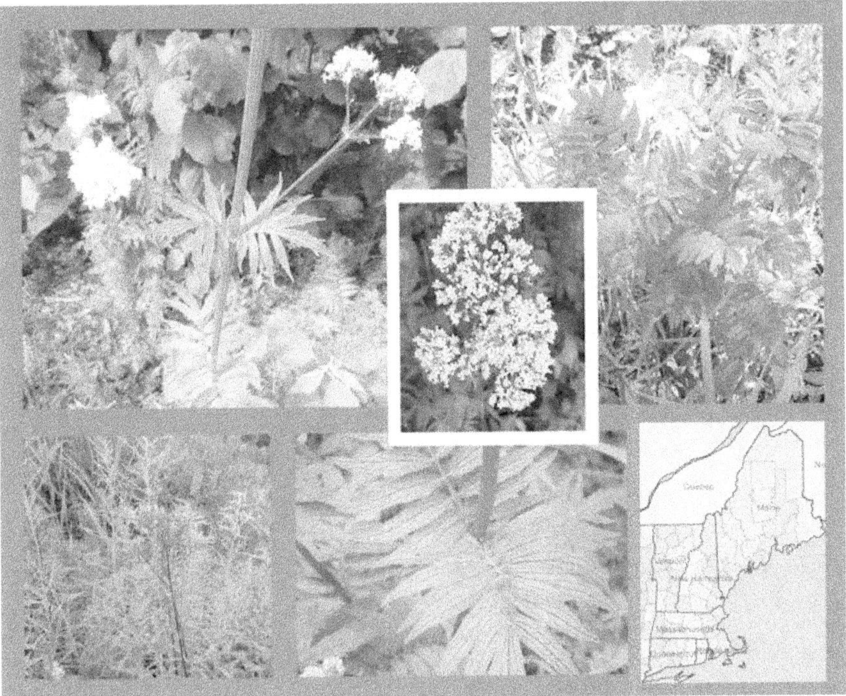

Valerian is a member of the Caprifoliaceae (honeysuckle) family and is also known as garden valerian, all-heal, and garden heliotrope. It can be found growing wild in damp meadows, marshes, and along stream banks. This herbaceous perennial has a rich history spanning centuries, revered for its medicinal properties. Since ancient times, it has been utilized for its sedative and calming effects, often brewed into teas or tinctures to aid sleep and alleviate anxiety. Valerian's reputation as a potent herbal remedy has endured through the ages, making it a staple in traditional medicine practices around the world.

Identification:

GROWTH / SIZE: typically grows in clumps, reaching heights of around 3 to 5 feet.

BARK / STEM / ROOT: Its stems are hollow and grooved, often reddish-brown in color. The roots are long and slender, emitting a distinct earthy aroma.

LEAF: the leaves are opposite, lance-shaped, and serrated, with a dark green color.

FLOWER: The flowers are small, fragrant, and white to pink in color. They grow in clusters at the top of tall stems in the summer.

FRUIT / SEED / NUT: After flowering, it produces small, oval-shaped fruits containing tiny seeds, ready for harvest in late summer to early fall.

Look-a-like(s): include meadowsweet and black cohosh.

Cautions: While Valerian is generally safe, be cautious of harvesting near polluted areas or roadsides due to potential contamination.

Culinary Uses: Valerian roots can be dried and used to make tea, tinctures, or even added to soups and stews for a unique flavor.

Medicinal Properties: Valerian is prized for its calming effects and is often used to alleviate anxiety, improve sleep, and soothe digestive issues.

Fun/Historical Fact(s): Valerian has been used since ancient times, with records dating back to ancient Greece and Rome. It was even used during World War II to reduce stress and anxiety in soldiers. Cats are attracted to the scent of valerian, much like catnip!

Dog Toxicity: While Valerian is not typically toxic to dogs, consuming large quantities may cause stomach upset or mild sedation. Monitor your furry friends closely if they ingest any.

Wild Mint
Mentha arvensis [MEN-THUH AR-VEN-SIS]

Wild Mint belongs to the Lamiaceae (mint) family and is also commonly referred to as Field Mint or Corn Mint. It thrives in moist soils along riverbanks, in meadows, and woodland edges, often spreading through rhizomes to form extensive colonies. It has been valued for its medicinal properties, used by indigenous peoples for its digestive benefits, and as a natural insect repellent. Early European settlers also recognized its culinary uses, incorporating it into teas, sauces, and desserts. Today, Wild Mint continues to enchant with its delicate beauty and versatile applications, embodying a timeless connection between humans and the bountiful flora of the natural world.

Identification:

GROWTH / SIZE: typically grows in clusters, reaching heights of about 1 to 2 feet.

BARK / STEM / ROOT: Its square stems are tinged with purple and covered in fine hairs. The fibrous roots spread horizontally just below the soil's surface.

LEAF: The leaves are opposite, toothed, and lance-shaped, with a vibrant green color and a wrinkled texture. They grow in pairs along the stem.

FLOWER: Its small, tubular flowers bloom in whorls around the stem, ranging in color from pale purple to white. They appear in mid to late summer.

FRUIT / SEED / NUT: After flowering, Wild Mint produces tiny nutlets containing its seeds. These nutlets are small and brown and typically ready for harvest in late summer or early fall.

Non-toxic Look-a-like(s): include Spearmint and Catnip, which share similar leaf shapes and growth patterns.

Toxic Look-a-like(s): include Pennyroyal and Dead Nettle, which may resemble Wild Mint but can cause harm if ingested.

Cautions: When foraging for Wild Mint, be cautious of potential contamination from pesticides or pollutants in urban areas. Always ensure you're harvesting from clean, safe locations.

Culinary Uses: Add fresh Wild Mint leaves to salads for a refreshing flavor. Use it to flavor drinks like iced tea or lemonade. Incorporate it into homemade mint sauces or dressings. Infuse it into syrups for cocktails or mocktails. Brew it into herbal teas for a soothing beverage.

Medicinal Properties: Brew a mint tea to aid digestion and soothe upset stomachs. Inhale mint steam to relieve congestion and clear sinuses. Apply crushed mint leaves topically to soothe bug bites and minor skin irritations. Use mint-infused water as a mouthwash for fresh breath and oral hygiene. Drink mint tea to alleviate headaches and reduce stress.

Fun/Historical Fact(s): Ancient Greeks and Romans used mint as a symbol of hospitality and wisdom. Mint was often strewn on floors to freshen the air in medieval times. Wild Mint has been used for centuries in traditional Native American medicine for its medicinal properties.

Dog Toxicity: Wild Mint is generally safe for dogs when consumed in small quantities. However, ingestion of large amounts can lead to gastrointestinal upset, including vomiting and diarrhea. It's always best to monitor your pet's consumption of any plant material and contact a veterinarian if you suspect poisoning.

Y arrow

Achillea millefolium [UH-KIL-EE-UH MILL-UH-FOH-LEE-UHM]

Yarrow belongs to the Asteraceae (aster/daisy) family and is renowned for its feathery leaves and clusters of small, delicate flowers. This versatile herb is also referred to as nosebleed plant, old man's pepper, and soldier's woundwort due to its historical uses in traditional medicine. In the wild, yarrows can be found thriving in various habitats including meadows, fields, and along roadsides. Its resilience allows it to flourish in diverse soil types and climates. Historically, yarrow has been valued for its medicinal properties, with documented use dating back thousands of years. Ancient civilizations such as the Greeks, Romans, and Native Americans utilized yarrow for its healing capabilities, employing it to staunch bleeding wounds, alleviate fevers, and treat various ailments.

Identification:

GROWTH/SIZE: A perennial herb, typically growing between 12-36 inches tall.

BARK/STEM/ROOT: The stems are erect, slender, and green, occasionally with a reddish tint. Yarrow roots are fibrous and spread horizontally in the soil.

LEAF: The leaves are feathery and finely divided, resembling a thousand leaflets, hence the species name "millefolium."

FLOWER: It has flat-topped clusters of small white to pinkish flowers. The inflorescence is a dense, umbrella-like cluster known as a corymb.

Fruit/Seed/Nut: The fruit is a small, dry, one-seeded achene that disperses easily in the wind.

Non-toxic Look-a-like(s):

Toxic Look-a-like(s): It can be mistaken for Poison Hemlock (*Conium maculatum*), which is a toxic plant. However, Yarrow has a distinct aroma, feathery leaves, and flat-topped flower clusters, while Poison Hemlock has smooth leaves and rounded flower clusters.

Cautions: Yarrow should be used cautiously, as some individuals may be allergic to it, causing skin irritation or other allergic reactions. Pregnant women should avoid using Yarrow, as it may stimulate uterine contractions.

Culinary Preparation: Yarrow leaves can be used fresh or dried as an herb, adding a slightly bitter, aromatic flavor to salads, soups, and teas.

Medicinal Properties: Traditionally, it's been used to treat various ailments, including wounds, fevers, and digestive issues. Modern herbal medicine uses Yarrow for its anti-inflammatory, antispasmodic, and astringent properties. It is often used in teas or tinctures to alleviate cold and flu symptoms, menstrual discomfort, or gastrointestinal problems.

Fun Fact: The name "Achillea" refers to the Greek hero Achilles, who, according to legend, used Yarrow to treat wounds sustained in battle.

Dog Toxicity: Yarrow is not considered toxic to dogs. However, some dogs may have an allergic reaction to the plant.

PAY IT FORWARD...

How many times have we relied on the experiences of others before diving into a new adventure? Countless, right? How gratifying does it feel when we can be that guiding light for someone else? Leaving a review isn't just a simple clickety-clack of your keyboard. Nope! It's a chance to share your wisdom, your "Ah-ha!" moments, and even your "Oops, shouldn't have eaten that" tales. By jotting down your thoughts, you're crafting a lighthouse for fellow plant enthusiasts, helping them navigate the vast array of edible plants.

Why We Need YOU!

In this digital age, there's an overabundance of information, but what's truly precious? Genuine experiences. Your insights are invaluable. By leaving an honest review, you ensure others get the most out of their edible journey without the pitfalls. Remember, your words could be the compass someone else is desperately seeking. Therefore, We're reaching out with a heartfelt plea: could you spare a few moments to leave an honest review? Your words will be the torch that lights up another enthusiast's path.

How to Review:

Scan the QR code below.

Pour your heart out! Let us know what you loved, what you learned, and any tips you might have.

Hit "Submit". Voilà!

The Ripple Effect

Every keystroke, every word, creates a ripple. By sharing your experiences, you're not just adding to a digital platform but making a real, tangible impact in someone's life. Your review could catalyze someone's passion or even help a novice avoid a potentially prickly situation.

Thanks and Happy Foraging,

Shannon Warner

PART FIVE
TREES AND NUTS

Eastern Hemlock

Tsuga canadensis [SOO-GUH KAN-UH-DEN-SIS]

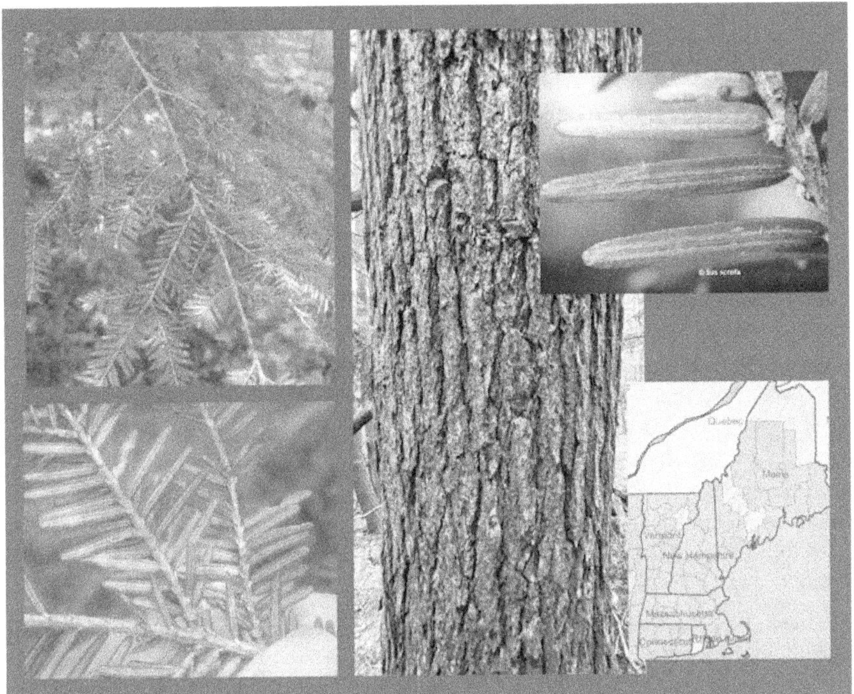

The Eastern Hemlock is a member of the Pinaceae (pine) family and is a majestic coniferous tree known for its graceful form and dense, evergreen foliage. Also referred to as Canadian hemlock or hemlock spruce, it flourishes in the cool, moist climates of eastern North America, it can be found in shaded ravines, along stream banks, and in moist forests. It has long been valued for its timber, used in construction, furniture making, and as a source of tannin for leather production. Additionally, indigenous peoples utilized its bark for medicinal purposes. Today, this iconic tree plays a crucial role in maintaining ecosystem stability and biodiversity in the forests of New England. However, it faces threats from invasive pests such as the hemlock woolly adelgid, underscoring the importance of conservation efforts to preserve this vital species.

Identification:

GROWTH / SIZE: typically grow tall and straight, reaching heights of up to 70-100 feet. They have a conical shape with dense foliage.

BARK / STEM / ROOT: The bark is deeply furrowed and reddish-brown in color. Their stems are slender and flexible, while their roots spread widely, anchoring the tree securely in the soil.

LEAF: The leaves are flat, needle-like, and arranged spirally around the twigs. They are dark green on top and paler underneath, giving the tree a lush appearance.

FLOWER: produce small, inconspicuous flowers that are pale yellow in color. They grow in clusters near the ends of the branches and bloom in spring.

FRUIT/SEED/NUT: The tree bears small, woody cones that are about 1 inch long. These cones mature in about a year and release tiny seeds that are dispersed by the wind. They are ready to harvest in late summer to early fall.

Non-Toxic Look-a-like(s): White Pine and Balsam Fir share similarities with Eastern Hemlocks in terms of needle-like foliage and overall appearance.

Toxic Look-a-like(s): Yew and Ground Hemlocks are toxic plants that resemble Eastern Hemlocks, especially in their needle-like leaves and growth patterns.

Cautions: While Eastern Hemlock has many uses, it's essential to be cautious when foraging as some parts of the tree, such as the needles and seeds, can be toxic if ingested in large quantities.

Culinary Uses: Brew tea from the young shoots for a refreshing beverage. Create a unique jelly from the tree's berries. Extract oil from the seeds for culinary purposes. Use young shoots in salads or as a garnish. Boil the inner bark to make a nourishing soup base.

Medicinal Properties: Hemlock tea can help soothe coughs and respiratory congestion. Poultices made from the bark can reduce swelling and inflammation. Consuming small amounts of hemlock seeds may aid in digestion. Hemlock-infused oil can be used topically to relieve muscle aches and pains. The leaves contain antioxidants that promote overall health and well-being.

Fun/Historical Fact(s): Eastern Hemlock was once extensively used in shipbuilding due to its durability and rot-resistant properties. Native American tribes utilized various parts of the Eastern Hemlock for medicinal and ceremonial purposes. Henry David Thoreau, the famous naturalist and writer, often wrote about the beauty of Eastern Hemlock in his works.

Dog Toxicity: Eastern Hemlock is toxic to dogs. Ingestion of any part of the tree can lead to symptoms such as vomiting, diarrhea, weakness, seizures, and potentially death. Immediate veterinary attention is necessary if a dog ingests any part of the plant.

Eastern White Pine

Pinus strobus [Pie-nuhs stroh-buhs]

The Eastern White Pine belongs to the Pinaceae (pine) family and is commonly known as the Northern White Pine or simply White Pine. This coniferous tree thrives in various habitats ranging from rocky slopes to moist lowlands. Historically, Eastern White Pine played a significant role in shaping the landscape and economy of the region. In the 17th and 18th centuries, it was a prized resource for shipbuilding due to its straight, tall trunk and lightweight yet durable wood. Today, the Eastern White Pine remains a cherished symbol of the northeastern United States, valued for its aesthetic appeal, ecological importance, and historical significance.

Identification:

GROWTH/SIZE: can tower up to an impressive 80 to 100 feet tall, with a straight trunk and a narrow, conical crown.

BARK/STEM/ROOT: Their bark is smooth and gray when young, becoming deeply furrowed and reddish-brown with age. The stems are slender and flexible, while the roots delve deep into the earth, providing stability.

LEAF: Their needles are soft and flexible, measuring around 2 to 5 inches long. They're grouped in bundles of five and have a bluish-green hue, arranged in a spiral fashion around the twig.

FLOWER: produce small, greenish-yellow flowers that cluster near the ends of the branches. They typically bloom in late spring to early summer.

Fʀᴜɪᴛ / Sᴇᴇᴅ / Nᴜᴛ: The tree bears cylindrical cones that are about 4 to 8 inches long. These cones start out green and turn brown as they mature. They usually ripen in their second year, releasing small winged seeds that are dispersed by the wind.

Non-toxic Look-a-like(s): Norway Spruce and Balsam Fir share similar needle arrangements and cone structures with Eastern White Pine.

Toxic Look-a-like(s): Yew and Ponderosa Pine may resemble Eastern White Pine, but beware! They're toxic if ingested.

Cautions: While Eastern White Pine itself isn't toxic, some look-a-like plants, like Yew, can be harmful if consumed. Always be certain of your plant identification before foraging or using any wild plants.

Culinary Uses: Brew a refreshing tea from young pine needles for a dose of Vitamin C. Use pine nuts in traditional pesto recipes for a unique twist. Flavor vinegar with pine needles for a zesty marinade or salad dressing. Create a sweet syrup by simmering pine needles with sugar and water. Grill pineapple skewers over pine wood for a smoky flavor.

Medicinal Properties: Pine needle tea can help alleviate coughs and congestion. Pine resin has anti-inflammatory properties, useful for soothing sore muscles and joints. Pine sap can be applied topically to minor cuts and scrapes to prevent infection. Pine needle extract is rich in antioxidants, supporting overall immune health. The scent of pine can promote relaxation and reduce stress.

Fun/Historical Fact(s): Eastern White Pine played a crucial role in American history, as it was highly sought after for ship masts during the colonial era. Its abundance led to the establishment of the "Pine Tree Riot" in 1772, a protest against British authority over the colonists' use of White Pine trees for lumber. The tallest Eastern White Pine on record stands at an impressive 230 feet tall! These trees can live for centuries, with some specimens reaching ages of 400 years or more.

Dog Toxicity: Thankfully, Eastern White Pine isn't toxic to our furry friends. So, your pup can safely romp around these majestic trees without worry!

H ophornbeam

Ostrya virginiana [O-STRAH-YUH VER-JIN-EE-AY-NUH]

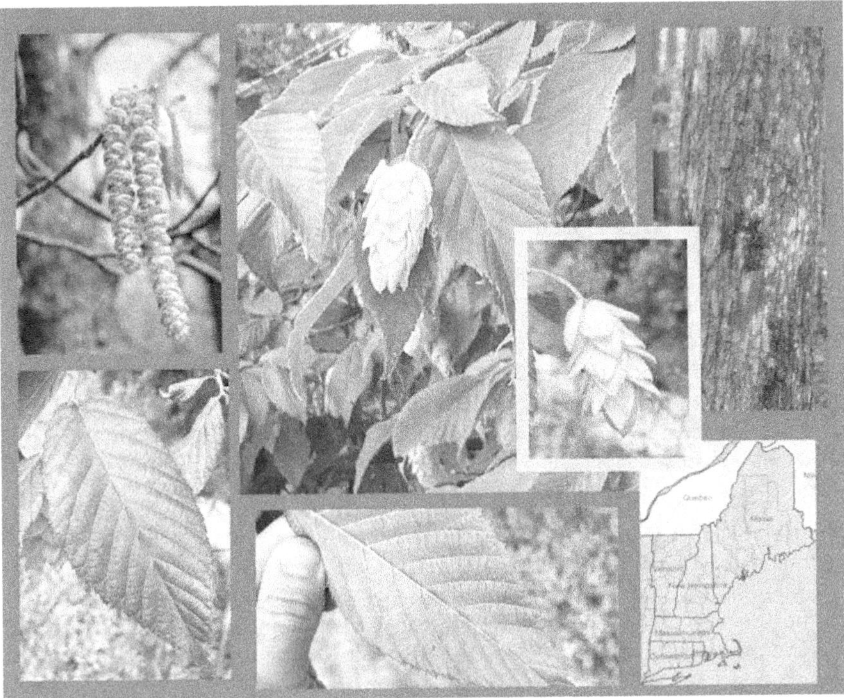

Hophornbeam, belonging to the Betulaceae (birch) family, is a sturdy and versatile deciduous tree native to the woodlands of North America. Also known as Ironwood or Musclewood due to its dense, tough wood, it often thrives in the wild, particularly in moist soils of mixed hardwood forests. Its distinctive hop-like fruits, hence the name "Hophornbeam," add to its visual charm. Historically, indigenous peoples utilized various parts of the tree for medicinal purposes, while European settlers recognized its value for tool handles and other implements due to its remarkable strength. Today, beyond its practical applications, the Hophornbeam stands as a resilient symbol of the region's rich natural heritage.

Identification:

GROWTH / SIZE: typically grows as a small to medium-sized tree, reaching heights of up to 30-50 feet. Its growth pattern is often irregular, with a spreading crown.

BARK / STEM / ROOT: The bark is grayish-brown and resembles muscles, often twisted and sinewy in appearance. The stems are slender and brown, with distinctive horizontal lenticels. The roots are shallow and widespread.

LEAF: The leaves are alternate, simple, and ovate with serrated edges. They are dark green in color and turn yellow in the fall. The leaves grow in an alternate pattern along the stem and are typically 2-4 inches long.

FLOWER: In spring, small, inconspicuous flowers cluster in hanging catkins. The flowers are greenish-yellow in color and have no petals. They bloom before the leaves emerge.

FRUIT/SEED/NUT: The fruit is a small, bladder-like structure containing nutlets. These nutlets are enclosed in papery bracts and are ready to harvest in late summer to early fall. They are brown in color and can be dispersed by wind.

Non-Toxic Look-a-likes: Beech trees and hornbeam trees share similar serrated leaves and grow in similar habitats.

Toxic Look-a-likes: Poison ivy and poison sumac can resemble hophornbeams in terms of their leaf shape and growth patterns, but they are toxic upon contact.

Cautions: When foraging for hophornbeam, proper identification is essential to avoid accidentally harvesting toxic look-alike plants. Additionally, be cautious of sharp branches or thorns while handling the tree.

Culinary Uses: Hophornbeam nuts can be roasted and eaten as a snack. The inner bark can be dried and ground into nutritious flour. Leaves can be used as a substitute for grape leaves in recipes like dolmas. Hophornbeam leaves can be brewed into tea for a mild, earthy flavor. The wood can be used for smoking meats, imparting a unique flavor.

Medicinal Properties: Hophornbeam bark has astringent properties and can be used topically to treat minor cuts and wounds. The inner bark infusion is believed to help alleviate diarrhea and stomach ailments. A decoction of hophornbeam leaves may soothe sore throats and respiratory issues. Hophornbeam tea is thought to have diuretic properties, aiding in detoxification. Poultices made from mashed hophornbeam nuts can be applied to reduce inflammation.

Fun/Historical Fact(s): Native American tribes utilized hophornbeam wood for making bows and tool handles due to its strength and flexibility. The name "hophornbeam" comes from the hard, hop-like fruits and the horn-like appearance of the tree's wood. Hophornbeam trees are often valued for their dense wood, which is resistant to rot and decay.

Dog toxicity: Hophornbeam is not known to be toxic to dogs. However, excessive consumption of nuts or bark may cause gastrointestinal discomfort in pets. If your dog ingests large quantities, watch for symptoms such as vomiting, diarrhea, or lethargy. If any adverse reactions occur, consult a veterinarian promptly.

Northern Red Oak

Quercus rubra [KWUR-kus ROO-bruh]

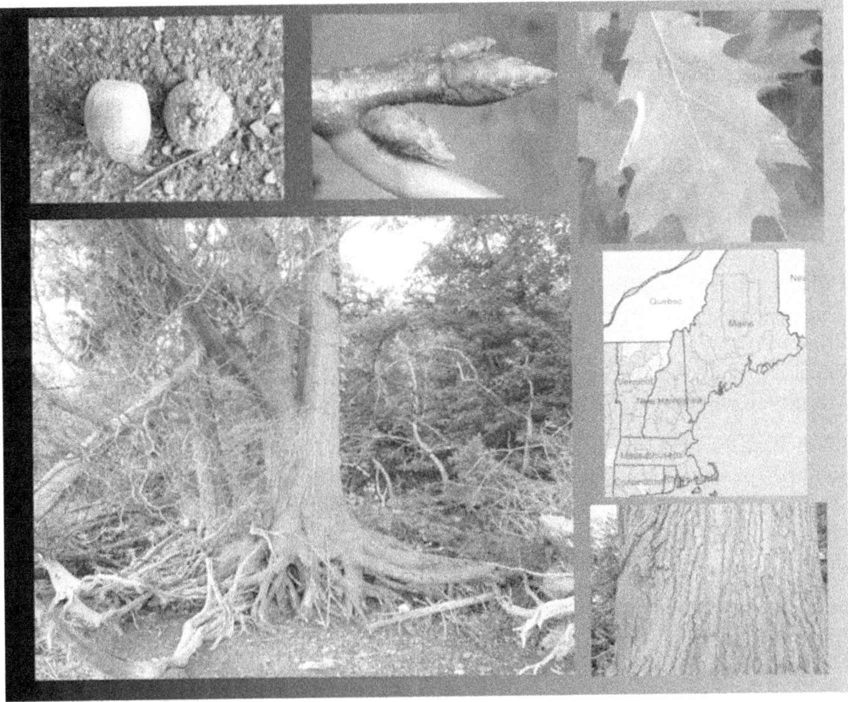

The Northern Red Oak, belonging to the Fagaceae (beech) family, is a majestic decid-uous tree native to North America, commonly known as champion oak, common red oak, or gray oak. In the wild, it thrives in rich, acidic soils. This resilient species can also be found in various habitats throughout Eastern North America, from southern Ontario and Quebec south to Georgia and west to Minnesota and Texas. Its history intertwines with the cultural and ecological tapestry of the region, serving as a valu-able timber source for Indigenous peoples and early European settlers, while also playing a crucial role in the forest ecosystems of the area, providing habitat and suste-nance for diverse wildlife.

Identification:

GROWTH/SIZE: typically grows tall and straight, reaching heights of up to 80 feet or more.

BARK/STEM/ROOT: The bark is dark and rough, with deep furrows and ridges. Its stems are slender and brown, while the roots spread widely underground.

LEAF: The leaves are simple and alternate, with lobed margins and a glossy green color. In the fall, they turn brilliant shades of red and orange.

FLOWER: In spring, it produces small, greenish-yellow flowers that grow in clusters. These flowers are inconspicuous but play a vital role in the tree's reproduction.

FRUIT/SEED/NUT: The fruit is an acorn, which is oval-shaped and usually brown with a cap covering about a quarter of its length. Acorns are ready to harvest in the fall when they ripen and fall from the tree.

Non-toxic Look-a-like(s): *White Oak (Quercus alba)* is similar in appearance, with lobed leaves and acorns, but it lacks the red hue of the Northern Red Oak's foliage. *Pin Oak (Quercus palustris)* Shares similar leaf shape and acorn characteristics but tends to have a more pyramidal growth pattern.

Toxic Look-a-like(s): Black Oak (Quercus velutina) resembles the Northern Red Oak in many ways but has hairier leaves and darker bark.

Cautions: When foraging for Northern Red Oak, be cautious of potential hazards like uneven terrain, wildlife, and poisonous plants like Poison Ivy.

Culinary Uses: Roasted Acorns: Remove the caps and shells, then roast the acorns for a nutty snack. Acorn Flour: Grind dried acorns into flour for baking. Oak Leaf Tea: Brew tea using dried oak leaves for a soothing drink. Oak Bark Infusion: Create an infusion from oak bark for flavoring or medicinal purposes. Pickled Acorns: Preserve acorns in a vinegar brine for a tangy treat.

Medicinal Properties: Oak bark can be used topically to reduce inflammation and soothe skin irritations. Oak leaf tea or bark infusion can help alleviate diarrhea and soothe sore throats. Acorns are rich in antioxidants, promoting overall health and wellness. Oak bark poultices can aid in wound healing and prevent infections. Consuming acorns in moderation may support digestion and gut health.

Fun/Historical Fact(s): Native American tribes, such as the Algonquian and Iroquois, used various parts of the Northern Red Oak for food, medicine, and tools. The Northern Red Oak is a symbol of strength and endurance, often planted as a commemorative tree in parks and public spaces. Some Northern Red Oak specimens can live for several hundred years, bearing witness to centuries of history and change in the New England region.

Dog Toxicity: While Northern Red Oak is not typically considered toxic to dogs, ingesting large quantities of acorns can cause gastrointestinal upset, including vomiting and diarrhea. It's essential to monitor pets and discourage excessive consumption of acorns. If any concerning symptoms occur, consult a veterinarian promptly.

Paper Birch

Betula papyrifera [BEH-TOO-LUH PAH-PUH-RIFF-ER-UH]

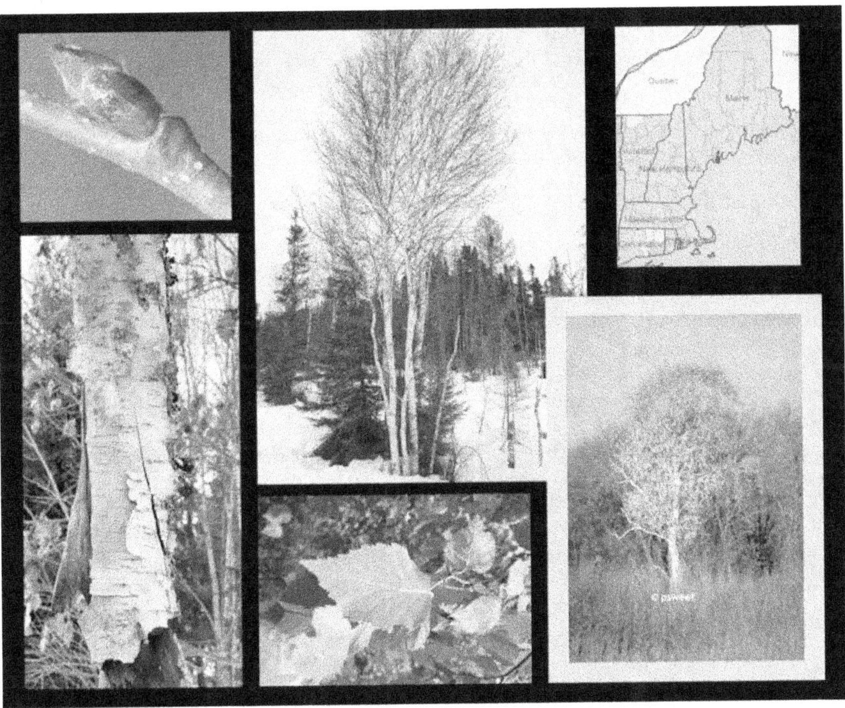

Paper Birch belongs to the Betulaceae (birch) family and is also commonly referred to as White Birch or Canoe Birch. This elegant tree thrives in the wild expanses, particularly in moist, well-drained soils, and is often found in forests, along streams, and in wetlands. Its distinctive white bark peels away in papery layers, hence its name. Historically, indigenous peoples across North America utilized various parts of the Paper Birch for medicinal, culinary, and practical purposes, including crafting canoes, baskets, and shelters. European settlers later adopted these uses and also valued the tree for its beauty and resilience. Today, Paper Birch remains a beloved fixture of the New England landscape, admired for its graceful form, striking bark, and ecological importance.

Identification:

GROWTH / SIZE: It usually grows between 65 to 100 feet tall, with a slender trunk and a graceful, open crown.

BARK / STEM / ROOT: The tree's show-stopping feature is its creamy-white, peeling bark that gives it a paper-like appearance. The bark naturally exfoliates in thin, horizontal strips, revealing a pinkish or orange-brown inner layer.

LEAF: The leaves are alternately arranged, oval to triangular, and measure 2 to 4 inches long. The leaf edges are double-toothed, and the leaf surface is a bright green, turning yellow in the fall.

FLOWER: It produces catkins in the spring, with separate male and female flowers on the same tree. Male catkins are long and pendulous, while female catkins are shorter and more upright.

FRUIT/SEED/NUT: The fruit is a small, winged nutlet dispersed by wind. The nutlets are enclosed in cone-like structures that disintegrate upon maturity.

Non-toxic Look-a-like(s): It may be confused with other birch species, like the European White Birch (*Betula pendula*), which also has white bark. However, the European White Birch has more drooping branches and a slightly different leaf shape.

Toxic Look-a-like(s):

Cautions: There are no specific cautions associated with Paperbark Birch.

Culinary Preparation: Paperbark Birch sap can be tapped and used as a refreshing drink or boiled down to make birch syrup. The tender young leaves and catkins can be eaten raw or cooked, adding a unique flavor to salads or stir-fries.

Medicinal Properties: Traditionally, Native Americans used Paperbark Birch for various medicinal purposes. The sap was believed to have detoxifying properties and treat skin conditions, while the inner bark was used to make a poultice for wounds and inflammations.

Fun Fact: The Paperbark Birch's lightweight and waterproof bark made it an ideal material for Native Americans to construct canoes, earning it the nickname "Canoe Birch."

Dog Toxicity: Paperbark Birch is not considered toxic to dogs.

R ed Spruce
Picea rubens [PEE-SEE-UH ROO-BENZ]

Red Spruce belongs to the Pinaceae (pine) family and is often referred to as Eastern Spruce or Yellow Spruce. In the wild, it thrives in cool, moist climates, particularly in high-elevation areas such as the Appalachian Mountains. Red Spruce has a rich history intertwined with the forests of this region, once dominating the landscape before extensive logging and environmental changes altered its habitat. However, concerted conservation efforts have aimed to restore its population and preserve its ecological significance, recognizing its importance in the biodiversity and ecosystem health of the area.

Identification:

GROWTH / SIZE: typically grow tall and straight, reaching heights up to 60-80 feet.

BARK / STEM / ROOT: The bark of mature trees is reddish-brown and scaly, while younger trees have smoother, purplish bark. The stems are slender and covered in short, stiff needles. The roots are extensive and shallow, spreading out to anchor the tree.

LEAF: The needles are sharp and prickly, arranged spirally around the branches. They are dark green in color, with a slender, cylindrical shape, and are about half an inch to an inch long.

FLOWER: it produces small, cylindrical cones that hang downwards from the branches.

These cones start out green and turn reddish-brown as they mature. They usually bloom in spring or early summer.

Fruit/Seed/Nut: The cones contain tiny seeds with papery wings, allowing them to be dispersed by the wind. They mature in late summer to early fall and are ready for harvest when the cones turn brown and start to open up.

Non-toxic Look-a-like(s): Balsam Fir (Abies balsamea) is similar in appearance, with short needles and upright cones. Eastern Hemlock (Tsuga canadensis) Shares a similar habitat and has short, flat needles.

Toxic Look-a-like(s): Yew (Taxus spp.) Resembles Red Spruce in shape but has red, berry-like fruits that are highly toxic.Oleander (Nerium oleander) is a tall shrub with similar needle-like leaves but produces pink or white flowers that are toxic if ingested.

Cautions: While Red Spruce itself is not toxic, be cautious when foraging as there may be look-alike plants nearby that are harmful if ingested. Also, avoid harvesting from polluted areas or private property without permission.

Culinary Uses: Red Spruce tips can be infused in vinegar or oil for a flavorful dressing. The inner bark can be dried and ground into nutritious flour. Young spruce shoots can be brewed into a refreshing tea. Spruce needles can be used as a seasoning for meats and soups. Coniferous jelly can be made from spruce tips and sugar.

Medicinal Properties: Red Spruce tea is known for its high vitamin C content and can help boost the immune system. The resin from the bark can be used as an antiseptic for wounds. Spruce bark poultices can help alleviate muscle pain and inflammation. Spruce needle infusions can aid in respiratory health and alleviate coughs. Red Spruce extracts may have antioxidant properties beneficial for overall health.

Fun/Historical Fact(s): Red Spruce played a significant role in early American history, as its wood was used for shipbuilding, particularly for masts. Native American tribes in the region used various parts of the Red Spruce for medicinal and ceremonial purposes. Red Spruce forests provide critical habitat for numerous wildlife species, including birds, mammals, and insects.

Dog toxicity: Red Spruce is not toxic to dogs. However, ingestion of large quantities of needles or bark may cause gastrointestinal upset, so it's best to discourage excessive chewing or consumption by pets.

Sugar Maple

Acer saccharum [AY-SER SAH-KAIR-UM]

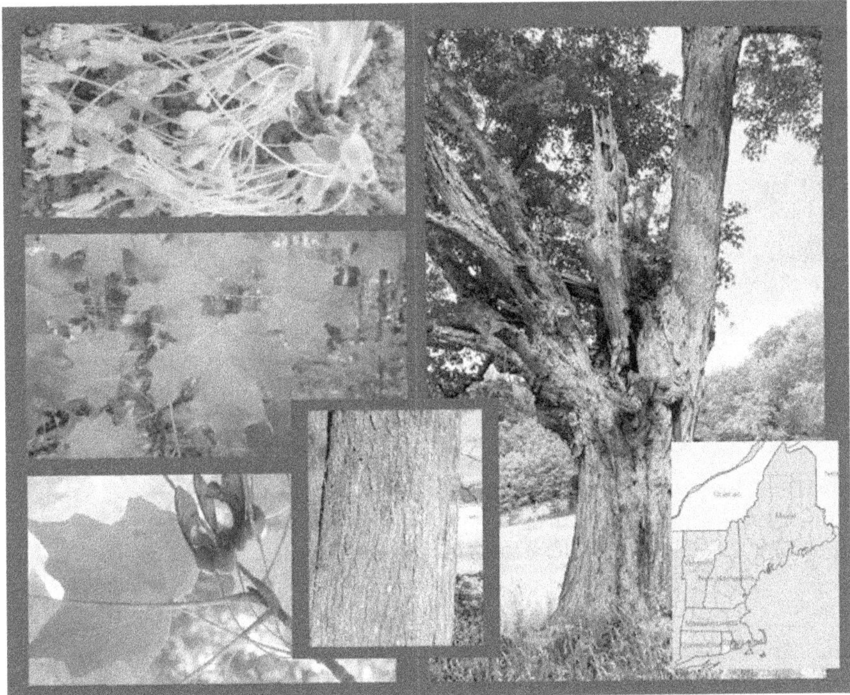

The Sugar Maple is a majestic deciduous tree belonging to the Aceraceae (maple) family. Commonly referred to as the rock maple, hard maple, or simply sugar tree, it is renowned for its stunning display of vibrant red, orange, and yellow foliage in the autumn. Native to the forests of eastern North America, the Sugar Maple thrives in a variety of soil types, often found in mixed hardwood forests alongside other iconic species like oak and beech. Its sap, rich in sucrose, has been harvested by indigenous peoples for centuries, serving as a vital source of sweetener and energy. Today, it remains a symbol of resilience and natural beauty, adorning landscapes and providing habitat for countless species across its range.

Identification:

GROWTH / SIZE: typically reaches heights of 80-100 feet, towering over the forest canopy.

BARK / STEM / ROOT: Its bark is gray and smooth when young, becoming rough and furrowed as it ages. The stems are slender and greenish-brown, while the roots spread out widely, anchoring the tree firmly.

LEAF: The leaves are typically 3-5 lobed, with serrated edges and vibrant green color, turning brilliant shades of red, orange, and yellow in the fall. They grow opposite each other on the twig and can be quite large, around 3 6 inches long.

Flower: In spring, it produces small clusters of greenish-yellow flowers. They aren't showy but play a crucial role in pollination. The tree relies on wind to spread its pollen.

Fruit/Seed/Nut: As summer turns to fall, the tree bears winged seeds called samaras, which twirl like helicopters as they fall to the ground. The seeds are ready to harvest when they turn brown and start to drop from the tree.

Non-toxic Look-a-like(s): Red Maple (Acer rubrum) and Silver Maple (Acer saccharinum) share similar leaves and growth habits.

Toxic Look-a-like(s): Boxelder (Acer negundo) and Norway Maple (Acer platanoides) have leaves that can resemble those of the Sugar Maple, but they are toxic to ingest.

Cautions: While Sugar Maple sap is delicious when processed into syrup, avoid ingesting the raw sap in large quantities, as it can cause stomach upset.

Culinary Uses: *Maple Syrup:* Boil down the sap into sweet, golden syrup. *Maple Sugar:* Further concentrate the syrup to make crystallized sugar. *Maple Glaze:* Use syrup as a base for glazing meats and vegetables. *Maple Candy:* Cook syrup to a specific temperature and pour it into molds for homemade treats. *Maple Flavored Beverages:* Add syrup to coffee, tea, or cocktails for a sweet twist.

Medicinal Properties: Maple sap contains compounds that may help reduce inflammation. Some studies suggest that maple syrup may have antioxidant properties. A poultice made from crushed leaves can aid in wound healing. Maple syrup, in moderation, may soothe digestive issues. Compounds in maple syrup could support bone health.

Fun/Historical Fact(s): The Sugar Maple leaf is featured prominently on the Canadian flag, symbolizing Canada's vast forests and maple syrup industry. The process of tapping maple trees for sap hasn't changed much since Native American times, showing the timeless connection between people and nature. Some of the oldest Sugar Maple trees in New England have been standing for over 200 years, witnessing generations of history.

Dog Toxicity: While Sugar Maple trees aren't considered toxic to dogs, ingesting large quantities of their seeds or leaves may cause mild gastrointestinal upset. Keep an eye on your furry friends during fall outings!

S wamp White Oak

Quercus bicolor [KWUR-ĸus BY-ĸə-ləʀ]

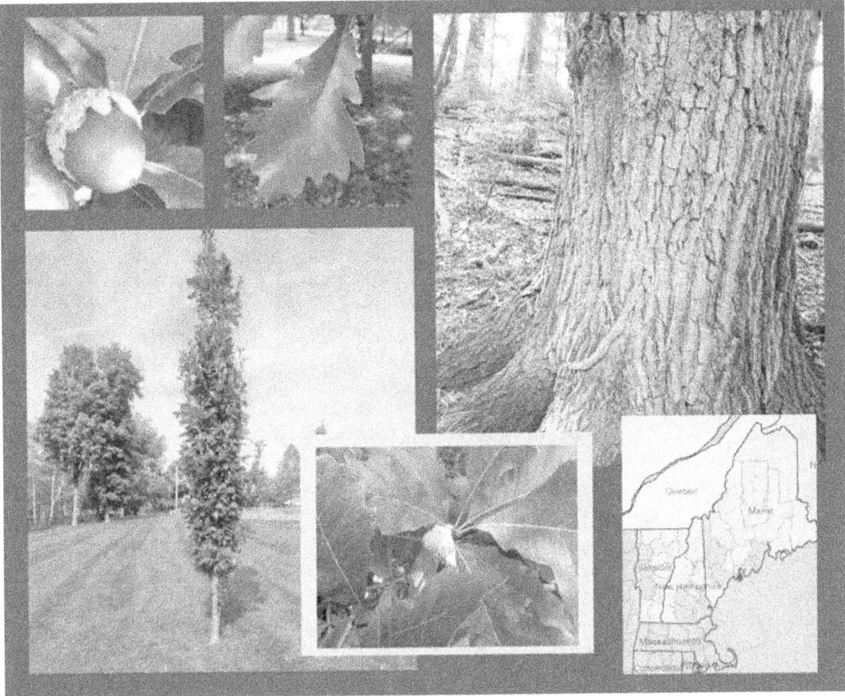

Swamp White Oak is a majestic deciduous tree belonging to the Fagaceae (beech) family. Also referred to as the Swamp Oak or Mud Oak, it thrives in wetlands and moist soils, particularly in low-lying areas, swamps, and along riverbanks. These resilient trees can be found scattered across habitats like floodplains, marshes, and riparian zones. With a history dating back centuries, Swamp White Oak has long been valued by indigenous peoples and settlers alike for its sturdy wood, which was traditionally used in construction, shipbuilding, and furniture making. Today, it continues to be appreciated for its ecological significance, providing habitat and food for various wildlife species while enhancing the natural beauty of its surroundings.

Identification:

GROWTH/SIZE: typically grows to be a medium to large-sized tree, reaching heights of up to 60-80 feet. Its growth pattern is relatively fast compared to other oak species.

BARK/STEM/ROOT: The bark is light gray to brown in color, often with shallow fissures and ridges. Its stems and roots are robust, providing stability and support to the tree.

LEAF: The leaves are distinctive, with a lobed shape and a shiny dark green color on the top surface, while the underside is paler. They typically grow in an alternate pattern along the branches and can range from 4 to 7 inches in length.

Flower: produces inconspicuous catkins. These greenish-yellow flowers appear in late spring to early summer.

Fruit/Seed/Nut: The fruit is the acorn, which is oval-shaped and about 1-2 inches long. It starts as green and gradually turns brown when mature, usually ready for harvest in the fall.

Non-Toxic Look-a-like(s): Northern Red Oak (Quercus rubra) is similar in appearance, with lobed leaves and acorns, but it is typically found in drier upland areas. Pin Oak (Quercus palustris) Resembles Swamp White Oak but prefers more acidic, poorly drained soils.

Toxic Look-a-like(s): Poison Ivy (Toxicodendron radicans) has leaves with a similar shape but grows as a vine and causes allergic reactions upon contact. Poison Sumac (Toxicodendron vernix) Resembles Swamp White Oak in leaf structure but contains urushiol, causing severe skin irritation.

Cautions: While Swamp White Oak itself is not toxic, foragers should be cautious of potential poisonous look-alike plants, such as Poison Ivy and Poison Sumac.

Culinary Uses: *Acorn Flour*: Ground acorns can be used to make flour for baking. *Acorn Coffee*: Roasted acorns can be ground and brewed as a coffee substitute. *Pickled Acorns*: Acorns can be pickled for a tangy snack. *Acorn Soup*: Acorns can be used to thicken soups and stews. *Acorn Pancakes*: Acorn flour can be used as a substitute for regular flour in pancake recipes.

Medicinal Properties: *Bark Infusion*: Used traditionally as a remedy for diarrhea and dysentery. *Leaf Poultice*: Applied topically to reduce inflammation and promote wound healing. *Acorn Tincture*: Used to alleviate digestive issues and improve appetite. *Acorn Decoction*: Consumed to boost energy and alleviate fatigue. *Bark Extract*: Used in traditional medicine to treat fevers and respiratory ailments.

Fun/Historical Fact(s): Swamp White Oak is an important species for wildlife, providing food and shelter for various animals, including deer, squirrels, and birds. Native American tribes used Swamp White Oak acorns as a food source and ground the bark into a powder for medicinal purposes. Swamp White Oak wood is highly valued for its strength and durability, making it popular for construction and furniture making.

Dog Toxicity: Swamp White Oak is not considered toxic to dogs. However, ingesting large quantities of acorns may cause gastrointestinal upset, including vomiting and diarrhea. It's essential to monitor your dog and prevent excessive consumption of acorns.

Y ellow Birch

Betula alleghaniensis [Buh-TOO-luh al-uh-ga-nee-EN-sis]

Yellow Birch belongs to the Betulaceae (birch) family and is commonly referred to as the Gray Birch or Swamp Birch. It thrives in the wild, particularly in moist woodlands, swamps, and along streamsides. This majestic tree, recognizable by its distinctive yellowish-brown bark that peels in thin, papery strips, has been a prominent feature of the region's forests for centuries. Native American tribes utilized various parts of the Yellow Birch for medicinal purposes and in crafting tools and containers. European settlers later admired its resilience and versatility, using its wood for furniture, flooring, and even wooden shoes. Today, Yellow Birch remains cherished for its beauty and practicality, valued both ecologically and economically across New England's diverse landscapes.

Identification:

Growth/Size: typically grows tall and straight, reaching heights of up to 80 feet or more. Its growth pattern is characterized by a single trunk with branches reaching outwards.

Bark/Stem/Root: The bark is distinctive, featuring a yellowish or bronze hue with horizontal lenticels. The stems are slender and flexible, while the roots extend deep into the soil, providing stability and nourishment to the tree.

Leaf: The leaves are ovate or elliptical in shape, with serrated edges. They showcase a vibrant green color in the spring and summer, turning into brilliant shades of yellow in the fall. The leaves grow alternately on the branches and can reach lengths of 3 to 5 inches.

FLOWER: In the spring, it produces small, inconspicuous flowers known as catkins. These pendulous flowers feature both male and female reproductive parts and bloom before the leaves fully emerge, adding a subtle charm to the tree.

FRUIT/SEED/NUT: The fruit consists of tiny winged seeds encased in cone-like structures called strobiles. These strobiles mature in late summer to early fall, turning from green to brown. When fully ripe, they release their seeds, ready for dispersal.

Non-toxic Look-a-like(s): Paper Birch (Betula papyrifera) and Sweet Birch (Betula lenta) share similarities in bark and leaf structure with Yellow Birch.

Toxic Look-a-like(s): Poison Ivy (Toxicodendron radicans) and Poison Hemlock (Conium maculatum) resemble Yellow Birch in certain aspects, but they pose significant health risks if ingested.

Cautions: While Yellow Birch is generally safe for foraging, be cautious of potential allergic reactions to the pollen or sap.

Culinary Uses: Yellow Birch sap can be tapped and boiled down to make a delicious syrup. The inner bark can be dried and ground into nutritious flour. Young leaves can be used to flavor teas or salads. The twigs can be infused into syrups or used as a seasoning for meats. The seeds can be roasted and eaten as a snack.

Medicinal Properties: Yellow Birch bark contains betulin, a compound with anti-inflammatory properties. Infusions made from Yellow Birch leaves can aid in digestion and alleviate cold symptoms. Poultices of mashed Yellow Birch leaves can soothe minor skin irritations. Chewing on Yellow Birch twigs can freshen your breath and promote oral health. Yellow Birch tea is believed to have diuretic properties and may support kidney function.

Fun/Historical Fact(s): Native Americans used Yellow Birch bark for making canoes and shelters due to its durability and flexibility. Early European settlers brewed tea from Yellow Birch leaves as a tonic to treat various ailments. The distinctive smell of Yellow Birch bark resembles that of wintergreen, making it a popular choice for flavoring candies and medicines.

Dog Toxicity: Yellow Birch is not toxic to dogs, and no toxic symptoms are associated with its ingestion. However, it's essential to monitor your pet's consumption of any plant material to prevent digestive upset.

PART SIX
MUSHROOMS AND FUNGI

The experience of mushroom foraging can be rewarding and fun. However, it is essential to correctly identify mushrooms before consuming them. Learning how to identify mushrooms by using field guides, taking foraging classes, or observing experienced foragers is critical. You should pay close attention to the cap, stem, and gills' shape, color, and texture. It is also crucial to consider the mushroom's habitat and the plants and trees it grows near.

Many poisonous mushrooms can cause severe illness or even death if ingested. Whenever you are foraging, stay away from mushrooms with white gills. Additionally, many poisonous mushrooms have red pigmentation on their cap or stem.

Whenever possible, be cautious and only consume mushrooms that an expert has positively identified. It would be best never to eat raw mushrooms because some toxic mushrooms can cause severe reactions. It is also important to remember that even though the mushroom is edible, some people will still experience allergic reactions. Therefore, starting small is essential when trying a new mushroom species.

It is generally recommended that dogs not be allowed to eat wild mushrooms, as it can be challenging to identify toxic species, and even a tiny amount of a poisonous mushroom can be harmful to a dog. It is best to err on the side of caution and keep your dog away from wild mushrooms.

American Matsutake

A merican Matsutake

Tricholoma magnivelare [TRIH-KOH-*LOH*-MUH MAG-NUH-VUH-*LAIR*-EE]

A fascinating mushroom found in the lush forests of the New England region of the United States. This unique fungus belongs to the Tricholomataceae family and goes by various names such as Pine Mushroom, American White Matsutake, and Alaskan Golden Chanterelle. American Matsutake thrives in specific habitats within the New England region, particularly in the states of Maine, New Hampshire, Vermont, Massachusetts, Connecticut, and Rhode Island. These mushrooms can be found nestled among coniferous trees, especially pine and spruce forests, where they form symbiotic relationships with the roots of these trees.

Identification:

GROWTH / SIZE: typically grows in clusters or singly, reaching heights of 2 to 6 inches.

CAP: The cap is convex when young, flattening out with maturity, ranging in color from creamy white to light brown. It can grow up to 3 to 6 inches in diameter.

HYMENIUM: The hymenium features crowded gills that are initially white but turn brown as the mushroom matures. They radiate from the stipe and are interconnected.

STIPE: The stipe, or stem, is firm and cylindrical, often slightly curved, and can reach lengths of 2 to 4 inches. Its color varies from white to pale brown.

SPORE PRINT: The spore print is typically white or creamy white, depending on the maturity of the mushroom.

Ecology: It has a distinct spicy and earthy aroma, reminiscent of cinnamon and pine. Its taste is described as robust and savory, making it a sought-after ingredient in culinary dishes. These mushrooms prefer well-drained, acidic soils and are commonly found in late summer to early autumn.

Non-toxic Look-a-like(s): Jack O'Lantern Mushroom and False Chanterelle, both of which share similar orange colors and grow in the same habitat.

Toxic Look-a-like(s): Death Cap Mushroom and Destroying Angel Mushroom, which bear resemblance in color and general appearance but are highly poisonous.

Cautions: When foraging for American Matsutake, it's crucial to accurately identify the mushroom to avoid consuming toxic look-a-likes. Additionally, always harvest from areas free of pesticides and pollutants.

Culinary Uses: Sautéed with garlic and butter for a flavorful side dish. Sliced thinly and added to soups or stews for depth of flavor. Grilled with olive oil and herbs for a smoky appetizer. Pickled to preserve and enhance their unique taste. Used as a topping for pizzas or in risottos for a gourmet touch.

Medicinal Properties: Boosts immune system function. Contains antioxidants that help combat oxidative stress. Supports digestive health and aids in detoxification. Exhibits anti-inflammatory properties, reducing inflammation in the body. May have anti-cancer effects, although further research is needed.

Fun/Historical Fact(s): American Matsutake has a rich cultural significance among Native American tribes, who revered it for its medicinal and culinary properties. In Japanese culture, the Matsutake mushroom is considered a symbol of autumn and is highly prized for its aromatic qualities. During World War II, American soldiers stationed in Japan developed a taste for Matsutake mushrooms, leading to increased demand for them in the United States.

B ear's Head
Hericium americanum [*HUH-RIH-SEE-UM UH-MAIR-UH-KAN-UHM*]

An intriguing mushroom species found in the lush forests of the New England region of the United States. This unique fungus belongs to the Hericiaceae family and goes by various charming names such as Lion's Mane, Hedgehog Mushroom, and Pom Pom Mushroom. You can stumble upon Bear's Head while exploring the forests of New England, particularly in states like Massachusetts, Vermont, New Hampshire, Connecticut, and Maine. These mushrooms can often be found on decaying hardwood trees such as oak and beech.

Identification:

Growth / Size:

CAP: It lacks a traditional mushroom cap. Instead, it has a densely packed mass of downward-hanging, white to cream-colored spines that resemble a shaggy, tooth-like structure or the mane of a lion.

HYMENIUM: The hymenium, or spore-producing surface, is located on the outer surface of the spines. As the mushroom matures, the spines may turn yellowish-brown or grayish.

STIPE: This mushroom typically does not have a well-defined stipe (stem), as the spines grow directly from the tree or substrate.

Spore print: The spore print is white, a crucial identifier distinguishing it from similar species.

Ecology & Season: Bear's Head has a mild, earthy scent and a delicate, slightly sweet taste, making it a sought-after delicacy for foragers and chefs alike. It thrives in cool, moist environments, often appearing in late summer to early fall. Harvesting should be done carefully to preserve the delicate nature of the mushrooms.

Non-toxic Look-a-like(s): The primary look-a-like for Bear's Head Tooth is another edible mushroom called the Comb Tooth (*Hericium coralloides*). The main difference is that the Comb Tooth has more extended, branched spines, while the Bear's Head Tooth has shorter, more compact spines.

Toxic **Look-a-like(s):**

Cautions: It's considered a safe and edible mushroom. However, always exercise caution when foraging mushrooms and consult an expert or a reliable field guide to ensure proper identification.

Culinary Preparation: Bear's Head Tooth has a delicate, seafood-like flavor reminiscent of crab or lobster. It can be sautéed in butter, added to soups, or used as a topping for pasta dishes. The mushroom's tender, meaty texture makes it a delicious and versatile ingredient in various recipes.

Medicinal Properties: Bear's Head Tooth has been used in traditional medicine for its potential anti-inflammatory, antioxidant, and cognitive-enhancing properties. Modern research is exploring its potential benefits for improving memory, supporting nerve regeneration, and promoting overall brain health.

Fun Fact: Bear's Head Tooth has been used in traditional Chinese medicine for centuries to treat various ailments, including stomach issues and ulcers. Today, it continues to be a popular functional food and dietary supplement in many parts of the world.

Candy Cap

Lactarius rubidus [LUH-KTEER-EE-UHS ROO-BAHY-DUHS]

The Candy Cap is a unique mushroom belonging to the family of Russulaceae (brittle gill or milk cap). What sets it apart from other mushrooms is its distinct maple syrup-like aroma when dried. It's also known by other names such as the Curry Milkcap or the Maple Sugar Mushroom. Candy Cap can be found in the dense woodlands of the New England region, particularly in states like Massachusetts, Vermont, and New Hampshire. It thrives in moist environments, often growing near oak and maple trees.

Identification:

GROWTH/SIZE: typically grow in clusters on the forest floor. They are small to medium-sized, with caps ranging from 2 to 5 centimeters in diameter.

CAP: The cap is convex when young, later flattening out with age. It has a distinctive curling edge and ranges in color from pale orange to deep reddish-brown.

HYMENIUM: The hymenium features closely packed gills that radiate from the stem. These gills are cream-colored when young, turning darker as the mushroom matures.

STIPE: The stipe is slender and cylindrical, often tapering towards the base. It shares the same color palette as the cap and can grow up to 8 centimeters tall.

SPORE PRINT: When the cap is placed on a piece of paper overnight, it leaves behind a spore print that is creamy to pale yellow in color.

ECOLOGY & SEASON: Candy Cap mushrooms exude a sweet, maple-like aroma that intensifies when dried. They are primarily found in deciduous forests and are most abundant during the fall months. Foragers and chefs alike highly prize these mushrooms for their unique flavor profile, which adds a touch of sweetness to both savory and dessert dishes.

Non-toxic Look-a-like(s): The False Chanterelle (Hygrophoropsis aurantiaca) and the Velvet Foot (Flammulina velutipes) share similar colors and growth patterns to Candy Cap mushrooms but can be distinguished by careful examination of their gills and spore prints.

Toxic Look-a-like(s): Beware of the Jack O'Lantern mushroom (Omphalotus olearius) and the Deadly Galerina (Galerina marginata), which resemble Candy Caps but are highly poisonous if ingested.

Cautions: When foraging for Candy Cap mushrooms, it's essential to be cautious and confident in your identification skills. Always consult a reliable field guide and, if unsure, seek guidance from experienced foragers.

Culinary Uses: Candy Cap mushrooms can be dried and ground into a flavorful powder, perfect for adding depth to sauces and soups. They can also be thinly sliced and sautéed with butter and herbs for a delicious topping on pasta or pizza. Candy Cap-infused cream makes for a delightful addition to desserts like ice cream and custards. Pickling Candy Cap mushrooms preserves their unique flavor for future culinary adventures. Incorporate them into baked goods such as cookies or muffins for a subtle hint of maple sweetness.

Medicinal Properties: Candy Cap mushrooms are believed to have immune-boosting properties and are often used in traditional herbal medicine. They may help regulate blood sugar levels and support overall metabolic health. Some studies suggest that the compounds found in Candy Caps could have anti-inflammatory effects. Infusions made from Candy Cap mushrooms are thought to promote relaxation and stress relief. When consumed in moderation, Candy Caps may aid in digestion and gut health.

Fun/Historical Fact(s): Native American tribes in the New England region used Candy Cap mushrooms both as a food source and in ceremonial rituals. During the colonial period, early settlers harvested Candy Caps for their unique flavor, often incorporating them into traditional dishes. Candy Cap mushrooms have gained popularity in modern cuisine, with chefs around the world experimenting with creative ways to showcase their sweet and earthy flavor.

Cauliflower

Sparassis crispa [SPAR-ASS-IS KRISS-PUH]

These unique fungi are part of the genus Sparassis and belong to the family Sparassidaceae. But don't let the scientific jargon intimidate you; these mushrooms are commonly known by various charming names like "cauliflower fungus," "sparassis," or simply "cauliflower mushroom." Let's dive into the intriguing story behind this fungal delight. Cauliflower mushrooms can be found flourishing in the damp, forested regions of the New England states, including Maine, Vermont, New Hampshire, Massachusetts, Connecticut, and Rhode Island. They prefer growing near the bases of hardwood trees such as oak, maple, and beech, often hiding amidst leaf litter and mossy patches.

Identification:

GROWTH / SIZE: Cauliflower mushrooms have a distinct growth pattern, appearing like large, fluffy masses resembling cauliflower heads. They can grow up to a foot or more in diameter.

CAP: The caps are intricately ruffled and can range from creamy white to pale yellow. They often have irregular shapes, resembling brain coral, and can grow up to several inches thick.

HYMENIUM: The hymenium is comprised of countless tiny spore-producing structures. They typically have a creamy white to pale yellow color and cover the undersides of the ruffled caps in a maze-like pattern.

Stipe: It has short, stout stipes that connect the caps to the substrate. The stipes are often hidden within the fungus's mass and can vary in color from white to pale yellow.

Spore Print: When mature, it produces a white to pale yellow spore print. This print is obtained by placing the mushroom cap gills or hymenium on a sheet of paper overnight.

Ecology & Season: Cauliflower mushrooms emit a pleasant, earthy fragrance and boast a mild, nutty flavor when cooked. They thrive in moist, cool environments and typically appear in late summer to early fall. Foragers can harvest them by gently detaching them from the base of trees.

Non-toxic Look-a-like(s): Lion's Mane and Bear's Head mushrooms, with their shaggy, white growths, resemble cauliflower mushrooms.

Toxic Look-a-like(s): While not common in New England, some toxic look-a-likes include certain species of Amanita mushrooms, which can resemble the ruffled appearance of cauliflower mushrooms but pose a serious health risk if consumed.

Cautions: As with all foraging endeavors, caution is paramount. Ensure proper identification before consuming any wild mushrooms, as misidentification can lead to serious illness or even death.

Culinary Uses: Sautéed with garlic and butter for a savory side dish. Added to soups and stews for a rich, umami flavor. Breaded and fried for a crispy appetizer. Sliced thin and added to salads for a unique texture. Pickled to preserve their delicate flavor for later use.

Medicinal Properties: Rich in antioxidants, cauliflower mushrooms may support immune health. They contain beta-glucans, which may have anti-inflammatory properties. Due to their fiber content, cauliflower mushrooms may aid in digestion. Some traditional medicine practices suggest they have anti-cancer properties. Used topically, they may help soothe skin irritations and promote healing.

Fun/Historical Fact(s): Cauliflower mushrooms have been prized in Asian cuisines for centuries, particularly in Chinese and Japanese cooking. In some cultures, these mushrooms are believed to possess mystical properties and are used in various spiritual rituals. Due to their unique appearance, cauliflower mushrooms have inspired artists and poets throughout history, appearing in paintings, literature, and even folklore tales.

C innabar Red Chanterelle

Cantharellus cinnabarinus [CAN-THUH-REL-US SIN-UH-BAR-IN-US]

A delightful mushroom found in the lush forests of New England. This unique fungi belongs to the Cantharellaceae family and goes by various names, including Cinnabar Chanterelle and Red Chanterelle. You can stumble upon the Cinnabar Red Chanterelle in the dense woodlands of New England, particularly in states like Maine, Vermont, New Hampshire, Massachusetts, Connecticut, and Rhode Island. Look for it amidst the damp undergrowth of deciduous and coniferous forests.

Identification:

GROWTH/SIZE: These mushrooms typically grow in clusters and can reach sizes ranging from a few centimeters to several inches.

CAP: The cap is vibrant red-orange, with a funnel-like shape and a slightly wavy margin. It can grow up to 5 inches in diameter.

HYMENIUM: The hymenium is smooth and ridged, with a deep orange to yellow coloration. It often exhibits a wrinkled appearance and extends from the cap to the stipe.

STIPE: The stipe is cylindrical, often tapering towards the base. It shares the same coloration as the cap and can range from 2 to 5 inches in height.

SPORE PRINT: When a Cinnabar Red Chanterelle releases its spores, it leaves behind a rusty orange spore print, which aids in its identification.

Ecology & Season: These mushrooms emit a fruity aroma reminiscent of apricots or peaches and boast a mildly peppery taste, making them a delightful addition to various dishes. They thrive in moist, shaded environments, particularly during the autumn months, offering foragers a bountiful harvest season.

Non-toxic Look-a-like(s): The Golden Chanterelle bears a resemblance to the Cinnabar Red Chanterelle, with a similar cap shape and coloration. Another non-toxic look-alike is the Smooth Chanterelle, which shares the same habitat and growth pattern.

Toxic Look-a-like(s): Beware of the Jack-O'-Lantern mushroom, which mimics the appearance of the Cinnabar Red Chanterelle but contains toxins harmful to humans. Additionally, the False Chanterelle may deceive foragers with its similar coloration and habitat.

Cautions: Exercise caution when foraging for Cinnabar Red Chanterelles, as mistaking them for toxic look-alikes can lead to adverse effects. Always consult a knowledgeable guide or expert before consuming wild mushrooms.

Culinary Uses: Sauté them with butter and garlic for a flavorful side dish. Incorporate them into creamy risotto or pasta dishes. Grill them with herbs and olive oil for a savory appetizer. Add them to omelets or frittatas for a gourmet breakfast. Preserve them by pickling or drying them for future culinary adventures.

Medicinal Properties: Cinnabar Red Chanterelles are believed to possess anti-inflammatory properties, aiding in the relief of arthritis and joint pain. They contain antioxidants that may promote overall immune health and combat oxidative stress. Extracts from these mushrooms are utilized in traditional medicine for their potential anti-cancer properties. They are rich in vitamins and minerals, contributing to improved overall wellness. Consuming Cinnabar Red Chanterelles may support digestive health and alleviate gastrointestinal discomfort.

Fun/Historical Fact(s): In European folklore, chanterelles were associated with good luck and prosperity, often considered a symbol of fortune. Ancient civilizations revered mushrooms for their mysterious growth habits and believed they held mystical properties. The Cinnabar Red Chanterelle's vibrant coloration has inspired artists and chefs alike, making it a sought-after delicacy in culinary circles.

Crown-tipped Coral
Artomyces pyxidatus [AHR-TOH-MY-SEES PIHK-SIH-DAY-TUHS]

These vibrant fungi are a fascinating sight in the forests of New England. They belong to the family Clavariaceae and go by various common names like Clavaria, Club Fungus, or Coral Fungus. Coral Mushrooms thrive in the rich forests of New England, particularly in states like Massachusetts, Vermont, and New Hampshire. You can find them nestled among leaf litter and decaying wood, often in shaded areas.

Identification:

GROWTH/SIZE: it displays a branching growth pattern, resembling coral formations, and can vary in size from a few inches to several feet tall.

CAP: Their caps come in an array of colors including white, pink, orange, or yellow. They have a distinctive shape, often resembling fingers or branches, and can range from small to large in size.

HYMENIUM: The hymenium is typically smooth and can be concave, convex, or wavy. It shares the color of the cap and grows in a branching or clustered pattern.

STIPE: The stipe is often slender and cylindrical, sometimes with a slightly thicker base. It shares the color of the cap and can have a smooth or slightly textured surface.

SPORE PRINT: When a Coral Mushroom's cap is placed on a piece of paper, it leaves behind a spore print. Spore prints can vary in color, typically matching the color of the mushroom, and are often white, pink, or yellow.

Ecology & Season: Coral Mushrooms have a mild taste and smell, making them appealing to foragers. They thrive in moist, cool environments and are commonly found in the late summer to early fall. They play a crucial role in forest ecosystems, aiding in the decomposition of organic matter.

Non-toxic Look-a-like(s): Some non-toxic fungi that resemble Coral Mushrooms include Ramaria species and Clavulina species, which also exhibit branching growth patterns and similar colors.

Toxic Look-a-like(s): Toxic look-a-likes include species like the Jack O'Lantern Mushroom (*Omphalotus illudens*) and the Clitocybe species, which may share similar colors but can cause gastrointestinal distress if ingested.

Cautions: When foraging for Coral Mushrooms, it's essential to be cautious of potential look-a-likes and ensure proper identification before consumption. Additionally, always harvest from clean, uncontaminated environments to avoid any risks.

Culinary Uses: Sautéed Coral Mushrooms with garlic and butter make a delightful side dish. Add chopped Coral Mushrooms to omelets or frittatas for a burst of flavor. Incorporate thinly sliced Coral Mushrooms into stir-fries or pasta dishes. Grill whole Coral Mushrooms with olive oil and herbs for a tasty appetizer. Use dried Coral Mushrooms to infuse soups and stews with a rich umami flavor.

Medicinal Properties: Coral Mushrooms contain antioxidants that may help support overall health. They are believed to have anti-inflammatory properties, potentially aiding in pain relief. Some traditional medicine practices suggest Coral Mushrooms for boosting the immune system. Extracts from Coral Mushrooms may have antimicrobial properties, useful in fighting infections. They are also studied for their potential anti-cancer properties, although more research is needed in this area.

Fun/Historical Fact(s): Coral Mushrooms have been admired for centuries for their unique appearance, often featured in artwork and literature. In some cultures, Coral Mushrooms are considered symbols of good luck and prosperity. These fungi have been used in traditional medicine practices around the world for their perceived health benefits.

H edgehog
Hydnum repandum [HI-DNUM REH-PAN-DUM]

A delightful resident of the New England region in the United States! Belonging to the Hydnaceae family, this charming fungus is also known by its common names like sweet tooth mushroom or pied de mouton in French. Let's take a closer look at this enchanting mushroom! Hedgehog Mushrooms can be found scattered across the forest floors of various New England states including Massachusetts, Vermont, New Hampshire, Connecticut, and Maine. They thrive in mixed woodlands, particularly under coniferous trees like pines and firs, and are often spotted during the fall season.

Identification:

GROWTH/SIZE: typically grow individually or in small groups. They usually measure around 2 to 4 inches in diameter.

CAP: The cap is convex to flattened, with a distinctive pale to light brown color. Its surface is covered in small spines or teeth, giving it a hedgehog-like appearance. Caps can vary in size but are generally between 1 to 3 inches wide.

HYMENIUM: The underside of the cap features a maze of spines or teeth that are creamy white to pale yellow in color. These tightly packed structures give the mushroom its unique appearance.

STIPE: The hedgehog mushroom's stipe, or stem, is short and stout, often off-center or eccentrically attached to the cap. It shares the same coloration as the cap and may have a slightly fuzzy texture.

Spore Print: When a mature Hedgehog Mushroom is placed on a piece of paper overnight, it leaves a spore print that is typically white to pale cream in color.

Ecology & Season: Hedgehog Mushrooms have a mildly sweet and nutty taste, making them a popular choice for culinary enthusiasts. They are best harvested during the fall months, usually from September to November, and can be found in both moist and dry forest environments.

Non-toxic Look-a-like(s): The Sweet Tooth Mushroom (Hydnum repandum) and the Bear's Head Mushroom (Hericium americanum) share similar growth patterns and habitats with Hedgehog Mushrooms.

Toxic Look-a-like(s): While not necessarily toxic, the Spiny Puffball (Lycoperdon echinatum) and the Jack-O'-Lantern Mushroom (Omphalotus illudens) resemble Hedgehog Mushrooms and should be avoided due to potential confusion.

Cautions: When foraging for Hedgehog Mushrooms, it's crucial to be mindful of potential look-a-likes and consult with an experienced forager or field guide to ensure accurate identification. Additionally, always avoid consuming mushrooms that you're not completely certain are safe and edible.

Culinary Uses: Sautéed Hedgehog Mushrooms with garlic and herbs make a delightful side dish. Add thinly sliced Hedgehog Mushrooms to risottos or pasta dishes for extra flavor and texture. Grill whole Hedgehog Mushrooms brushed with olive oil and seasonings for a tasty appetizer. Incorporate chopped Hedgehog Mushrooms into omelets or frittatas for a savory breakfast option. Use dried Hedgehog Mushrooms to infuse soups, stocks, and sauces with rich umami flavor.

Medicinal Properties: Hedgehog Mushrooms are believed to possess anti-inflammatory properties and may help alleviate symptoms of arthritis and other inflammatory conditions. Extracts from Hedgehog Mushrooms have shown the potential to boost immune function and support overall health. Some traditional medicine practices suggest Hedgehog Mushrooms as a remedy for digestive issues and stomach ailments. The high fiber content of Hedgehog Mushrooms can promote digestive health and regularity when consumed as part of a balanced diet. Compounds found in Hedgehog Mushrooms may have antioxidant effects, protecting cells from oxidative damage and supporting overall well-being.

Fun/Historical Fact(s): The Hedgehog Mushroom gets its name from the spiny structures on the underside of its cap, which resemble the spines of a hedgehog. In European folklore, Hedgehog Mushrooms were believed to bring good luck and prosperity to those who found them in the wild. Hedgehog Mushrooms have been used in culinary traditions around the world for centuries, prized for their unique flavor and texture.

Lion's Mane

Hericium erinaceus [HUH-RIH-see-UM ER-UH-NAY-see-UHS]

Lion's Mane Mushroom, scientifically known as Hericium erinaceus, goes by various charming names like "bearded tooth mushroom" or "monkey head mushroom." This funky-looking fungus has been popping up in the lush forests of the New England region for ages, delighting foragers and curious minds alike. You can stumble upon Lion's Mane Mushroom while wandering through the wooded areas of New England, particularly in states like Massachusetts, Vermont, and New Hampshire. Look for them nestled on decaying hardwood trees, often in the cooler and damper parts of the forest.

Identification:

GROWTH/SIZE: typically grows in a cascading, pom-pom-like formation, reaching sizes ranging from a few inches to over a foot in diameter.

CAP: The cap is soft and white, resembling a furry ball or a cluster of tiny icicles. It can vary in size but usually ranges from small to medium-sized.

HYMENIUM: Underneath the furry exterior lies a soft, white layer of spines that hang down. They form a somewhat irregular pattern and can be seen as the mushroom matures.

STIPE: Unlike traditional mushrooms, Lion's Mane lacks a distinct stipe or stem. Instead, it appears to be directly attached to the tree, with its spines cascading downward.

Spore Print: When collected and left to print, Lion's Mane Mushroom's spore print is white, matching its overall coloration.

Ecology & Season: Lion's Mane Mushrooms emit a faint seafood-like aroma and boast a delicate, almost lobster-like taste when cooked. They thrive in old-growth forests, especially on decaying hardwood trees like oak and beech. You can usually find them in late summer to early fall, making them a delightful addition to autumn foraging adventures.

Non-toxic Look-a-like(s): Pom Pom Mushroom (Hericium pomponium) and Bear's Head Tooth Mushroom (Hericium americanum) share similar tooth-like structures and grow on trees, but they lack the distinctive furry appearance of Lion's Mane.

Toxic Look-a-like(s): Be cautious of similar-looking fungi like the Shaggy Mane (Coprinus comatus) and the Spiny Puffball (Lycoperdon echinatum), which may bear resemblance but can cause gastrointestinal distress if consumed.

Cautions: While Lion's Mane Mushroom is generally safe to forage, be sure to properly identify it to avoid any potential look-a-like confusion. Always consult with a knowledgeable forager or mycologist if uncertain.

Culinary Uses: Sautéed with butter and garlic, it makes a savory side dish. It can also be added to soups and stews for a rich umami flavor. It can also be grilled or roasted as a meat substitute for vegetarian dishes. It can also be pickled for a tangy and crunchy appetizer. Finally, it can be used as a topping for pizzas or pasta dishes for a gourmet twist.

Medicinal Properties: Supports cognitive function and brain health. Enhances nerve regeneration and may alleviate nerve-related conditions. Boosts the immune system and aids in fighting off infections. May help reduce inflammation and promote digestive health. Exhibits potential anti-cancer properties and supports overall well-being.

Fun/Historical Fact(s): Lion's Mane Mushroom has been revered for centuries in traditional Chinese medicine for its believed cognitive-enhancing and longevity properties. In Japanese culture, it is often referred to as "yamabushitake," which translates to "mountain priest mushroom," associated with wisdom and spiritual enlightenment. Some foragers affectionately call it "the pom-pom of the woods" due to its fluffy appearance, resembling the cheerleading accessory.

R eishi

Ganoderma lucidum [GUH-NO-DER-MUH LOO-SID-UM]

A fascinating fungus found right here in the New England region of the United States. Reishi Mushroom, scientifically known as *Ganoderma lucidum*, goes by several common names like Lingzhi or the "Mushroom of Immortality" due to its long history of use in traditional medicine. Reishi Mushrooms can be found and foraged in specific areas across New England, particularly in wooded areas with hardwood trees. States like Massachusetts, Vermont, and Connecticut consider it native to their regions.

Identification:

GROWTH/SIZE: typically grow in a shelf-like pattern on the sides of hardwood trees, reaching sizes ranging from 8 to 14 inches in diameter.

CAP: The cap is usually reddish-brown with a shiny, lacquered appearance. It's shaped like a fan or kidney, and its size can vary depending on the maturity of the mushroom.

HYMENIUM: The underside of the cap features a porous surface, often whitish to yellowish in color, with a maze-like or pored structure. As the mushroom grows, these pores can become more defined.

STIPE: Reishi mushrooms have a stubby or nonexistent stipe, with the cap directly attached to the substrate. The stipe's color matches the cap, and its texture can be tough and woody.

Spore Print: When a mature Reishi mushroom releases its spores, it leaves behind a rusty brown spore print. The shape of the spores is typically elliptical, and they are microscopic in size.

Ecology & Season: Reishi mushrooms have a unique aroma, often described as slightly woody or earthy. They have a bitter taste and thrive in temperate forests, particularly in areas with rich soil and plenty of moisture. Harvest season for Reishi mushrooms typically spans from late summer to early autumn.

Non-Toxic Look-a-like(s): Turkey Tail (*Trametes versicolor*) and Artist's Conk (*Ganoderma applanatum*) share similar shelf-like growth patterns and can sometimes resemble Reishi mushrooms.

Toxic Look-a-like(s): False Tinder Fungus (*Phellinus igniarius*) and Jack O'Lantern Mushroom (*Omphalotus olearius*) can be mistaken for Reishi mushrooms, but they are toxic and should be avoided.

Cautions: When foraging for Reishi mushrooms, be cautious of potential look-a-likes, especially toxic species. Always double-check your identification before consumption.

Culinary Uses: Reishi mushroom tea: Simmer-dried Reishi slices in hot water for a soothing and earthy tea. Reishi mushroom powder: Grind dried Reishi mushrooms into a fine powder to add to soups, smoothies, or baked goods. Reishi mushroom broth: Boil Reishi slices with other herbs and vegetables to create a flavorful broth for cooking. Reishi mushroom tincture: Prepare a tincture using alcohol and dried Reishi mushrooms for a concentrated medicinal extract. Reishi mushroom stir-fry: Sauté fresh Reishi slices with garlic and vegetables for a nutritious and savory dish.

Medicinal Properties: Reishi mushrooms are believed to boost the immune system and promote overall health. Compounds found in Reishi mushrooms may help reduce inflammation and alleviate symptoms of certain conditions. Consuming Reishi mushrooms may support relaxation and stress reduction. Reishi mushrooms are thought to have detoxifying properties that support liver function. Reishi mushrooms contain antioxidants that can help combat oxidative stress and protect against cellular damage.

Fun/Historical Fact(s): Reishi mushrooms have been revered in traditional Chinese medicine for over 2,000 years for their purported health benefits. Due to their rarity and perceived medicinal properties, they were reserved for royalty and nobility in ancient times. The name "Reishi" translates to "divine" or "spiritual" mushroom in Japanese, highlighting its esteemed status in Asian cultures.

Shaggy Mane

Coprinus comatus [COH-PRIH-NUHS KOH-MAH-TUHS]

This fascinating fungus has quite a story to tell. Known scientifically as Coprinus comatus, it belongs to the family Agaricaceae. But don't let the scientific jargon scare you off – you might also hear it called "Lawyer's Wig" or "Shaggy Ink Cap" due to its unique appearance. You can find the Shaggy Mane Mushroom sprouting up in various locations across the New England region of the United States. Keep an eye out for it in wooded areas, grassy fields, and even along roadsides. It's native to states like Massachusetts, Vermont, New Hampshire, Maine, and Connecticut.

Identification:

GROWTH / SIZE: typically grows in clusters or solitary patches. It can reach heights of 4 to 6 inches.

CAP: The cap is quite distinctive, shaped like a bell or an elongated cylinder. It starts off white and gradually turns grayish-brown as it matures. The cap is covered in shaggy scales, giving it a unique texture.

HYMENIUM: is initially white and turns pinkish-brown as the mushroom matures. It's gilled, with the gills starting off white and eventually turning black and deliquescing (turning to ink) as the mushroom matures.

STIPE: The stipe is tall and slender, often with a slightly bulbous base. It's white and fibrous, with a texture similar to delicate paper.

Spore Print: When you take a spore print of the Shaggy Mane Mushroom, you'll notice it's black in color, forming a distinctive pattern on the paper.

Ecology & Season: The Shaggy Mane Mushroom has a unique ecology. Its mild, earthy smell and taste make it a delightful addition to various dishes. You'll often find it growing in rich soil, especially in the fall months. For optimal flavor, it's best to harvest it when it's young and firm.

Non-toxic Look-a-like(s): The Parasol Mushroom and the Shaggy Parasol have similar appearances to the Shaggy Mane Mushroom, but they lack the ink-like substance that the Shaggy Mane produces.

Toxic Look-a-like(s): Be cautious of the Common Ink Cap and the Magpie Fungus, as they closely resemble the Shaggy Mane Mushroom. However, consuming them can lead to gastrointestinal distress.

Cautions: When foraging for Shaggy Mane Mushrooms, avoid picking specimens that are past their prime. Consuming them after they've started to liquefy can lead to unpleasant digestive issues.

Culinary Uses: Sauté them with garlic and butter for a simple and delicious side dish. Add them to omelets or quiches for a flavorful twist. Incorporate them into pasta dishes for an earthy flavor boost. Grill them and serve as a savory appetizer. Make a creamy mushroom soup for a comforting meal.

Medicinal Properties: Shaggy Mane Mushrooms are believed to have antibacterial properties, aiding in immune system support. They contain compounds that may help regulate blood sugar levels. Some studies suggest they possess anti-inflammatory properties. Consuming Shaggy Mane Mushrooms may contribute to improved digestion. Extracts from these mushrooms have shown the potential to inhibit tumor growth in preliminary research.

Fun/Historical Fact(s): The Shaggy Mane Mushroom earned its nickname "Inky Cap" because its gills dissolve into an inky black substance as it matures. It's believed that Native Americans used Shaggy Mane Mushrooms for both culinary and medicinal purposes. The Mushroom is known for its rapid growth, sometimes appearing overnight after rainfall.

Shiitake

Lentinula edodes [LEN-TIN-YOO-LUH EH-DOE-DEEZ]

Fascinating fungi with a rich history in the New England region of the United States. Belonging to the family Lentinulaceae, these mushrooms have been cherished for centuries for their culinary and medicinal properties. In addition to being called shiitake, they're also known as black forest mushrooms or oakwood mushrooms. Shiitake mushrooms can be found and foraged in specific areas across the New England region, including dense forests, particularly those with oak trees. States where they are native include Massachusetts, Connecticut, Rhode Island, Vermont, New Hampshire, and Maine.

Identification:

GROWTH/SIZE: typically grow in clusters on decaying hardwood logs, reaching sizes ranging from 5 to 10 centimeters in diameter.

CAP: The cap is convex when young, flattening out as it matures. It is usually brown in color with white edges and ranges from 5 to 10 centimeters in diameter.

HYMENIUM: The underside of the cap features closely spaced gills that are creamy white when young, turning a darker color as the mushroom matures. The gills are usually straight and narrow, radiating from the stipe.

STIPE: The stipe is firm and cylindrical, often with a slightly bulbous base. It is white to light brown in color, growing to heights of 5 to 10 centimeters.

Spore Print: When a shiitake mushroom's cap is placed on a piece of paper, it leaves behind a creamy white spore print that reflects the color of the mushroom's gills.

Ecology & Season: Shiitake mushrooms have a distinctive earthy aroma and a savory taste, making them a popular choice in various cuisines. They thrive in moist environments and are typically harvested in the spring and fall seasons. These mushrooms play a crucial role in forest ecosystems, aiding in the decomposition of dead wood.

Non-toxic Look-a-like(s): The maitake mushroom and the oyster mushroom share similar growth patterns and habitats with shiitake mushrooms, but they have distinct differences upon close inspection.

Toxic Look-a-like(s): Deadly galerina and the death cap mushroom bear some resemblance to shiitake mushrooms, but they can be identified by their different cap shapes and colors.

Cautions: When foraging for shiitake mushrooms, it's essential to be cautious and confident in your identification skills. Mistaking them for toxic look-a-likes can lead to severe illness or even death.

Culinary Uses: Shiitake mushrooms can be enjoyed in various culinary creations, including stir-fries, soups, stews, and pasta dishes. They can be sautéed, grilled, roasted, or even dried for later use. Their rich, umami flavor adds depth to vegetarian and meat-based dishes alike.

Medicinal Properties: In traditional medicine, shiitake mushrooms are believed to have immune-boosting properties and are used to support overall health. They contain compounds that may help lower cholesterol, reduce inflammation, and support cardiovascular health. Additionally, shiitake mushrooms are rich in vitamins, minerals, and antioxidants.

Fun/Historical Fact(s): Shiitake mushrooms have been cultivated in East Asia for over a thousand years, prized for their flavor and health benefits. In Japanese folklore, shiitake mushrooms were believed to have medicinal properties and were often given as gifts to promote longevity and good health. Today, shiitake mushrooms are enjoyed worldwide and are a staple ingredient in many international cuisines.

Turkey Tail
Trametes versicolor [TRUH-MEE-TEEZ VUR-SI-KUH-LUR]

This fascinating fungus has quite the story to tell. Belonging to the Polyporaceae family, it goes by many names, including Trametes versicolor or Coriolus versicolor. Its colorful fan-shaped caps resemble the tail feathers of a turkey, hence the name! You can spot Turkey Tail Mushrooms adorning the landscape in various spots across the New England region of the United States. Keep an eye out for them while foraging in wooded areas, particularly in states like Maine, Vermont, New Hampshire, Massachusetts, Rhode Island, and Connecticut, where they are native.

Identification:

GROWTH/SIZE: typically grow in clusters on decaying logs or stumps, reaching sizes of up to 4 inches in diameter.

CAP: Their caps showcase a vibrant array of colors, ranging from shades of brown, tan, white, and even blue or green. They are fan-shaped, with wavy edges, and can vary in size within the cluster.

HYMENIUM: The underside of the cap features a porous surface, often displaying contrasting colors to the cap, with tiny pores where spores are produced.

STIPE: Attached to the substrate, the stipe is tough and fibrous, often dark-colored and branching out irregularly.

Spore Print: When you take a spore print by placing the cap on a piece of paper, you'll notice that the spores are white, creating a characteristic pattern.

Ecology & Season: Turkey Tail Mushrooms exude a mild, earthy aroma and offer a slightly bitter taste. They thrive in moist, forested environments, playing essential roles in decomposition. You can typically find them in the autumn months, though they may persist year-round in suitable conditions.

Non-toxic Look-a-like(s): Some non-toxic look-alikes include the False Turkey Tail (Stereum ostrea) and the Many-zoned Polypore (Coriolus versicolor), which share similar growth patterns and colors.

Toxic Look-a-like(s): Toxic look-alikes include the poisonous Jack O'Lantern Mushroom (Omphalotus illudens) and the deadly Destroying Angel (Amanita bisporigera), which may resemble Turkey Tail Mushrooms in appearance but pose significant health risks.

Cautions: When foraging for Turkey Tail Mushrooms, be cautious of potential confusion with toxic look-alikes. Always consult reliable sources or an experienced forager if you're unsure about identification.

Culinary Uses: Brew as tea for immune support. Grinding into powder for encapsulation. Add to soups or stews for flavor and nutritional benefits. Infuse in alcohol to make tinctures. Incorporate into stir-fries or pasta dishes for added texture.

Medicinal Properties: Boosting the immune system. Supporting digestive health. Providing antioxidant benefits. Assisting in cancer therapy. Alleviating inflammation and allergies.

Fun/Historical Fact(s): Turkey Tail Mushrooms have been used for centuries in traditional Chinese medicine for their health-boosting properties. They have also been extensively studied for their potential role in cancer treatment and prevention. These mushrooms have a rich cultural significance in various indigenous communities, often symbolizing longevity and resilience.

Velvet Foot

Flammulina velutipes [FLAM-YOO-LEE-NUH VEL-OO-TIE-PEEZ]

This delightful fungus, scientifically known as Flammulina velutipes, boasts several common names, including Enoki Mushroom, Velvet Stem, and Golden Needle Mushroom. Venture into the wooded areas of New England, and you might just stumble upon this gem. Native to states like Massachusetts, Vermont, and Maine, the Velvet Foot Mushroom thrives in cool, damp environments like forests and woodlands.

Identification:

GROWTH/SIZE: This mushroom typically grows in clusters on decaying wood, reaching heights of up to 3-7 centimeters.

CAP: the cap ranges from golden to chestnut brown in color. Its smooth surface glistens with moisture, and it can span 2-8 centimeters in diameter.

HYMENIUM: features closely spaced gills that are creamy white to pale yellow in color. They radiate from the stipe and may exhibit a slightly serrated edge.

STIPE: The stipe is slender and velvety in texture, often displaying a yellow-brown hue. It can grow up to 4-9 centimeters tall and is sometimes curved or irregular in shape.

SPORE PRINT: When the cap is placed on a sheet of paper, it leaves behind a spore print that is white to pale yellow in color, helping with identification.

ECOLOGY & SEASON: With a subtle nutty aroma and a mild, earthy taste, the Velvet Foot Mushroom adds a delightful touch to soups, stir-fries, and pasta dishes. It thrives in the colder months, typically appearing from late fall to early spring, making it a cherished find for foragers.

Non-toxic Look-a-like(s): The Enoki Mushroom (Flammulina velutipes var. enoki-take) and the Velvet Shank (Flammulina velutipes var. minor) bear resemblance to the Velvet Foot Mushroom, with similar cap shapes and growth patterns.

Toxic Look-a-like(s): Beware of the deadly Galerina Marginata and the Conocybe filaris, which mimic the appearance of the Velvet Foot Mushroom but can pose serious health risks if consumed.

Cautions: Exercise caution when foraging for mushrooms, as misidentification can lead to illness or poisoning. Always consult a reliable field guide or experienced forager before consuming any wild mushroom.

Culinary Uses: Sautéed with garlic and butter for a savory side dish. Added to creamy soups and stews for a rich flavor. Tossed into stir-fries with vegetables and noodles. Grilled or roasted with herbs and olive oil for a tasty appetizer. Pickled or preserved to enjoy throughout the year.

Medicinal Properties: Boosts immune function and supports overall health. Contains antioxidants that may help combat inflammation. Supports digestive health and may aid in weight management. Rich in vitamins and minerals, contributing to overall well-being. Traditionally used in Eastern medicine to promote longevity and vitality.

Fun/Historical Fact(s): The Velvet Foot Mushroom has been cultivated in Japan for centuries and is a staple in traditional Asian cuisine. In Chinese folklore, this mushroom is associated with good fortune and prosperity, making it a popular ingredient in celebratory dishes. The Enoki Mushroom variety of Flammulina velutipes is often grown commercially and sold fresh or canned in grocery stores worldwide.

PART SEVEN
SEAWEED

B ladderwrack
Fucus vesiculosus [FYOO-KUS VEH-SIK-YOO-LOH-SUS]

Bladderwrack is a fascinating, nutrient-rich seaweed with a name that might make you giggle. A Fucaceae (wrack) family member, Bladderwrack, goes by other names, such as Rockweed, Black Tang, or Sea Oak. It's a shoreline superstar, preferring the colder waters of the North Atlantic. You'll find this seaweed rocking the coastlines of North America and Europe, latched onto rocky shores, and flaunting its distinct appearance.

Identification:

GROWTH/SIZE: It can reach lengths of up to 35 inches and is often found in dense, intertidal clusters.

BLADE: Its blades are flat, branching, and olive-green to brownish in color. The small, gas-filled bladders that help the seaweed float closer to the water's surface set Bladderwrack apart.

STIPE: The stipe is short, branching, and tough, connecting the blades to the holdfast.

HOLDFAST: The holdfast is a root-like structure that securely anchors it to rocks and other surfaces in its marine habitat.

Non-toxic Look-a-like(s): Knotted Wrack (*Ascophyllum nodosum*) is a non-toxic look-a-like, but it has a single, long, branching stipe, unlike Bladderwrack's shorter stipe.

Toxic **Look-a-like(s):**

Cautions: Always harvest it from clean, uncontaminated waters and wash it thoroughly before consuming. Remember that it is high in iodine, which may cause issues for individuals with thyroid problems.

Culinary Preparation: Bladderwrack is a versatile ingredient enjoyed in soups, salads, or seasoning. Dried and ground into a powder adds a unique umami flavor to your dishes.

Medicinal Properties: Bladderwrack has been traditionally used for its high iodine content, which supports thyroid health. Modern research has discovered its potential benefits for weight loss, digestion, and skin health.

Fun/Historical Fact(s): Bladderwrack was the source of iodine, discovered in 1811, and used to treat goiter, a thyroid gland enlargement.

Dog Toxicity: There is no specific toxicity of Bladderwrack for dogs.

Dead Man's Fingers

Codium fragile [KOH-dee-um FRAJ-il]

A unique plant found in the New England region of the United States! This plant belongs to the botanical family Alcyoniaceae and goes by several common names, including Knobbed Whelk, Stubby Rose Coral, and Sponge Coral. Dead Man's Fingers can be found in various locations along the rocky shores of New England, particularly in Maine, New Hampshire, Massachusetts, Rhode Island, and Connecticut. Foragers often discover them nestled within tide pools or attached to rocks just above the waterline.

Identification:

Growth/Size: Dead Man's Fingers typically grow in clusters, forming compact masses ranging from a few inches to several feet in size.

Blade: The blade of Dead Man's Fingers is cylindrical or club-shaped, with a rough texture and a dark brown or blackish color. It can vary in size but is usually around 2 to 6 inches long.

Stipe: The stipe, or stem-like structure, of Dead Man's Fingers is short and stubby, often resembling fingers or knobs. It is usually a similar color to the blade and can be up to several inches long.

Float: Dead Man's Fingers lack a float as they are attached directly to the substrate.

HOLDFAST: The holdfast of Dead Man's Fingers is a flattened, disc-shaped structure that adheres firmly to rocks or other hard surfaces. It is typically dark brown or black and can range from a few inches to several inches in diameter.

Non-toxic Look-a-like(s): Sea fingers (Codium fragile) and Sea lettuce (Ulva lactuca) share a similar appearance to Dead Man's Fingers but are not toxic.

Toxic Look-a-like(s): While not common in the New England region, it's essential to distinguish Dead Man's Fingers from toxic species like Manchineel (Hippomane mancinella) and Deadly Nightshade (Atropa belladonna), which can be harmful if ingested.

Cautions: When foraging for Dead Man's Fingers, be cautious not to mistake them for toxic species. Additionally, avoid harvesting specimens from polluted waters or areas with heavy metal contamination, as they can accumulate toxins.

Culinary Uses: Dead Man's Fingers can be dried and ground into a powder to add flavor to soups and stews. They can be pickled or fermented for a tangy addition to salads or sandwiches. Incorporate chopped Dead Man's Fingers into seafood dishes like chowders or pasta sauces. Use them as a garnish for sushi or seafood platters. Infuse oils or vinegars with Dead Man's Fingers for a unique flavor twist in dressings or marinades.

Medicinal Properties: Dead Man's Fingers have anti-inflammatory properties and can be used topically to soothe skin irritations or sunburn. Infusions or teas made from Dead Man's Fingers may help alleviate digestive issues like bloating or indigestion. Poultices made from mashed Dead Man's Fingers can be applied to bruises or minor wounds to promote healing. The high calcium content in Dead Man's Fingers may support bone health when consumed regularly. Some traditional remedies suggest using Dead Man's Fingers to reduce swelling and pain associated with arthritis.

Fun/Historical Fact(s): Dead Man's Fingers get their name from their resemblance to the decomposed digits of a human hand, adding a spooky allure to their coastal habitats. Native American tribes in the region once used Dead Man's Fingers in ceremonial rituals and as a natural remedy for various ailments. Early European settlers believed Dead Man's Fingers possessed mystical properties and incorporated them into folklore and superstitions surrounding the sea.

Dog Toxicity: Dead Man's Fingers are not known to be toxic to dogs. However, consuming large quantities may cause gastrointestinal upset in pets, such as vomiting or diarrhea. It's best to keep curious canines away from this marine plant.

G ulfweed
Sargassum natans [S*AR*-*GAS*-*UM NUH*-*TANZ*]

Gulfweed, scientifically known as Sargassum, belongs to the Sargassaceae family. It's commonly referred to as "seaweed" or "sargassum." This unique plant has a rich history, often associated with the mysterious Sargasso Sea, where vast mats of it drift. In the New England region, Gulfweed can be found along the coastlines of states like Massachusetts, Rhode Island, Connecticut, New Hampshire, and Maine. It's native to these areas and can be foraged in specific coastal locations.

Identification:

GROWTH / SIZE: Gulfweed typically grows in large floating mats, with individual specimens ranging from a few inches to several feet in length.

BLADE: The blades of Gulfweed are olive-green to golden-brown in color, often with a slightly wrinkled appearance. They are elongated and strap-like, varying in size from small to medium.

STIPE: The stipe, or stem, of Gulfweed is cylindrical and flexible, ranging from yellowish to brown in color. It grows in a branching pattern, supporting the blades.

FLOAT: Gulfweed features distinctive air bladders, known as floats, which are round or oval in shape and filled with gas. They help the plant stay afloat and can range in color from yellowish to golden-brown.

HOLDFAST: The holdfast of Gulfweed is a root-like structure that anchors the plant to rocks or other substrates. It's brownish in color and has a branched or tangled appearance.

Non-toxic Look-a-like(s): include other types of seaweed like bladderwrack and kelp, which share similar growth patterns and habitats.

Toxic Look-a-like(s): include certain species of green algae, which may resemble Gulfweed but should be avoided due to their potential harmful effects.

Cautions: When foraging Gulfweed, be cautious of harvesting from polluted waters or areas with heavy boat traffic, as the plant may absorb contaminants. Additionally, be aware of potential allergic reactions to seaweed.

Culinary Uses: Gulfweed can be used in various culinary preparations, including salads, soups, stir-fries, and sushi rolls. It can also be dried and ground into a powder for seasoning or used as a wrap for seafood dishes.

Medicinal Properties: Medicinally, Gulfweed is believed to have antioxidant, anti-inflammatory, and detoxifying properties. It can be used topically in skincare products or consumed as a dietary supplement to support overall health and wellness.

Fun/Historical Fact(s): Gulfweed played a significant role in maritime history, as it was often encountered by sailors navigating the Atlantic Ocean. The Sargasso Sea, where Gulfweed is abundant, is known as a unique ecosystem and a spawning ground for various marine species. Gulfweed has inspired myths and legends, with some tales describing it as the remnants of lost continents or the hair of mythical sea creatures.

Dog Toxicity: Gulfweed is generally not toxic to dogs. However, consuming large quantities may lead to gastrointestinal upset, such as vomiting or diarrhea. It's advisable to monitor pets and seek veterinary assistance if any adverse symptoms occur.

Irish Moss

Chondrus crispus [KON-DRUS KRIS-PUS]

Irish Moss, scientifically known as Chondrus crispus, is a fascinating marine plant that has been cherished in the New England region for centuries. Also referred to as Carrageen Moss, it belongs to the family Gigartinaceae. Its common names reflect its various uses and historical significance in the area. Irish Moss can be found along the rocky coastlines of New England, particularly in areas such as Maine, Massachusetts, and Rhode Island. It thrives in cool, intertidal zones, clinging to rocks just beneath the water's surface. Native to these regions, it has been a vital part of the coastal ecosystem for generations.

Identification:

GROWTH / SIZE: Irish Moss typically forms dense mats, growing up to 20 centimeters in height.

BLADE: The blade of Irish Moss is thin and membranous, ranging in color from green to reddish-purple. It's often lobed and can reach lengths of 10-20 centimeters.

STIPE: The stipe, or stem-like structure, is cylindrical and may be slightly flattened. It matches the color of the blade and can grow to around 2-10 centimeters in length.

FLOAT: Irish Moss may feature small, balloon-like structures, known as floats, which help it stay buoyant. These floats are typically spherical and vary in size, often matching the color of the blade.

HOLDFAST: The holdfast of Irish Moss is disc-shaped and attaches firmly to rocks. It can range in size from a few centimeters to several inches and is usually brown or reddish-brown in color.

Non-toxic Look-a-like(s): include various species of red algae, such as dulse (Palmaria palmata) and laver (Porphyra spp.), which share similar growth habits and colors.

Toxic Look-a-like(s): include species like Desmarestia spp. and Dictyota spp., which can be mistaken for Irish Moss but may cause adverse effects if consumed.

Cautions: While Irish Moss itself is non-toxic, foragers should be cautious of harvesting from polluted waters or areas with industrial runoff. Additionally, proper identification is crucial to avoid harvesting toxic look-a-likes.

Culinary Uses: Irish Moss is commonly used as a thickening agent in soups and stews. It can be blended into smoothies or juices for added nutritional value. Irish Moss can be simmered and sweetened to create a nutritious gelatin-like dessert. It is often added to baked goods such as bread and cookies for texture and nutrients. Irish Moss can be used to make a traditional Irish drink called "carrageen moss pudding."

Medicinal Properties: Irish Moss is rich in vitamins and minerals, making it a popular remedy for boosting immunity. It is believed to have anti-inflammatory properties and can soothe digestive issues. Irish Moss is often used topically to promote skin health and hydration. It may help alleviate symptoms of respiratory conditions like coughs and bronchitis. Irish Moss has been traditionally used to support thyroid health and regulate metabolism.

Fun/Historical Fact(s): Irish Moss has been harvested for centuries in Ireland and other coastal regions for its culinary and medicinal benefits. During the Irish Potato Famine in the 19th century, Irish Moss became a valuable source of nutrition for many families. The carrageenan extracted from Irish Moss is used as a stabilizer and thickening agent in a variety of commercial products, including dairy alternatives and cosmetics.

Dog Toxicity:

Irish Moss is generally considered safe for dogs in small amounts. However, consuming large quantities may lead to gastrointestinal upset, including vomiting and diarrhea. It's best to avoid allowing dogs to ingest large amounts of Irish Moss. If symptoms persist or worsen, veterinary attention should be sought.

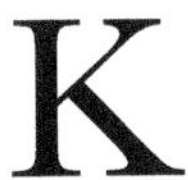# Knotted Wrack

Ascophyllum nodosum [UH-SKOH-FIL-UHM NOH-DOH-SUM]

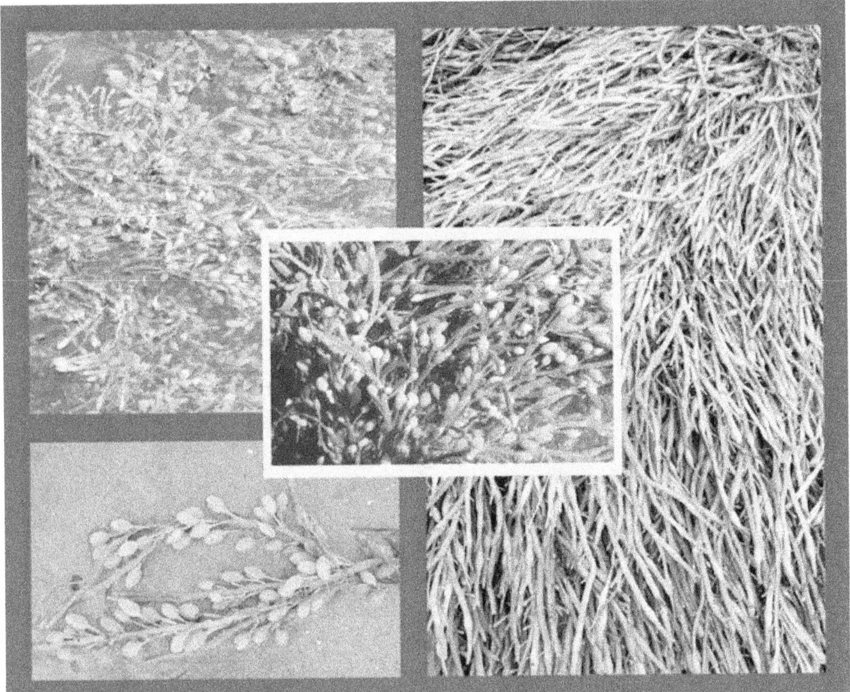

Knotted Wrack, known scientifically as Ascophyllum nodosum, is a fascinating plant that has long been part of the coastal ecosystem in New England. This seaweed, also commonly referred to as egg wrack or rockweed, belongs to the Fucaceae family. Its history intertwines with the coastal communities, where it has been harvested for various purposes for centuries. Knotted Wrack can be found along the rocky shores and intertidal zones of the New England region, thriving in the cold waters of the Atlantic Ocean. Specific areas where it can be foraged include the coasts of Maine, New Hampshire, Massachusetts, Rhode Island, and Connecticut. It is considered native to all these states.

Identification:

GROWTH/SIZE: Knotted Wrack exhibits a robust growth pattern, forming dense clusters along the rocky substrate. It can reach lengths of up to several feet, depending on environmental conditions.

BLADE: The blade of Knotted Wrack is typically olive-green to brown in color, with a broad and strap-like shape. It can grow up to several inches wide and is often intricately divided, giving it a distinctive appearance.

STIPE: The stipe, or stem-like structure, of Knotted Wrack is sturdy and cylindrical, ranging in color from light brown to dark olive-green. It grows upright from the substrate, with occasional branching, and can vary in length.

FLOAT: Knotted Wrack features air bladders, or floats, along the length of the stipe. These floats are usually spherical to elliptical in shape, with a smooth surface, and are filled with gases to provide buoyancy. They are typically brown or yellowish-brown in color and aid in keeping the seaweed afloat.

HOLDFAST: The holdfast of Knotted Wrack serves to anchor the seaweed to rocks or other substrates. It is disc-shaped, with a rough texture, and can vary in size depending on the age and size of the plant. The color may range from light brown to dark.

Non-toxic Look-a-like(s): Bladder wrack (Fucus vesiculosus) and Channelled wrack (Pelvetia canaliculata) share similarities with Knotted Wrack in terms of appearance, but they are non-toxic and safe for consumption.

Toxic Look-a-like(s): Sargassum weed and Dead Man's Fingers (Codium fragile) are toxic look-a-like plants. They resemble Knotted Wrack in appearance but should be avoided due to their toxicity.

Cautions: When foraging for Knotted Wrack, it's essential to ensure the water quality of the harvesting area and avoid polluted or contaminated sites. Additionally, be mindful of local regulations regarding seaweed collection to maintain sustainable practices.

Culinary Uses: Salads: Fresh Knotted Wrack can be rinsed and added to salads for a nutritious boost. **Soup Base:** Boil Knotted Wrack to create a flavorful broth for soups and stews. **Seasoning:** Dried and powdered Knotted Wrack can be used as a seasoning for various dishes. **Smoothies:** Blend Knotted Wrack into smoothies for added minerals and vitamins. **Wraps:** Use blanched Knotted Wrack leaves as a healthy alternative to traditional wraps.

Medicinal Properties: Rich in Iodine: Knotted Wrack is a natural source of iodine, which supports thyroid health. **Antioxidant:** It contains antioxidants that may help reduce inflammation and oxidative stress. **Detoxifying:** Consuming Knotted Wrack may aid in detoxifying the body by eliminating heavy metals. **Skin Health:** Topical applications of Knotted Wrack extracts may promote skin hydration and healing. **Digestive Aid:** It is believed to have prebiotic properties, supporting gut health and digestion.

Fun/Historical Fact(s): Sailors in the past used Knotted Wrack as a remedy for scurvy due to its high vitamin C content. Native American tribes along the New England coast utilized Knotted Wrack for various medicinal and culinary purposes. Knotted Wrack plays a crucial role in coastal ecosystems, providing habitat and food for numerous marine organisms.

Dog toxicity: Knotted Wrack is not known to be toxic to dogs. However, ingestion of large quantities may lead to gastrointestinal upset, so it's best to monitor your pet's consumption. If any unusual symptoms occur, consult a veterinarian promptly.

Nori
Porphyra tenera [PY-ROH-PEE-UH TEH-NAIR-UH]

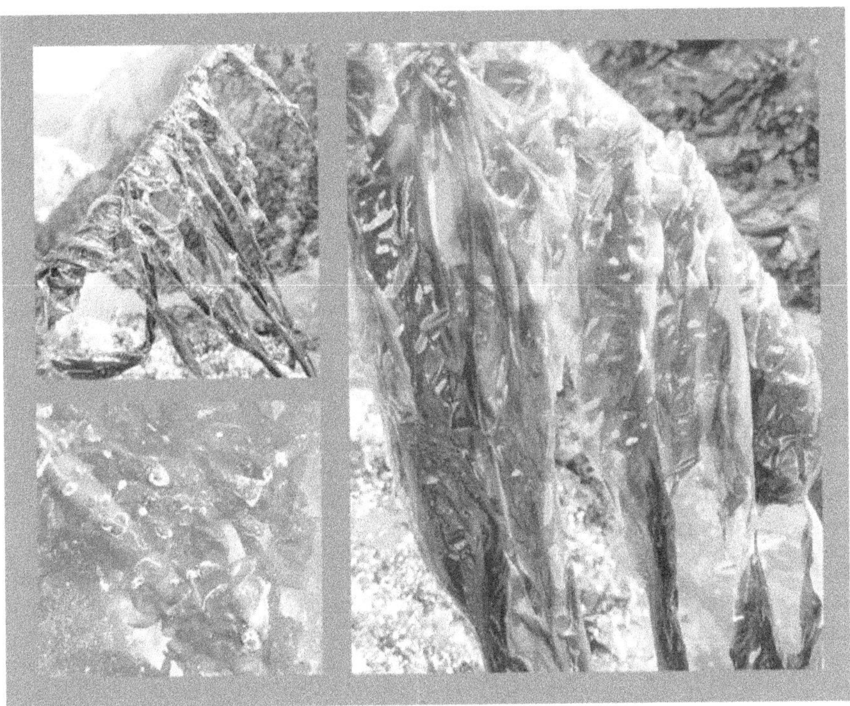

Nori belongs to the red algae family, scientifically known as *Porphyra* and commonly referred to as laver. This nutrient-packed marine plant has been a part of Asian cuisine for centuries and has recently gained popularity in Western dishes. Nori thrives along the rocky shores and tidal pools of New England, particularly in Maine, Massachusetts, and Rhode Island. You can often find it clinging to rocks during low tide, waiting to be harvested by adventurous foragers.

Identification

GROWTH/SIZE: Nori typically grows in thin, delicate sheets that can range from a few inches to several feet in length.

BLADE: The blade of Nori is flat and ribbon-like, with a dark green to reddish-brown coloration. It can vary in size but is generally smooth and slightly translucent.

STIPE: Attached to the blade, the stipe of Nori is small and often goes unnoticed. It is thin, cylindrical, and matches the color of the blade.

FLOAT: Nori lacks a distinct float structure as it grows directly attached to rocks.

HOLDFAST: Nori anchors itself to rocks with a small holdfast, which resembles a disc-shaped structure. It is typically brownish in color and can vary in size.

Non-toxic Look-a-like(s): Sea lettuce (*Ulva lactuca*) and Dulse (*Palmaria palmata*) share a similar appearance to Nori but are safe for consumption.

Toxic Look-a-like(s): Avoid confusing Nori with toxic species like Dead Man's Fingers (*Codium fragile*) and Green Fleece (*Caulerpa taxifolia*), which can cause digestive issues if ingested.

Cautions: When foraging Nori, be cautious of pollution in coastal waters, as contaminated seaweed can be harmful if consumed.

Culinary Uses: Nori can be dried and roasted to make crispy seaweed snacks. It's a popular ingredient in sushi rolls, providing a unique umami flavor. Use Nori as a wrap for rice balls or sandwiches. Add shredded Nori to soups or stews for added depth of flavor. Blend Nori into a seasoning mix to sprinkle over salads or roasted vegetables.

Medicinal Properties: Nori is rich in vitamins, minerals, and antioxidants, supporting overall health. It may help regulate thyroid function due to its iodine content. Consuming Nori regularly can aid in digestion and promote gut health. Some studies suggest that Nori may have anti-inflammatory properties. Applied topically, Nori extract can hydrate and nourish the skin.

Fun/Historical Fact(s): Nori has been cultivated in Japan for over 300 years and was originally harvested from natural coastal habitats. In ancient China, Nori was prized for its medicinal properties and was believed to promote longevity. Nori production in New England has increased in recent years, as chefs and home cooks alike discover its versatility in Western cuisine.

Dog Toxicity: Nori is not toxic to dogs. However, consuming large quantities may cause gastrointestinal upset, such as vomiting or diarrhea. It's best to limit your furry friend's consumption to avoid any discomfort.

Oarweed

Laminaria digitata [LAH-MUH-*NAIR*-EE-UH DIH-JIH-*TAH*-TUH]

Oarweed is a captivating brown seaweed in the Laminariaceae (kelp) family. This nautical gem has a few other names, such as Tangleweed, Fingered Tangle, and Sea Girdles, which perfectly capture its maritime charm. Oarweed can be found abundantly along the rocky shores of New England, particularly in coastal areas of Maine, Massachusetts, New Hampshire, Rhode Island, and Connecticut. It is native to these states and is commonly foraged by locals.

Identification:

GROWTH/SIZE: Oarweed typically grows in dense patches and can reach lengths of up to several feet.

BLADE: Its blade is large, broad, and ribbon-like, with a deep olive-green color. It can grow up to 6 feet in length and is intricately divided into segments.

STIPE: The stipe, or stem-like structure, is sturdy and flexible, with a golden-brown hue. It can grow quite long and features a slightly ribbed texture.

FLOAT: Oarweed possesses small, round floats called pneumatocysts, which help it stay buoyant. These floats are usually light brown or yellowish and are attached along the length of the blade.

HOLDFAST: The holdfast is the root-like structure that anchors the seaweed to rocks or other substrates. It is disc-shaped and dark brown in color, firmly securing the plant in place.

Non-toxic Look-a-like(s): Sugar kelp (*Saccharina latissima*) and bladderwrack (*Fucus vesiculosus*) share similar appearances to oarweed, with long, ribbon-like blades and similar colors.

Toxic Look-a-like(s): While there are no toxic look-a-likes that closely resemble oarweed, caution should be taken to distinguish it from potentially harmful species such as wireweed (*Sargassum muticum*) and dead man's fingers (*Codium fragile*).

Cautions: When foraging for oarweed, it's essential to avoid areas with pollution or contamination, as seaweed can absorb toxins from its environment. Additionally, ensure proper identification to avoid harvesting toxic look-a-like species.

Culinary Uses: Rinse and dry the blades to use as a nutritious addition to salads. Boil or steam the blades and serve as a side dish seasoned with herbs and spices. Incorporate chopped oarweed into soups, stews, or chowders for added flavor and texture. Blend dried oarweed into powder and use as a seasoning or thickening agent in cooking. Fry small pieces of oarweed to make crispy seaweed snacks.

Medicinal Properties: Rich in vitamins and minerals, it supports overall health and wellbeing. Its high iodine content promotes thyroid function and hormone regulation. The mucilage found in oarweed can soothe digestive issues such as inflammation and irritation. Applied topically, oarweed extracts may help alleviate skin conditions like eczema and psoriasis. Some studies suggest that oarweed may have antioxidant and anti-inflammatory properties, offering potential health benefits.

Fun/Historical Fact(s): Native American tribes along the New England coast historically used oarweed for various purposes, including food, medicine, and fertilizer. In the 19th century, oarweed harvesting became an important industry in coastal communities, providing employment and valuable resources. Oarweed is a vital habitat for diverse marine life, including fish, crustaceans, and mollusks, contributing to the rich biodiversity of coastal ecosystems.

Dog toxicity: Oarweed is not toxic to dogs, and there are no reported toxic symptoms associated with its consumption. However, it's essential to ensure that dogs don't consume large quantities of seaweed, as it may cause gastrointestinal discomfort due to its high fiber content. As with any new food, moderation is key when introducing oarweed to your pet's diet.

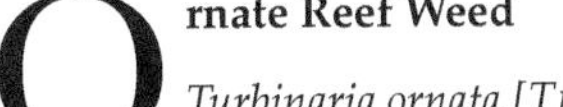

Ornate Reef Weed

Turbinaria ornata [Tur-bin-AIR-ee-uh or-NAH-tuh]

This fascinating aquatic plant is a beloved resident of the New England region in the United States. Commonly referred to as "Ornate Reef Weed," this plant has quite a rich history in the coastal ecosystems of the area. Ornate Reef Weed can be found in abundance along the rocky coastlines and shallow waters of New England. Specifically, it thrives in areas with moderate water movement and ample sunlight. States such as Maine, New Hampshire, Massachusetts, Rhode Island, and Connecticut boast the native presence of this remarkable seaweed.

Identification:

GROWTH/SIZE: Ornate Reef Weed typically grows in dense clusters, forming intricate underwater forests. It can reach lengths of up to two feet, providing essential habitat and food for various marine creatures.

BLADE: The blades of Ornate Reef Weed are beautifully intricate, with a delicate reddish-brown hue. They are ribbon-like in shape, ranging from 2 to 4 inches in width and adorned with intricate patterns.

STIPE: Attached to the blades, the stipe of Ornate Reef Weed is slender and flexible. It showcases a similar reddish-brown coloration, growing in a graceful, swaying manner. Stipes can reach lengths of up to one foot.

FLOAT: This seaweed lacks distinct air bladders or floats. Instead, it relies on its buoyant structure and the surrounding water for support.

HOLDFAST: Anchoring itself to rocky substrates, the holdfast of Ornate Reef Weed is small and disc-shaped. Its coloration matches that of the stipe and blade, providing a seamless integration into its coastal habitat.

Non-toxic Look-a-like(s): Bladder Wrack (*Fucus vesiculosus*): Similar in appearance, with ribbon-like blades, but lacks the intricate patterns of Ornate Reef Weed. Irish Moss (*Chondrus crispus*): Another red seaweed commonly found in the region, but its blade structure differs from that of Ornate Reef Weed.

Toxic Look-a-like(s): Devil's Fingers (*Clathrus archeri*): Not a seaweed but a fungus, this organism shares the name "fingers" but is vastly different in appearance and habitat.

Cautions: While Ornate Reef Weed is generally safe for foraging and consumption, it's crucial to avoid areas with potential pollution or contaminants. Always gather seaweed from clean, unpolluted waters, and be mindful of local regulations regarding harvesting.

Culinary Uses: Rinse and chop Ornate Reef Weed for a nutritious addition to salads, adding a unique texture and flavor. Simmer the seaweed in broths or stews to infuse them with its savory essence. Incorporate thinly sliced Ornate Reef Weed into sushi rolls for an authentic touch of the ocean. Blend fresh seaweed into fruit or vegetable smoothies for a boost of vitamins and minerals. Preserve Ornate Reef Weed by pickling it with vinegar, spices, and herbs for a tangy treat.

Medicinal Properties: Ornate Reef Weed is a valuable source of essential minerals like iodine, calcium, and magnesium, supporting overall health. Consuming this seaweed may help promote healthy digestion and alleviate gastrointestinal discomfort. Applied topically or ingested, Ornate Reef Weed may contribute to skin health, thanks to its abundance of antioxidants and vitamins. The iodine content in Ornate Reef Weed can benefit thyroid function and hormone regulation. Preliminary research suggests that compounds found in this seaweed may possess anti-inflammatory properties, potentially aiding in the management of inflammatory conditions.

Fun/Historical Fact(s): Native American tribes along the New England coast have long revered Ornate Reef Weed for its nutritional and medicinal benefits, incorporating it into various traditional dishes and remedies. Early European settlers in the region also utilized this seaweed, often referring to it as "sea lettuce," for its resemblance to terrestrial lettuce varieties. Ornate Reef Weed plays a vital role in the coastal ecosystem, providing habitat and food for a diverse array of marine life, including fish, crustaceans, and mollusks.

Dog Toxicity: Ornate Reef Weed is generally not considered toxic to dogs. However, excessive consumption may lead to gastrointestinal upset, such as vomiting or diarrhea. It's best to monitor your pet's intake and consult a veterinarian if any concerning symptoms arise.

S ea Belt
Laminaria saccharina [*SUH-KAR-EE-NUH LUH-TIS-UH-MUH*]

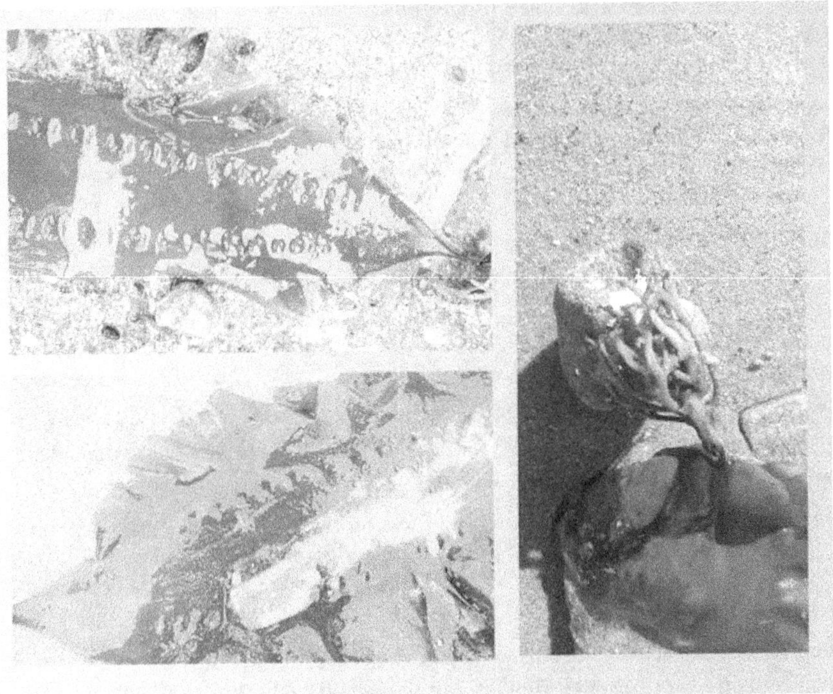

A coastal treasure found in the New England region of the United States. This unique plant has quite a history! Belonging to the botanical family Fucaceae, Sea Belt goes by several common names, including Rockweed, Bladderwrack, and Kelp. Sea Belt can be found and foraged along the rocky coastlines of New England, particularly in areas with cool, nutrient-rich waters. States such as Maine, New Hampshire, Massachusetts, Rhode Island, and Connecticut boast Sea Belt as a native species.

Identification:

Growth/Size: Sea Belt exhibits a robust growth pattern, often forming dense colonies along rocky shores. It can reach lengths of several feet, depending on environmental conditions.

Blade: The blade of Sea Belt is typically olive-green to brown in color, with a distinctive strap-like shape. It can grow to be quite large, sometimes reaching over a foot in length. The blade is smooth and leathery to the touch.

Stipe: The stipe, or stem-like structure, of Sea Belt is usually brown and somewhat flattened. It grows in a branching pattern, with smaller blades attached along its length. The size of the stipe varies but can reach several inches in diameter.

Float: Sea Belt often features gas-filled bladders, or floats, which help it stay buoyant and close to the water's surface. These floats are round or oval-shaped and may be olive-green or yellowish-brown in color. They can range in size from small peas to marbles.

HOLDFAST: The holdfast of Sea Belt is a root-like structure that anchors the plant to rocks or other substrates. It is typically brown and can be quite intricate in shape, forming a secure attachment to the substrate. The size of the holdfast varies but is generally proportional to the size of the plant.

Non-toxic Look-a-like(s): Rockweed (Ascophyllum nodosum): Similar in appearance to Sea Belt, with olive-green blades and brown stipes. Irish Moss (Chondrus crispus): Another seaweed with a similar growth pattern and coloration, but with smaller, more delicate blades.

Toxic Look-a-like(s): Sargassum: Resembles Sea Belt in color and shape but can be toxic if ingested, causing gastrointestinal upset.

Cautions: When foraging Sea Belt, be cautious of potential contamination from pollutants in coastal waters. Additionally, avoid harvesting from areas with heavy boat traffic or industrial pollution.

Culinary Uses: Seaweed salad with sesame dressing. Sea Belt chips, roasted with olive oil and sea salt. Sea Belt broth for soups and stews. Blanched Sea Belt as a side dish with seafood. Sea Belt wraps for sushi or sandwiches.

Medicinal Properties: Supports thyroid function due to its iodine content. Improves digestion and gut health. Boosts immune function with its high vitamin C content. Promotes healthy skin and hair. May aid in weight management by promoting feelings of fullness.

Fun/Historical Fact(s): Native American tribes along the New England coast used Sea Belt for various purposes, including as a food source and medicinal remedy. During the Irish Potato Famine in the 19th century, Sea Belt was harvested and used as a supplement to alleviate food shortages. Sea Belt plays a crucial role in coastal ecosystems, providing habitat and food for various marine species.

Dog toxicity: Sea Belt is generally not toxic to dogs in small amounts. However, consuming large quantities may cause gastrointestinal upset, including vomiting and diarrhea. It's best to keep pets away from Sea Belt to avoid any potential digestive issues. If ingestion occurs, monitor your dog closely and consult a veterinarian if symptoms persist or worsen.

# Sea Colander

Scytosiphon lomentaria [UH-GAIR-UHM KRIH-BROH-SUHM]

Sea Colander is a part of the Phaeophyceae (brown algae) family. Also known as Agarum, this lovely seaweed flaunts a unique net-like structure, making it the darling of the underwater world. Sea colander can be found along the rocky shores and intertidal zones of the New England coast, particularly in Maine, Massachusetts, New Hampshire, Rhode Island, and Connecticut. These states consider it native to their coastal areas.

Identification:

GROWTH/SIZE: Sea colander typically grows in dense patches attached to rocks. It can reach lengths of up to 6 feet and spreads out horizontally in a fan-like manner.

BLADE: The blade of sea colander is broad and deeply lobed, resembling a colander or sieve. It is typically brownish in color, with a leathery texture. Blades can grow up to 2 feet long and are sturdy enough to withstand the force of ocean waves.

STIPE: The stipe, or stem-like structure, of sea colander is thick and cylindrical. It attaches firmly to rocks and can grow up to 1 foot in length. The color varies from brown to olive green, and its surface may have small bumps or ridges.

FLOAT: Sea colander doesn't have a float as it stays anchored to rocks.

HOLDFAST: The holdfast of sea colander is a root-like structure that anchors the plant to rocky substrates. It is typically disc-shaped, with numerous branching extensions that grip onto rocks tightly. The holdfast is brownish in color and can be several inches in diameter.

Non-toxic Look-a-like(s): Bladder wrack (*Fucus vesiculosus*) and rockweed (*Ascophyllum nodosum*) resemble sea colander in appearance but are not toxic. They also have broad blades and attach to rocks along the shoreline.

Toxic Look-a-like(s): While not common along the New England coast, certain species of red algae such as *Heterosiphonia crispella* and *Polysiphonia spp.* can resemble sea colander. However, they may contain toxins harmful to humans if ingested.

Cautions: When foraging for sea colander, be cautious of harvesting from polluted waters or areas with industrial runoff, as it may contain contaminants harmful to health.

Culinary Uses: Rinse sea colander thoroughly to remove excess salt. Use it fresh in salads for a salty, oceanic flavor. Dry sea colander and grind it into powder to use as a seasoning. Add chopped sea colander to soups or stews for a rich umami taste. Incorporate sea colander into seafood dishes like sushi rolls or seafood pasta.

Medicinal Properties: Sea colander is rich in iodine, which supports thyroid function. It contains antioxidants that help reduce inflammation. Sea colander is a good source of vitamins and minerals, including vitamin K and calcium, which promote bone health. It may have antibacterial properties beneficial for oral health. Consuming sea colander may aid digestion due to its high fiber content.

Fun/Historical Fact(s): Native American tribes along the New England coast used sea colander for food and medicinal purposes. In the 19th century, sea colander was harvested commercially for its alginate content, which was used in various industrial processes. Sea colander plays a vital role in coastal ecosystems, providing habitat and food for marine organisms.

Dog Toxicity: Sea colander is not known to be toxic to dogs. However, ingestion of large amounts may cause gastrointestinal upset, including vomiting and diarrhea. It's best to prevent dogs from consuming large quantities of sea colander to avoid any potential digestive issues. If your dog shows symptoms of illness after consuming sea colander, consult a veterinarian promptly.

Sea Comb

Plocamium cartilagineum [PLO-KAY-MEE-UM KAR-TI-LAJ-IN-EE-UM]

A fascinating plant found along the coastal regions of New England! This unique marine species, scientifically known as *Ascophyllum nodosum*, goes by various common names including rockweed, knotted wrack, and Norwegian kelp. Let's dive into its story and discover more about this coastal gem. Sea Comb thrives in the rocky intertidal zones of the New England coast, making its home along the shores of Maine, New Hampshire, Massachusetts, Rhode Island, and Connecticut. Foragers can often find it clinging to rocks or floating in shallow waters during low tide.

Identification:

GROWTH/SIZE: Sea Comb typically grows in dense patches and can reach lengths of up to six feet.

BLADE: Its blades are olive-brown in color, with a distinctive strap-like shape and irregular edges. They can vary in size but are generally broad and flat, providing ample surface area for photosynthesis.

STIPE: The stipe, or stem-like structure, is sturdy and flexible, branching out irregularly. It is also brownish in color, often with small air bladders that help the plant float.

FLOAT: Sea Comb's floats, or air bladders, are round to oval-shaped, filled with gas to aid buoyancy. They are typically brown or yellowish-brown in color and can vary in size depending on the plant's age and environmental conditions.

HoldFast: The holdfast is the root-like structure that anchors Sea Comb to rocks or other substrates. It is tough and fibrous, often branching out to securely grip onto surfaces. Its color ranges from dark brown to black.

Non-toxic Look-a-like(s): Bladderwrack (*Fucus vesiculosus*) and Irish moss (*Chondrus crispus*) share similar habitats and physical characteristics with Sea Comb but are non-toxic.

Toxic Look-a-like(s): Dead Man's Fingers (*Codium fragile*) and Green Algae (*Ulva spp.*) can resemble Sea Comb but are toxic if ingested.

Cautions: When foraging for Sea Comb, be cautious of possible contamination from polluted waters, and avoid areas near industrial sites or heavy boat traffic.

Culinary Uses: Rinse fresh Sea Comb thoroughly to remove any debris. Steam or blanch the blades for a few minutes until tender. Add to salads for a nutritious boost. Incorporate into soups or stews for a hint of oceanic flavor. Dry and grind Sea Comb into a powder to use as a seasoning or thickening agent.

Medicinal Properties: Rich in iodine, Sea Comb may support thyroid health. Contains antioxidants that help combat inflammation. May aid digestion and promote gut health. Applied topically, Sea Comb extracts may help soothe skin irritations. Provides essential minerals like calcium and magnesium for overall wellness.

Fun/Historical Fact(s): Native Americans utilized Sea Comb for various purposes, including as fertilizer and as a food source. In the 18th century, coastal communities in New England used Sea Comb as insulation in their homes. Sea Comb plays a vital role in coastal ecosystems, providing habitat and food for numerous marine species.

Dog toxicity: Sea Comb is not known to be toxic to dogs. However, excessive ingestion may cause gastrointestinal upset. Monitor your pet's consumption and consult a veterinarian if any unusual symptoms occur.

S ea Lettuce
Ulva lactuca [UL-vuh lak-TOO-kuh]

Sea Lettuce is a vibrant marine algae found along the shores of the New England region in the United States. This sea vegetable has a rich history, being used by coastal communities for centuries. Its common names include Green Laver, Green Seaweed, and Atlantic Lettuce. Sea Lettuce thrives in the rocky intertidal zones of New England's coastline, particularly along the shores of Maine, New Hampshire, Massachusetts, Rhode Island, and Connecticut. It can be foraged during low tide from exposed rocks and tidal pools.

Identification:

GROWTH / SIZE: Sea Lettuce typically grows in thin, sheet-like structures that can range from a few inches to several feet in size.

BLADE: The blades of Sea Lettuce are bright green, translucent, and thin, resembling lettuce leaves. They can vary in shape from round to oval and can grow up to a few inches wide.

STIPE: Sea Lettuce lacks a true stipe; instead, it attaches to rocks or other substrates with a holdfast. However, its attachment structure is usually small and inconspicuous.

FLOAT: Sea Lettuce does not have float structures.

HOLDFAST: The holdfast of Sea Lettuce is small and disc shaped, often blending in with the substrate. It anchors the algae to rocks or other surfaces.

Non-toxic Look-a-like(s): Green Algae: Some non-toxic green algae species can resemble Sea Lettuce, but they lack its distinctive lettuce-like appearance. **Bladder Wrack:** While not closely resembling Sea Lettuce, bladder wrack is another common seaweed found in the same habitats.

Toxic Look-a-like(s): Green Hair Algae: This algae, while resembling Sea Lettuce in color, has a finer texture and different growth pattern.

Cautions: When foraging Sea Lettuce, be cautious of contamination from polluted waters, which can make the algae unsafe for consumption. Additionally, ensure proper identification to avoid harvesting toxic look-a-like species.

Culinary Uses: Rinse Sea Lettuce thoroughly and toss it into salads for a fresh oceanic flavor. Wrap sushi rolls with Sea Lettuce for added texture and taste. Use Sea Lettuce as a garnish for seafood soups and chowders. Add chopped Sea Lettuce to stir-fries for a nutritious boost. Incorporate Sea Lettuce into seafood dishes for a complementary taste.

Medicinal Properties: Sea Lettuce is packed with essential minerals like iron, calcium, and iodine. Consuming Sea Lettuce may support healthy digestion due to its fiber content. Some traditional medicine practices suggest Sea Lettuce for its potential detoxifying properties. Applied topically, Sea Lettuce may help soothe minor skin irritations. Sea Lettuce can serve as a natural supplement to boost overall nutrient intake.

Fun/Historical Fact(s): Sailors in the past consumed Sea Lettuce to prevent scurvy due to its high vitamin C content. Native American tribes along the New England coast have used Sea Lettuce as both food and medicine for generations. Sea Lettuce plays a vital role in marine ecosystems, providing habitat and food for various sea creatures.

Dog Toxicity: Sea Lettuce is not known to be toxic to dogs. However, consumption in large quantities may cause gastrointestinal upset, so it's best to monitor your pet's intake if they encounter it while near the shore. If you notice any unusual symptoms in your dog after ingestion, consult with a veterinarian promptly.

PART EIGHT
POISONOUS

B ulbous Buttercup

Ranunculus bulbosus [RUH-NUN-KYUH-LUS BUL-BOH-SUS]

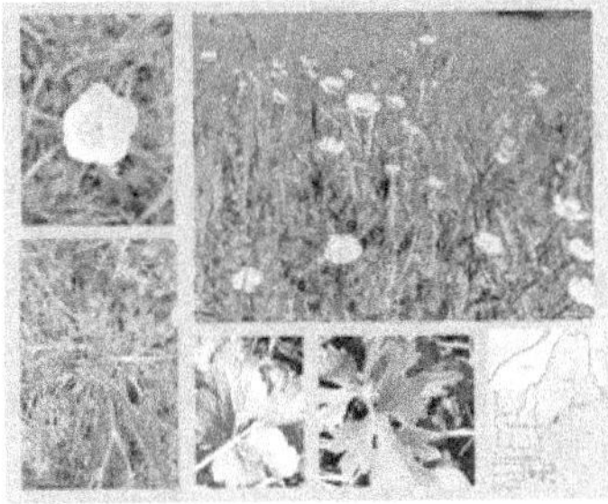

Bulbous Buttercup, scientifically known as Ranunculus bulbosus, is a common poisonous plant found in the New England region of the United States. This perennial herbaceous plant is characterized by its bright yellow flowers and deeply lobed, shiny green leaves. It typically grows in fields, meadows, and along roadsides, often thriving in moist soils during the spring and early summer months.

Despite its charming appearance, the Bulbous Buttercup contains toxic compounds known as protoanemonin glycosides throughout its foliage, stems, and bulbs. When ingested by humans or animals, these compounds can cause a range of toxic effects. Symptoms of toxicity may include severe gastrointestinal irritation, such as abdominal pain, nausea, vomiting, and diarrhea. In more severe cases, ingestion of Bulbous Buttercup can lead to oral ulcers, excessive salivation, and even paralysis if consumed in large quantities. Due to its toxicity, it's crucial to avoid handling or consuming any part of the Bulbous Buttercup plant and to keep grazing animals away from areas where it grows abundantly. If ingestion occurs, immediate medical attention should be sought to mitigate potential health risks.

White Baneberry

Actaea pachypoda [AK-TEE-UH PUH-KIP-UH-DUH]

In the lush woodlands of the New England region, the White Baneberry, also known as Doll's Eyes or Actaea pachypoda, stands as a striking yet perilous sight. This perennial herbaceous plant bears distinctive clusters of white berries with black dots, resembling eerie doll's eyes, hence its ominous moniker. While its appearance may be intriguing, White Baneberry harbors toxicity within its deceptively innocent facade. The plant contains cardiogenic toxins, specifically protopine alkaloids, which can cause severe symptoms if ingested.

Consuming any part of the White Baneberry plant, particularly its berries, can lead to gastrointestinal distress, including nausea, vomiting, and diarrhea. However, the most concerning aspect of its toxicity lies in its impact on the cardiovascular system. The cardiogenic toxins present in White Baneberry can induce cardiac arrest, arrhythmias, and potentially fatal complications if ingested in significant quantities. Therefore, it's crucial for hikers, foragers, and gardeners alike to recognize White Baneberry and exercise caution to prevent accidental ingestion. With its striking appearance masking a hidden danger, White Baneberry serves as a reminder of nature's intricate balance between beauty and peril.

F alse Hellebore

Veratrum viride [VUH-RAT-RUM VUH-RY-DY]

False Hellebore, also known as Veratrum viride, is a highly toxic plant found in the New England region of the United States, particularly in damp, wooded areas and along stream banks. This plant is characterized by its large, broad leaves arranged in a rosette formation and clusters of small, greenish-white flowers on tall stalks. Despite its lush appearance, False Hellebore poses a significant threat to humans and animals due to the potent toxins contained within its tissues.

The toxicity of False Hellebore stems from alkaloids such as veratridine and jervine, which disrupt the normal function of the nervous system and the heart. Ingesting any part of the plant, including leaves, stems, and roots, can lead to severe poisoning. Symptoms of toxicity may include nausea, vomiting, abdominal pain, excessive salivation, dizziness, weakness, slow heart rate, low blood pressure, seizures, and in severe cases, coma or death. It's crucial to avoid handling or consuming False Hellebore and to keep pets and livestock away from areas where it grows to prevent accidental ingestion and poisoning. If poisoning is suspected, immediate medical attention should be sought, and any affected animals should be taken to a veterinarian as soon as possible for treatment.

Fly Agaric

Amanita muscaria [UH-MAN-IH-TUH MUH-SKAIR-EE-UH]

The Fly Agaric Mushroom, scientifically known as Amanita muscaria, is a striking and widely recognizable fungus found in the forests of the New England region of the United States. With its vibrant red cap adorned with white spots, this mushroom is both captivating and dangerous. Despite its alluring appearance, the Fly Agaric Mushroom is highly toxic and should never be consumed.

Its toxicity stems from several compounds, including muscimol and ibotenic acid, which can cause a range of symptoms when ingested. These symptoms include nausea, vomiting, diarrhea, hallucinations, delirium, seizures, and even coma in severe cases. The toxic effects of the Fly Agaric Mushroom can be attributed to its impact on the central nervous system, leading to altered perceptions and potentially life-threatening complications. Due to its toxicity and potential for fatal outcomes, it's crucial to educate oneself on the distinguishing features of the Fly Agaric Mushroom and avoid ingesting it under any circumstances. If accidental ingestion occurs or symptoms of toxicity manifest, seeking immediate medical attention is imperative to mitigate the risks associated with this poisonous fungus.

I ndian Tobacco

Lobelia inflata [LOH-BEE-LEE-UH IN-FLAY-TUH]

Indian Tobacco, scientifically known as Lobelia inflata, is a poisonous plant native to the New England region of the United States. Despite its name, Indian Tobacco is not related to true tobacco but rather belongs to the bellflower family. This herbaceous plant is characterized by small, tubular flowers that range in color from pale blue to violet. Its leaves are lance-shaped and arranged alternately along the stem. Indian Tobacco typically grows in open fields, meadows, and disturbed areas, thriving in sandy or loamy soils.

The toxicity of Indian Tobacco is primarily attributed to its alkaloid content, particularly lobeline. Ingesting any part of the plant, especially the leaves and seeds, can lead to poisoning in humans and animals. Symptoms of toxicity include nausea, vomiting, diarrhea, dizziness, confusion, sweating, rapid heartbeat, and in severe cases, convulsions and respiratory failure. Due to its toxicity, Indian Tobacco should be avoided and not ingested under any circumstances. If accidental ingestion occurs, immediate medical attention is necessary to address symptoms and prevent further complications. Additionally, pet owners should be cautious as Indian Tobacco can pose a risk to animals if consumed.

Jack-in-the-Pulpit

Arisaema triphyllum [UH-RISS-EE-MUH TR-EYE-FILL-UM]

In the lush woodlands of the New England region, an intriguing but potentially dangerous plant known as Jack-in-the-Pulpit (Arisaema triphyllum) lurks beneath the forest canopy. This perennial herbaceous plant, belonging to the Araceae family, is easily recognizable by its distinctive structure resembling a miniature pulpit, with a hooded spathe (the "pulpit") enclosing a spadix (the "Jack"). Despite its charming appearance, Jack-in-the-Pulpit harbors toxic compounds, particularly calcium oxalate crystals, in all parts of the plant. These compounds serve as a natural defense mechanism against herbivores, deterring animals from consuming their foliage or berries.

While Jack-in-the-Pulpit adds a touch of wild beauty to the forest floor, caution must be exercised, especially for curious foragers or unsuspecting wildlife. Ingesting any part of the plant can lead to severe toxicity, causing symptoms such as burning and swelling of the mouth, throat, and digestive tract. Additionally, contact with the plant's sap can result in skin irritation or dermatitis. The toxic effects of Jack-in-the-

Pulpit underscore the importance of proper plant identification and awareness of potential hazards while exploring the enchanting landscapes of New England's woodlands.

J imsonweed

Datura stramonium [DUH-TOO-RUH STRUH-MOH-NEE-UHM]

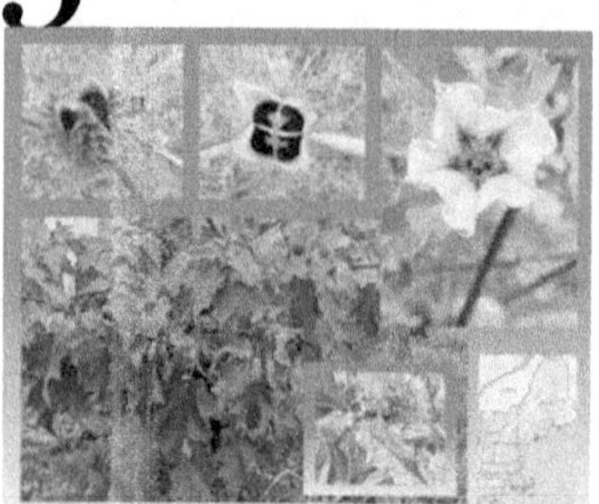

Jimsonweed, scientifically known as Datura stramonium, is a poisonous plant found in the New England region of the United States. This plant, also referred to as Devil's snare or Thornapple, is known for its distinctive trumpet-shaped flowers and spiky seed pods. Jimsonweed is a member of the nightshade family and contains potent alkaloids such as atropine, scopolamine, and hyoscyamine, which are responsible for its toxicity.

The plant can grow up to several feet tall with large, dark green leaves that have irregular, toothed edges. Its flowers are typically white or pale purple and have a strong, unpleasant odor. The spiky seed pods contain numerous small, black seeds. All parts of the Jimsonweed plant are toxic if ingested, with the seeds being particularly dangerous. Symptoms of toxicity include hallucinations, delirium, blurred vision, rapid heartbeat, dry mouth, fever, and in severe cases, convulsions and coma. Due to its high toxicity and potential for fatal poisoning, it is essential to avoid contact with Jimsonweed and to seek medical attention immediately if ingestion is suspected.

Monkshood

Aconitum napellus [UH-KOH-NUH-TUHM NUH-PEL-US]

Monkshood, also known as Aconitum, is a highly poisonous plant found in the New England region of the United States. This perennial herbaceous plant is characterized by its tall spikes of hooded, deeply lobed flowers, typically ranging in color from deep blue to purple. Monkshood is native to moist woodland areas, making it prevalent in parts of New England, particularly in shady, damp forests.

The toxicity of Monkshood is primarily due to the presence of alkaloids, including aconitine, which can have severe effects on the nervous system and heart. All parts of the plant, including the leaves, flowers, and roots, contain these potent toxins. Ingesting even small amounts of Monkshood can lead to symptoms such as nausea, vomiting, abdominal pain, dizziness, and numbness or tingling in the mouth and extremities. In more severe cases, ingestion can cause respiratory paralysis, cardiac arrhythmias, and even death. Due to its high toxicity, handling Monkshood without gloves or consuming it accidentally can result in serious health complications, making it crucial to exercise caution and avoid contact with this dangerous plant.

SHANNON WARNER

P oison Sumac

Toxicodendron vernix [Tox-i-co-DEN-dron VER-niks]

In the lush landscapes of New England, among the verdant foliage, hides a less-than-friendly neighbor: Poison Sumac (Toxicodendron vernix). Unlike its benign relatives, such as the staghorn sumac known for its tangy lemonade-like beverage, Poison Sumac carries a potent venom that can swiftly ruin an outdoor adventure. This shrub or small tree stands out with its distinctive clusters of leaflets arranged in rows of 7-13 on red stems. Each leaflet is oblong and smooth-edged, showcasing glossy green hues that transition to fiery reds and oranges in the fall.

While its vibrant appearance might tempt the unsuspecting, contact with any part of Poison Sumac – leaves, stems, or roots – spells trouble. The culprit behind its toxicity lies in an oily resin called urushiol, which is also found in its more well-known cousins, Poison Ivy and Poison Oak. Upon skin contact, urushiol triggers an allergic reaction in most people, leading to painful rashes, itching, swelling, and blisters. Inhaling smoke from burning Poison Sumac can also cause severe respiratory irritation. To avoid the unpleasant aftermath of a Poison Sumac encounter, it's essential to steer clear of its presence and promptly wash any exposed skin with soap and water if contact occurs. If symptoms of toxicity persist or worsen, seeking medical attention is crucial to ensure proper treatment and relief.

Water Hemlock

Cicuta maculata [sih-KYOO-tuh mak-yoo-LAH-tuh]

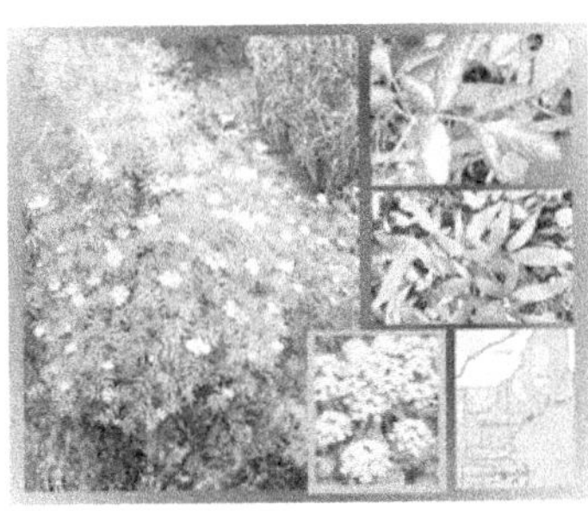

In the lush landscapes of New England, a peril lurks amidst the verdant foliage - Water Hemlock, a highly poisonous plant that poses a grave danger to both humans and animals alike. This deadly botanical menace, scientifically known as Cicuta maculata, boasts clusters of small white flowers and lacy, fern-like leaves, often camouflaging itself among other vegetation. Its innocent appearance belies its deadly nature, as every part of the Water Hemlock plant contains potent neurotoxins, particularly cicutoxin.

Ingestion of even small amounts of Water Hemlock can lead to severe and often fatal consequences. The toxins in this plant interfere with the nervous system, causing symptoms such as tremors, seizures, nausea, vomiting, abdominal pain, dilated pupils, and respiratory failure. Swift medical attention is imperative in cases of Water Hemlock poisoning, as its effects can rapidly escalate, leading to coma or death if left untreated. Given its prevalence in wetlands, marshes, and along stream banks in New England, it's crucial for outdoor enthusiasts, hikers, and foragers to exercise caution and familiarize themselves with the distinguishing features of Water Hemlock to avoid accidental ingestion and potential tragedy.

B ittersweet Nightshade
Solanum dulcamara [*SOH-LAY-NUM DUHL-KUH-MAIR-UH*]

Bittersweet Nightshade, scientifically known as Solanum dulcamara, is a toxic plant found in the New England region of the United States. This perennial vine belongs to the nightshade family and is characterized by its distinctive purple flowers, red berries, and elongated leaves. Often growing in wooded areas, along fences, or in neglected areas, Bittersweet Nightshade can be easily mistaken for harmless vines due to its attractive appearance.

However, all parts of the Bittersweet Nightshade plant contain toxic compounds, including solanine and glycoalkaloids, which can be harmful if ingested. Symptoms of toxicity from Bittersweet Nightshade consumption may include nausea, vomiting, abdominal pain, diarrhea, drowsiness, confusion, and hallucinations. In severe cases, ingestion of this plant can lead to convulsions, respiratory depression, and even death. Due to its toxicity, it's crucial to be able to recognize Bittersweet Nightshade and avoid accidental ingestion, especially in areas frequented by children and pets. If ingestion occurs, immediate medical attention is necessary to mitigate the effects of poisoning.

American Matsutake Mushroom Rice

Prep Time: 10 minutes *Cooking Time:* 20 minutes

Serving: serves 2-3 people as a side dish or 1-2 people as a main course.

Ingredients:

- 1 cup Japanese short-grain rice
- 2 cups water
- 1 American Matsutake mushroom, cleaned and sliced
- 2 cloves garlic, minced
- 1 tablespoon soy sauce
- 1 tablespoon mirin (Japanese sweet rice wine)
- 1 tablespoon sesame oil
- Salt to taste

Optional: Chopped green onions or parsley for garnish

Instructions:

1. Rinse the rice under cold water until the water runs clear. Drain well.
2. In a rice cooker or a pot, combine the rinsed rice and water. Cook the rice according to your rice cooker's instructions or bring to a boil, then reduce heat to low, cover, and simmer for about 15-20 minutes, or until the rice is cooked and fluffy.
3. While the rice is cooking, heat the sesame oil in a skillet over medium heat. Add the sliced Matsutake mushroom and minced garlic, and sauté for about 3-4 minutes until the mushrooms are tender and aromatic.
4. Once the mushrooms are cooked, add the soy sauce and mirin to the skillet. Stir well to combine and let it simmer for another 2 minutes.
5. When the rice is done cooking, fluff it with a fork and transfer it to a serving bowl.
6. Pour the cooked Matsutake mushroom mixture over the rice and gently toss to combine.
7. Taste and adjust the seasoning with salt if needed.

Serve the Matsutake Mushroom Rice hot, garnished with chopped green onions or parsley if desired.

Black Huckleberry Pie

Ingredients:

- 4 cups fresh black huckleberries
- 1 cup granulated sugar
- 1/4 cup all-purpose flour
- 1 tablespoon lemon juice
- 1/2 teaspoon ground cinnamon (optional)
- 1/4 teaspoon ground nutmeg (optional)
- 2 tablespoons butter, cut into small pieces
- 1 double crust pie pastry (store-bought or homemade)

Instructions:

1. Preheat your oven to 400°F (200°C).
2. In a large mixing bowl, gently combine the black huckleberries, sugar, flour, lemon juice, and spices (if using). Stir until the berries are evenly coated.
3. Roll out half of the pie pastry and line a 9-inch pie dish with it. Trim any excess pastry hanging over the edges.
4. Pour the black huckleberry mixture into the pastry-lined pie dish, spreading it out evenly.
5. Dot the top of the berry mixture with the pieces of butter.
6. Roll out the remaining pie pastry and place it over the filling. Seal the edges by crimping with a fork or your fingers. Cut a few slits in the top crust to allow steam to escape during baking.
7. Optionally, you can brush the top crust with milk or beaten egg for a golden finish.
8. Place the pie on a baking sheet to catch any drips, and then bake in the preheated oven for about 40-45 minutes, or until the crust is golden brown and the filling is bubbling.
9. Once baked, remove the pie from the oven and allow it to cool on a wire rack before serving.
10. Serve the black huckleberry pie warm or at room temperature, optionally topped with a scoop of vanilla ice cream or a dollop of whipped cream.

Cranberry Chutney

Prep Time: 10 minutes

Cook Time: 20-25 minutes

Servings: Makes about 2 cups of cranberry chutney, serving approximately 8 people.

Ingredients:

- 12 ounces (about 3 cups) fresh cranberries
- 1 medium apple, peeled, cored, and chopped
- 1/2 cup raisins
- 1/2 cup chopped onion
- 1/2 cup packed brown sugar
- 1/2 cup apple cider vinegar
- 1/2 cup water
- 1 teaspoon grated fresh ginger
- 1/2 teaspoon ground cinnamon
- 1/4 teaspoon ground cloves
- 1/4 teaspoon salt

Instructions:

1. In a medium saucepan, combine all the ingredients: cranberries, chopped apple, raisins, onion, brown sugar, apple cider vinegar, water, ginger, cinnamon, cloves, and salt.
2. Stir the mixture well to combine.
3. Bring the mixture to a boil over medium-high heat, then reduce the heat to low and simmer, uncovered, for about 20-25 minutes, stirring occasionally, until the cranberries burst and the chutney thickens.
4. Remove the saucepan from the heat and let the chutney cool to room temperature.
5. Once cooled, transfer the cranberry chutney to a serving bowl or airtight container. You can serve it immediately, or refrigerate it for a few hours to allow the flavors to meld.

Goldenrod Eggs

Prep Time: Approximately 20 minutes

Servings: serves 4 people as a main dish or can be adjusted to serve more as a side dish or appetizer.

Ingredients:

- 8 large eggs
- 2 tablespoons butter
- 2 tablespoons all-purpose flour
- 1 cup milk
- Salt and pepper to taste
- 1 cup finely chopped Canadian Goldenrod leaves (washed and dried)

Instructions:

1. Place the eggs in a pot and cover them with water. Bring the water to a boil over medium-high heat. Once boiling, reduce the heat to low and let the eggs simmer for 10-12 minutes. Remove the eggs from the pot and let them cool. Once cooled, peel the eggs and separate the yolks from the whites.
2. In a saucepan, melt the butter over medium heat. Once melted, stir in the flour to create a roux. Cook the roux for 1-2 minutes, stirring constantly, until it becomes golden brown. Gradually whisk in the milk until the mixture is smooth. Continue cooking, stirring constantly, until the sauce thickens, about 5-7 minutes. Season with salt and pepper to taste.
3. Finely chop the cooked egg whites and set them aside. Mash the egg yolks with a fork and stir them into the sauce until well combined. Add the chopped Canadian Goldenrod leaves to the sauce, reserving some for garnish if desired. Gently fold in the chopped egg whites.
4. Spoon the Goldenrod Eggs mixture over toast, biscuits, or your choice of bread. Garnish with additional chopped Canadian Goldenrod leaves if desired.

Serve hot and enjoy!

Hophornbeam Seed Energy Bites

Prep Time: Approximately 15 minutes (plus additional time for drying and toasting seeds, if desired)

Servings: Makes about 12-16 energy bites, depending on size.

Ingredients:

- 1 cup Hophornbeam seeds
- 1 cup rolled oats
- 1/2 cup peanut butter (or any nut/seed butter of your choice)
- 1/4 cup honey or maple syrup
- 1/4 cup mini chocolate chips (optional)
- 1 teaspoon vanilla extract
- Pinch of salt

Instructions:

1. Start by collecting Hophornbeam seeds. Remove any outer husks or debris and thoroughly rinse the seeds under cold water. Spread them out on a baking sheet and allow them to dry completely, either by air-drying or using a low oven temperature.
2. In a large mixing bowl, combine the toasted Hophornbeam seeds, rolled oats, peanut butter, honey or maple syrup, mini chocolate chips (if using), vanilla extract, and a pinch of salt. Stir everything together until well combined.
3. Using clean hands, scoop out about a tablespoon of the mixture and roll it between your palms to form a small ball. Repeat with the remaining mixture until you have used it all up. You should get approximately 12-16 energy bites, depending on the size.
4. Place the energy bites on a plate or baking sheet lined with parchment paper. Place them in the refrigerator for at least 30 minutes to firm up. Once chilled, they are ready to serve.

Optional: Preheat your oven to 300°F (150°C). Spread the dried Hophornbeam seeds on a baking sheet in a single layer. Toast them in the oven for about 10-15 minutes or until they are lightly golden and fragrant. Remove from the oven and let them cool completely.

Note: These energy bites can be stored in an airtight container in the refrigerator for up to one week. They make a nutritious and convenient snack for on-the-go or as a pre/post-workout treat. Enjoy!

J ewelweed Tincture

Prep Time: 10 minutes

Servings: The number of servings will vary depending on the size of the glass jar used and the amount of jewelweed collected.

Ingredients:

- Fresh jewelweed plants (leaves, stems, and flowers)
- High-proof alcohol (such as vodka or grain alcohol)

Equipment:

- Clean glass jar with a tight-fitting lid
- Scissors or knife
- Measuring cup or scale
- Cheesecloth or fine mesh strainer
- Funnel
- Dark glass bottles for storing the tincture

Instructions:

1. Gather fresh jewelweed plants. It's best to harvest them when they are in full bloom for maximum potency. Make sure to collect the leaves, stems, and flowers.
2. Wash the jewelweed thoroughly under cold running water to remove any dirt or debris.
3. Chop the jewelweed into small pieces using scissors or a knife. The size of the pieces doesn't need to be uniform, but smaller pieces will allow for better extraction of the plant's constituents.
4. Fill a clean glass jar with the chopped jewelweed, leaving some space at the top.
5. Pour the high-proof alcohol over the jewelweed until it is completely covered. Make sure the alcohol has a high enough concentration to effectively extract the plant's properties.
6. Seal the jar tightly with the lid and shake it gently to ensure the plant material is well coated with the alcohol.
7. Store the jar in a cool, dark place for at least 4-6 weeks, shaking it occasionally to agitate the mixture.
8. After the designated extraction period, strain the tincture through a cheesecloth or fine mesh strainer to remove the plant material. You may need to use a funnel to transfer the tincture into a clean, dark glass bottle for storage.
9. Label the bottle with the date and contents of the tincture.

Note: can be used externally as a natural remedy for poison ivy, insect bites, and other skin irritations. It should be applied topically to the affected area as needed.

L ion's Mane Mushroom Stir Fry

Prep Time: 10 minutes - Cook Time: 15 minutes

Servings: 4

Ingredients:

- 1 lb fresh Lion's Mane mushrooms, sliced into 1/4 inch thick pieces
- 1 red bell pepper, sliced
- 1 green bell pepper, sliced
- 1 yellow onion, sliced
- 3 garlic cloves, minced
- 2 tbsp soy sauce
- 1 tbsp hoisin sauce
- 1 tbsp cornstarch
- 1 tbsp sesame oil
- 1 tbsp vegetable oil
- Salt and pepper to taste
- 2 green onions, sliced (optional)

Instructions:

1. Mix soy sauce, hoisin sauce, cornstarch, and 1/4 cup of water in a small bowl. Set aside.
2. Heat vegetable oil in a wok or large skillet over high heat. Add Lion's Mane mushrooms and stir-fry for 2-3 minutes until they start to brown. Remove from pan and set aside.
3. Add sesame oil to the same pan and stir-fry bell peppers and onion for 3-4 minutes until they are slightly tender.
4. Add garlic and stir-fry for another minute.
5. Add the sauce mixture to the pan and stir until it thickens.
6. Add the Lion's Mane mushrooms back into the pan and stir until everything is coated in the sauce.
7. Season with salt and pepper to taste.
8. Top with sliced green onions (optional) and serve hot.

This Lion's Mane Mushroom Stir Fry is a quick and easy recipe that is perfect for a healthy weeknight dinner. Enjoy!

Poverty Oatgrass Porridge

Prep Time: Approximately 5-10 minutes for cleaning and preparation, plus 20-30 minutes for cooking.

Servings: This recipe makes approximately 2-3 servings, depending on portion size.

Ingredients:

- 1 cup Poverty Oatgrass seeds
- 3 cups water
- Optional: sweeteners such as honey, maple syrup, or sugar
- Optional: toppings such as fresh fruits, nuts, or cinnamon

Instructions:

1. Begin by harvesting Poverty Oatgrass seeds. You can find them in the wild or purchase them from specialty suppliers if available.
2. Thoroughly clean the harvested seeds to remove any debris or impurities.
3. In a medium saucepan, bring 3 cups of water to a boil.
4. Once the water is boiling, add 1 cup of cleaned Poverty Oatgrass seeds to the saucepan.
5. Reduce the heat to low and let the seeds simmer in the water for about 20-30 minutes, or until they become tender and the water is absorbed. Stir occasionally to prevent sticking.
6. If desired, add sweeteners such as honey, maple syrup, or sugar to taste, and mix well.
7. Once the porridge reaches your desired consistency and sweetness, remove it from the heat and transfer it to serving bowls.
8. Garnish the porridge with your choice of toppings, such as fresh fruits, nuts, or a sprinkle of cinnamon, for added flavor and texture.

Note: Poverty Oatgrass porridge may have a chewier texture compared to traditional oatmeal due to the nature of the grass seeds. Adjust the cooking time and water ratio to achieve your desired consistency.

Sea Belt Salad

Prep Time: Approximately 20 minutes (including rehydrating time for dried seaweed)

Ingredients:

- 100g (about 3.5 oz) fresh Sea Belt seaweed
- 1 tablespoon sesame oil
- 1 tablespoon soy sauce
- 1 teaspoon rice vinegar
- 1 teaspoon honey or maple syrup
- 1 clove garlic, minced
- 1 teaspoon grated ginger

Optional toppings: sesame seeds, sliced scallions, chili flakes

Instructions:

1. Rinse the Sea Belt seaweed under cold water to remove any debris. If the seaweed is dried, rehydrate it in cold water for about 10-15 minutes until it becomes soft. Drain and squeeze out excess water.
2. In a small bowl, whisk together sesame oil, soy sauce, rice vinegar, honey or maple syrup, minced garlic, and grated ginger to make the dressing.
3. In a mixing bowl, combine the prepared Sea Belt seaweed with the dressing. Toss gently to coat the seaweed evenly with the dressing.
4. Transfer the dressed Sea Belt salad to serving plates. Garnish with optional toppings such as sesame seeds, sliced scallions, or chili flakes for added flavor and texture.

Sea Buckthorn Berry Smoothie

Prep Time: Approximately 10 minutes

Servings: 2

Ingredients:

- 1 cup fresh Sea Buckthorn berries
- 1 ripe banana
- 1/2 cup Greek yogurt
- 1/2 cup orange juice

Optional: 1 tablespoon honey (depending on taste)

Optional: Ice cubes

Optional: Fresh mint leaves for garnish

Instructions:

1. Rinse the Sea Buckthorn berries thoroughly under cold water and remove any stems or debris.
2. In a blender, combine the Sea Buckthorn berries, ripe banana, Greek yogurt, and orange juice.
3. If desired, add honey for extra sweetness.
4. Blend all the ingredients until smooth and creamy. If you prefer a colder smoothie, you can also add a few ice cubes to the blender.
5. Taste the smoothie and adjust sweetness or tartness by adding more honey or orange juice if needed.
6. Once the desired consistency and taste are achieved, pour the smoothie into glasses.
7. Garnish with fresh mint leaves for a refreshing touch.

Serve immediately and enjoy!

Sea Lettuce Sheet

Prep Time: Approximately 15-20 minutes

Servings: This recipe yields one sea lettuce sheet.

Ingredients:

- Fresh sea lettuce (enough to make one sheet)
- Water (for rinsing)

Optional: Seasonings such as sesame oil, soy sauce, or rice vinegar for flavoring

Instructions:

1. Begin by rinsing the sea lettuce thoroughly under cold running water to remove any sand or debris.
2. If desired, blanch the sea lettuce quickly in boiling water for about 10-15 seconds. This step helps to soften the sea lettuce and brighten its color, but it's not necessary if you prefer a more raw texture.
3. After rinsing or blanching, gently pat the sea lettuce dry with paper towels or a clean kitchen towel to remove excess moisture.
4. Lay out a clean, flat surface such as a cutting board or baking sheet. Arrange the sea lettuce leaves side by side, slightly overlapping, to form a single layer. Press them gently together to help them adhere.
5. **(optional):** If you prefer a crispy texture, you can dry the sea lettuce sheet further by placing it in a dehydrator or a low-temperature oven (around 200°F or 90°C) for about 1-2 hours until completely dry and crisp.
6. Once the sea lettuce sheet is dry, use kitchen scissors or a sharp knife to trim any uneven edges and cut it into desired shapes and sizes.
7. If desired, drizzle the sea lettuce sheet with a small amount of sesame oil, soy sauce, or rice vinegar for added flavor. You can also sprinkle it with sesame seeds or other seasonings of your choice.

Ideas: Sea lettuce sheets can be used in various ways, such as wrapping sushi rolls, making seaweed snacks, or adding crispy texture to salads and soups. They can also be crumbled and used as a garnish or flavoring for seafood dishes, rice bowls, or noodle dishes.

Shaggy Mane Mushrooms with Garlic and Butter

Prep Time: approximately 15 minutes.

Servings: serves 2-4 people as a side dish or appetizer.

Ingredients:

- 1 pound fresh Shaggy Mane mushrooms
- 2-3 cloves of garlic, minced
- 2 tablespoons butter
- Salt and pepper to taste

Optional: chopped parsley for garnish

Instructions:

1. Gently brush off any dirt or debris from the Shaggy Mane mushrooms using a soft brush or cloth. Avoid washing them with water as they can absorb moisture easily.
2. Cut the Shaggy Mane mushrooms into thin slices, discarding any tough or discolored parts.
3. In a large skillet, melt the butter over medium heat. Add the minced garlic and sauté for 1-2 minutes until fragrant.
4. Add the sliced Shaggy Mane mushrooms to the skillet, stirring to coat them evenly with the butter and garlic. Cook for 5-7 minutes, stirring occasionally, until the mushrooms are tender and lightly browned.
5. Season the mushrooms with salt and pepper to taste, adjusting the seasoning as needed.
6. Transfer the cooked Shaggy Mane mushrooms to a serving dish, garnish with chopped parsley if desired, and serve immediately.

Stinging Nettle Tincture

Prep Time: around 15-20 minutes to gather and chop the nettle leaves and stems, and then a few minutes to fill the jar and add alcohol.

Stinging nettle tincture is commonly used to support various health issues such as allergies, inflammation, urinary tract health, and more.

Ingredients:

- Fresh stinging nettle leaves and stems
- High-proof alcohol (such as vodka or brandy)

Equipment:

- Clean glass jar with a tight-fitting lid
- Fine mesh strainer or cheesecloth
- Dark glass dropper bottles for storage

Instructions:

1. Gather fresh stinging nettle leaves and stems. Wear gloves to protect your hands from the stinging hairs.
2. Rinse the nettle leaves and stems under cold water to remove any dirt or debris. Allow them to air dry or gently pat them dry with a clean towel.
3. Chop the nettle leaves and stems into small pieces. This increases the surface area, allowing for better extraction of the plant's medicinal compounds.
4. Place the chopped nettle leaves and stems into a clean glass jar, filling it about halfway.
5. Pour the high-proof alcohol (vodka or brandy) over the nettle plant material until it is completely covered, ensuring there are no air pockets.
6. Secure the lid tightly on the jar and label it with the date of preparation. Store the jar in a cool, dark place, such as a pantry or cupboard.
7. Allow the nettle mixture to steep in the alcohol for at least 4 to 6 weeks, shaking the jar gently every few days to agitate the contents and facilitate extraction.
8. After the steeping period, strain the mixture through a fine mesh strainer or cheesecloth into a clean bowl or another jar. Squeeze out as much liquid as possible from the nettle plant material.
9. Transfer the strained nettle tincture into dark glass dropper bottles for storage. Label the bottles with the tincture name and date of preparation.

Sugar Maple Syrup

Prep Time: It typically takes several hours to boil down the sap to syrup consistency.

Servings: On average, 40 gallons of sap will yield approximately 1 gallon of syrup. Therefore, the number of servings will vary accordingly.

Ingredients:

- Fresh sap from sugar maple trees (typically harvested in late winter to early spring)
- Large cooking pot
- Candy thermometer
- Fine mesh strainer or cheesecloth
- Sterilized glass bottles or jars for storage

Instructions:

1. Tap sugar maple trees in late winter or early spring when daytime temperatures are above freezing but nighttime temperatures are still below freezing. Collect the clear sap from the trees using taps and buckets or a tubing system.
2. Pour the collected sap into a large cooking pot. Boil the sap over medium to high heat until it reaches a temperature of 219°F (104°C) or until it reaches the consistency of syrup. This process can take several hours and requires constant monitoring. Skim off any foam that forms on the surface.
3. Once the sap has reached the desired consistency, remove it from the heat. Let it cool slightly, then strain it through a fine mesh strainer or cheesecloth to remove any impurities or sediment.
4. Pour the filtered syrup into sterilized glass bottles or jars for storage. Seal the containers tightly.
5. Use sugar maple syrup as a topping for pancakes, waffles, French toast, oatmeal, or other breakfast foods. It can also be used as a sweetener in baking and cooking recipes.

Enjoy your homemade sugar maple syrup on a variety of dishes, and savor the unique flavor of this natural sweetener!

Teaberry Ice Cream

Prep Time: Approximately 15 minutes, plus chilling and freezing time

Servings: Makes about 1 quart of Teaberry Ice Cream (approximately 4 servings)

Ingredients:

- 2 cups heavy cream
- 1 cup whole milk
- 3/4 cup granulated sugar
- 1/4 teaspoon salt
- 1 teaspoon vanilla extract
- 1/4 cup fresh or frozen teaberries (chopped)
- 1/2 teaspoon teaberry extract (adjust to taste)
- 2-3 drops red food coloring (optional, for color)

Instructions:

1. In a medium saucepan, combine the heavy cream, whole milk, granulated sugar, and salt. Heat the mixture over medium heat, stirring occasionally, until it reaches a gentle simmer. Remove from heat.
2. Stir in the vanilla extract and teaberry extract. If desired, add a few drops of red food coloring to achieve a pink color for the ice cream.
3. Transfer the mixture to a bowl and let it cool to room temperature. Once cooled, cover the bowl and refrigerate for at least 4 hours or overnight to chill completely.
4. Once the mixture is chilled, pour it into an ice cream maker and churn according to the manufacturer's instructions until it reaches a soft-serve consistency.
5. During the last few minutes of churning, add the chopped teaberries to the ice cream mixture and continue churning until evenly distributed.
6. Transfer the churned ice cream to a freezer-safe container and freeze for at least 4 hours or until firm.

Serve the Teaberry Ice Cream scooped into bowls or cones, and enjoy the unique flavor of Eastern Teaberry!

Vegan Irish Moss Pudding

Prep Time: 12-24 hours (for soaking Irish Moss), 30 minutes (for cooking and blending)

Servings: makes approximately 4 servings.

Ingredients:

- 1/4 cup dried Irish Moss
- 2 cups water
- 1/2 cup coconut milk (or any plant-based milk of your choice)
- 1/4 cup maple syrup (or sweetener of your choice, adjust to taste)
- 1 teaspoon vanilla extract
- Pinch of salt

Optional: cinnamon, nutmeg, or other spices to taste

Instructions:

1. Rinse the dried Irish Moss thoroughly to remove any debris. Soak the Irish Moss in water for 12-24 hours, changing the water a few times to remove excess salt. The Irish Moss will expand and soften during soaking.
2. After soaking, drain the Irish Moss and place it in a pot with 2 cups of water. Bring to a boil, then reduce heat and simmer for 15-20 minutes, or until the Irish Moss is completely dissolved and the liquid has thickened.
3. Once the Irish Moss mixture has cooled slightly, transfer it to a blender. Add the coconut milk, maple syrup, vanilla extract, salt, and any optional spices. Blend until smooth and creamy.
4. Pour the pudding mixture into serving cups or bowls. Refrigerate for at least 1-2 hours, or until set and chilled.
5. Serve the Irish Moss pudding cold, optionally garnished with fresh fruit, coconut flakes, or a sprinkle of cinnamon.

This vegan pudding is not only delicious but also packed with nutrients from the Irish Moss, making it a healthy and satisfying dessert or snack option.

Velvet Foot Soup

Prep Time: Approximately 10 minutes

Cook Time: Approximately 20-25 minutes

Servings: makes about 4 servings.

Ingredients:

- 200g (about 7 oz) velvet foot mushrooms
- 1 onion, finely chopped
- 2 cloves garlic, minced
- 4 cups vegetable or chicken broth
- 1 tablespoon olive oil
- Salt and pepper to taste
- Fresh parsley or chives for garnish (optional)

Instructions:

1. Clean the velvet foot mushrooms thoroughly, removing any dirt or debris. Trim the tough ends of the stems if necessary, but retain most of the tender stems and caps.
2. Heat olive oil in a large pot over medium heat. Add the chopped onion and minced garlic, sautéing until softened and fragrant, about 3-4 minutes.
3. Add the cleaned velvet foot mushrooms to the pot, stirring well to combine with the onions and garlic. Cook for an additional 5 minutes, allowing the mushrooms to release their moisture and develop flavor.
4. Pour the vegetable or chicken broth into the pot, stirring to combine with the mushrooms, onions, and garlic. Bring the mixture to a gentle simmer.
5. Allow the soup to simmer for about 15-20 minutes, or until the mushrooms are tender and the flavors have melded together. Season with salt and pepper to taste.
6. Once the soup is cooked to your liking, remove it from the heat and let it cool slightly before serving.
7. Ladle the velvet foot soup into bowls and garnish with fresh parsley or chives if desired. Serve hot and enjoy!

This soup is not only flavorful but also packed with nutrients from the velvet foot mushrooms, making it a comforting and nourishing dish for any occasion. Feel free to customize the recipe by adding other vegetables or herbs according to your taste preferences.

# Yarrow Tea

Prep time: 5 minutes

Servings: 2

Ingredients:

- 1 tablespoon dried yarrow flowers and leaves
- 2 cups water
- honey or lemon (optional)

Instructions:

1. Bring the water to a boil in a pot or kettle.
2. Add the dried yarrow flowers and leaves to the boiling water.
3. Reduce heat to low and let the mixture simmer for 5-10 minutes.
4. Strain the yarrow tea into a teapot or pitcher.
5. Add honey or lemon to taste, if desired.

Serve hot, and enjoy!

Note: Yarrow tea can also be enjoyed cold by letting it cool and adding ice cubes. It is important to consult a healthcare professional before using yarrow tea as a remedy, as it may interact with certain medications or cause allergic reactions in some individuals.

Yarrow tea is a popular herbal remedy used to treat various health issues such as fever, colds, and flu.

Yarrow Tincture

Prep time: 10 minutes

Servings: 30-40 servings

Ingredients:

- 1 cup of fresh yarrow leaves and flowers
- 1 pint of 100-proof vodka or grain alcohol

Tools:

- A quart-sized mason jar with a lid
- Cheesecloth or a fine-mesh strainer
- A small funnel
- An amber glass dropper bottle

Directions:

1. Rinse the yarrow leaves and flowers and dry them thoroughly.
2. Chop the yarrow leaves and flowers into small pieces and place them in the mason jar.
3. Pour the vodka or grain alcohol over the yarrow until it is completely covered.
4. Seal the mason jar with the lid and shake it vigorously for a few seconds.
5. Store the jar in a cool, dark place for 4-6 weeks, shaking it daily to ensure that the yarrow is fully infused into the alcohol.
6. After 4-6 weeks, strain the mixture through cheesecloth or a fine-mesh strainer into a clean bowl or jar.
7. Transfer the yarrow tincture into an amber glass dropper bottle using the funnel.
8. Store the bottle in a cool, dark place, and use it as needed.

To use the yarrow tincture, place a few drops under your tongue or mix it with a small amount of water. Start with a small amount and gradually increase as needed.

Note: As with any herbal preparation, it's important to consult with a healthcare provider before using yarrow tincture, especially if you're pregnant or nursing, or have a medical condition or are taking any medication.

Yellow Birch Glazed Salmon

Prep time: 10 minutes

Servings: 4

Ingredients:

- 4 salmon fillets (about 6 ounces each)
- 1/4 cup Yellow Birch syrup
- 2 tablespoons soy sauce
- 2 cloves garlic, minced
- 1 tablespoon grated fresh ginger
- 1 tablespoon olive oil
- Salt and pepper to taste

Optional: chopped green onions, sesame seeds

Instructions:

1. Preheat your oven to 375°F (190°C).
2. In a small bowl, whisk together the Yellow Birch syrup, soy sauce, minced garlic, and grated ginger. This will be your glaze.
3. Place the salmon fillets on a baking sheet lined with parchment paper or aluminum foil. Drizzle the olive oil over the salmon and season with salt and pepper.
4. Brush the Yellow Birch glaze generously over the tops of the salmon fillets, reserving some for later.
5. Bake the salmon in the preheated oven for about 12-15 minutes, or until the fish is cooked through and flakes easily with a fork.
6. Once the salmon is cooked, remove it from the oven and brush with the remaining Yellow Birch glaze.

Serve the glazed salmon hot, garnished with chopped green onions and sesame seeds if desired.

AFTERWORD

In wrapping up "Wild Edible Plants of New England," I can't help but feel a sense of awe and gratitude for the journey we've taken together through the landscapes of this beautiful region. This book has been more than just a field guide; it's been a companion, opening our eyes to the wonders of nature right in our own backyard.

As we've flipped through its pages, we've discovered the stories of familiar and new plants, each a testament to the resilience and interconnectedness of life in the wild. From the sweet tang of wild blueberries to the delicate crunch of fiddleheads, every plant has its own tale woven into New England's ecosystems.

Yet, the impact of this book extends far beyond the practical knowledge of foraging and cooking. It has instilled in us a deeper understanding of our role in the natural world, urging us to tread lightly and with reverence for the land and its inhabitants. It has taught us how to harvest wild edibles and why it's crucial to do so responsibly, ensuring the preservation of these bounties for future generations.

As we gently close the cover of 'Wild Edible Plants of New England,' let's carry its profound teachings into the vast wilderness and beyond. Let's continue to venture, unearth, and treasure nature's precious offerings graciously bestowed upon us. Above all, let's remember to pause, to inhale deeply, and to relish the exquisite beauty and abundance of our natural world with all the gratitude and awe it deserves.

PLANT INDEX

PART TEN
APPENDIX

UNIVERSAL EDIBILITY TEST

If you are in an unfamiliar area or a survival situation, you may be unable to identify edible plants. In this case, you'd want to use the universal edibility test. As the name suggests, this test will help determine whether a plant is edible. It should only be used as a last resort, as you should ideally never be in a situation where you can't find an identifiable plant or mushroom. Always check the edibility of your harvest, even if you're sure it's safe to eat. This is important when foraging and Identifying an edible plant you've never tried before.

Everyone will come across this scenario at some point. Even if you're confident that you've identified an edible plant, only try a small amount first. Even something safe to eat can make you feel unwell if you have digestive issues. Sometimes a food you haven't tried before doesn't agree with you, and you don't want to discover this after having a large portion. It's also possible to have an undiagnosed food allergy. Suppose you eat a lot of plant food on an empty stomach. In that case, you can quickly end up with cramps, nausea, diarrhea, or other gastrointestinal issues. An upset stomach is a quick way to ruin an otherwise enjoyable foraging trip.

Step 1: Fast for eight hours. You likely haven't eaten for at least eight hours in a survival situation like this. Still, it's essential to start on an empty stomach so that you know whether or not the plant you are testing is what has made you unwell. You can and should drink plenty of clean water, if possible.

Step 2: Check for common poisonous traits. Most toxic plants have distinguishing characteristics that are unlikely to be found on edible plants. These include shiny, waxy leaves, spines, fine hairs, milky sap, umbrella-shaped flowers, and green or white berries. If it looks like dill or parsley, avoid it, and steer clear of anything that smells like almonds. Not every plant with these characteristics is toxic, edible dandelions have milky sap, for example, but it's an excellent rule of thumb. Rule out anything with those traits.

Step 3: Once you find a plant without any of those traits, ensure you can find plenty of specimens. Remember, the edibility test takes time, so there's not much point in going through the whole process if you can't find any more plants of that type. When you find a likely plant, break it down into sections: flower, leaf, stem, etc. Not every plant part is edible, even if one part is. For example, potato tubers are edible, but the plant's stem is toxic. You will need to test every aspect of the plant individually.

Step 4: Now, it's time to start testing. Select a plant part and rub it on your skin. Most people rub it on their inner forearm, the inside of their elbow, or their outer lip. Wait for fifteen minutes. Continue with the test if you don't experience tingling, burning, or other adverse reactions. If any of the above persist, you will want to choose a different plant part.

Step 5: If all is well from the step above, do a taste test with the same plant part. Put it in your mouth and don't chew or swallow; leave it for five minutes. Spit it out and wash your mouth if you have any adverse reactions. Do the same if you taste bitterness, soapy flavors, or experience numbness. If nothing happens, continue with the test.

Step 6: Do a more extensive taste test. Now put the plant part in your mouth and chew for five minutes. Wait for any of the adverse effects mentioned above and spit out excess saliva (don't swallow anything yet). If everything seems okay after five minutes, swallow the plant part. Now the waiting begins. You need to fast for another eight hours before the next step.

Step 7: If you haven't experienced any digestive issues, you can prepare and eat one tablespoon of the plant part. If possible, it's usually safer to cook the plant part. If there are no poisoning symptoms after another eight hours of waiting, you can be sure this plant part is edible as you prepared. It would be best if you still didn't gorge yourself, but at least you have a relatively dependable food source. You'll reduce the chance of accidental poisoning by sticking with small amounts and waiting eight hours between tasting and eating. Suppose you have significant gastrointestinal symptoms in a survival situation, like vomiting or diarrhea. In that case, you may not be able to seek medical attention.

<u>*Glossary*</u>

<u>*Plant Families*</u>

Actinidiaceae [AK-TIN-UH-DIE-UH-SEE-EE] - This flowering plant family has three genera and about 355 species. It consists of shrubs, small trees, and lianas. It is primarily tropical and is particularly common in Southeast Asia.

Anacardiaceae [AN-UH-KAR-DEE-AY-SEE-EE] - The cashew or sumac family of flowering plants includes 83 genera and 860 species. Several species bear drupes and sometimes produce *urushiol*, which can cause skin irritation.

Apiaceae [AY-PEE-AY-SEE-EE] - These primarily aromatic flowering plants are known as the celery, carrot, and parsley family, or umbellifers. They are named after the genus Apium.

Araliaceae [UH-RAH-LEE-AY-SEE-EE] - This family includes approximately 43 genera and about 1500 flowering plants; most are woody, and some are herbaceous.

Asparagaceae [UH-SPAR-UH-GAY-SEE-EE] - the asparagus family of flowering plants based on the edible garden asparagus, *Asparagus officinalis*.

Aspleniaceae [AS-PLEE-NEE-AY-SEE-EE] - The spleenwort family **is** a family of ferns

Asteraceae [AS-TER-AY-SEE-EE] - The Compositae family was first described in the year 1740. They are called daisies, sunflowers, asters, composites, or sunflowers. With more than 32,000 species and 1,900 genera, it is the world's largest flowering plant group, rivaled only by the Orchidaceae family.

Berberidaceae [BER-BUH-RID-UH-SEE-EE] - Generally known as the Barberry family, this group of flowering plants contains 18 genera.

Brassicaceae [BRAS-IH-KAY-SEE-EE] - These medium-sized flowering plants are economically important. They are commonly known as the mustards, crucifers, or cabbage family.

Caryophyllaceae [KAR-EE-OH-FUH-LAY-SEE-EE] - The carnation family is a family of flowering plants with about 2,625 known species.

Elaeagnaceae [EE-LEE-AG-NAY-SEE-EE] - The Oleaster family comprises small trees and shrubs.

Ericaceae [EH-RI-KAY-SEE-EE] - The heath or heather family consists of flowering plants that flourish in acidic and infertile environments. Cranberries, blueberries, huckleberries, rhododendrons (including azaleas), and a wide range of heaths and heathers are examples of well-known members.

Euphorbiaceae [YOO-FOR-BEE-AY-SEE-EE] - Among flowering plants, the spurge family is one of the largest. They are also commonly known as euphorbias in English, their genus name. Most spurges are herbs, such as Euphorbia paralias, but some are shrubs or trees, particularly in the tropics.

Lamiaceae [LAY-MEE-AY-SEE-EE] The mint or deadnettle family is aromatic in all parts. They include widely used culinary herbs like basil, mint, rosemary, sage, savory, marjoram, oregano, hyssop, thyme, lavender, and perilla. Catnip, salvia, bee balm, wild dagga, and oriental motherwort are medicinal herbs.

Malvaceae [MAL-VAY-SEE-EE] - The Mallow family of flowering plants is estimated to contain 244 genera and 4225 known species. Among its well-known members are okra, cotton, cacao, and durian.

Menispermaceae [MEN-EE-SPER-MAY-SEE-EE]- The moonseed family comprises 440 species, most of which are found in low-lying tropical regions, with some species also found in temperate and arid regions.

Morchellaceae [MOR-KEL-EE-AY-SEE-EE]- This family includes the well-known morel mushrooms, which are highly prized for their culinary value. Members of the Morchellaceae family are characterized by their distinctive fruiting bodies, which typically have a sponge-like, honeycomb appearance. These fungi are found in a variety of habitats, often in forests, and are known to form symbiotic relationships with trees, helping in nutrient exchange. They are ascomycetes, meaning they produce spores in specialized cells called asci.

Oxalidaceae [OKS-UH-LUH-DAY-SEE-EE] - The wood sorrel family comprises five genera of herbaceous plants, shrubs, and small trees, with about 570 species in the Oxalis genus.

Plantaginaceae [PLAN-TUH-JIH-NAY-SEE-EE] - The Plantain family and order Lamiales include common flower species such as snapdragon and foxglove.

Polygonaceae [PUH-LIG-UH-NAY-SEE-EE] - The knotweed or smartweed-buckwheat family is an informal name for a family of flowering plants. There are about 1200 species within about 48 genera. Members of this family are found worldwide, but they are most abundant in the North Temperate Zone.

Portulacaceae [POR-CHUH-LUH-KAY-SEE-EE]- The purslane family is a family of flowering plants with 115 species in one genus, Portulaca.

Ranunculaceae [RUH-NUN-KYOO-LAY-SEE-EE]- the buttercup or crowfoot family is a family of over 2,000 known flowering plants in 43 genera distributed worldwide.

Rosaceae [ROH-ZAY-SEE-EE] - The rose family includes 4,828 species of flowering plants.

Viburnaceae [VY-BUR-NAY-SEE-EE] - was previously known as the Adoxaceae family and is commonly known as the Moschatel family. About 150–200 species belong to this family of flowering plants.

<u>*Plant Types*</u>

Annual [AN-YOO-UHL] - Plants without a permanent woody stem. They are usually flowering garden plants or potherbs.

Deciduous [DIH-SIJ-OO-UHS] - After the growing season, the plant sheds leaves and turns dormant.

Dioecious [DAHY-EE-SHUHS] - having the male and female organs in separate and distinct individuals, having different sexes.

Herbaceous [HUR-BEY-SHUHS] - low-growing plants with soft green stems. Their above-ground growth is often seasonal.

Monoecious [MUH-NEE-SHUHS] - having the stamens and the pistils in separate flowers on the same plant.

Perennial [PUH-REN-EE-UHL] - It usually lasts for more than two years. These plants don't have a lot of woody growth.

Plant Parts

Achene [UH-KEEN] - a small, dry, one-seeded fruit that does not open to release the seed.

Anther [AN-THER] - the pollen-bearing part of a stamen.

Filament [FIL-UH-MUHNT] - the stalklike portion of a stamen, supporting the anther.

Ligulate [LIG-YUH-LIT] - strap-shaped, such as the ray florets of daisy family plants.

Peltate [PEL-TEYT] - fixed to the stalk by the center or by some point distinctly within the margin.

Petiole [PET-EE-OHL] - the slender stalk by which a leaf is attached to the stem; leafstalk.

Pistil [PIS-TL] - the ovule-bearing or seed-bearing female organ of a flower, consisting when complete of the ovary, style, and stigma.

Pith - The soft central cylinder of tissue in the plant's stem.

Sepal [SEE-PUHL] - The outer parts of the flower (often green and leaf-like) that enclose a developing bud.

Sessile [SES-IL] - attached directly by its base without a stalk or peduncle.

Stamen [STEY-MUHN] - the pollen-bearing organ of a flower, consisting of the filament and the anther.

Staminodia [STAM-UH-NOH-DEE-UH] - A stamen that is sterile or abortive.

Whorled - The arrangement of like parts around a point on an axis, such as leaves or flowers;

Leaf Types

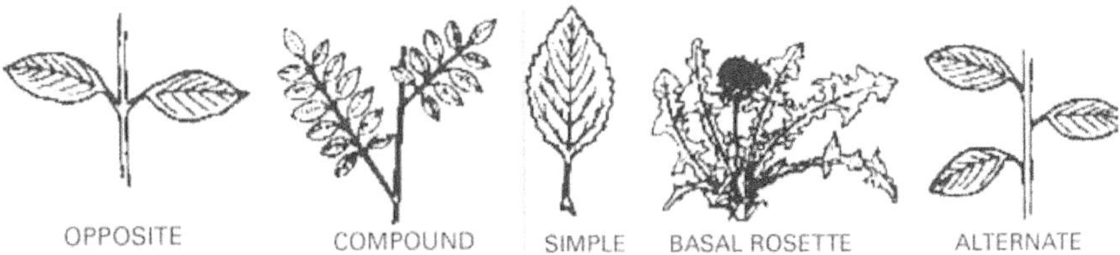

Alternate - The leaves are single at each node and spiral upwards along the stem.

Basal leaf - a leaf that grows lowest on the stem of a plant or flower.

Compound - composed of two or more leaflets that are attached to a single leaf stalk or petiole.

Opposite - When two leaves are attached at the same node, one on either side of the stem.

Palmate [PAL-MEYT] - Having four or more lobes or leaflets.

Palmately compound - A petiole's tip is attached to a leaflet.

Pinnate [PIN-EYT] - Each side of a stalk is divided into leaflets

Rosette [ROH-ZET] - a circular arrangement of leaves or structures resembling leaves.

Simple - Leaves with a single, undivided lamina

Tripinnately compound - Leaf made up of three pinnate parts.

Leaf Shapes

Cordate [KAWR-DEYT] - heart-shaped.

Elliptical [IH-LIP-TI-KUHL] - Planar, shaped like a flattened circle, symmetrical about the long and short axes, tapering equally to the tip and the base; oval.

Lanceolate [AN-SEE-UH-LEYT] - shaped like the head of a lance, having a rounded base and a tapering apex.

Long-pointed - Lying close and flat and pointing toward the plant's apex or structure.

Oblanceolate [OB-LAN-SEE-*UH*-LIT] - having a rounded apex and a tapering base.

Oblong [OB-LAWNG]- Having a length a few times greater than the width, with sides almost parallel and ends rounded.

Ovate [OH-VEYT] - egg-shaped, having such a shape with a broader end at the base.

Triangular - Planar with three sides.

Wedge - narrowly triangular, wider at the apex, and tapering toward the base.

Flower Types

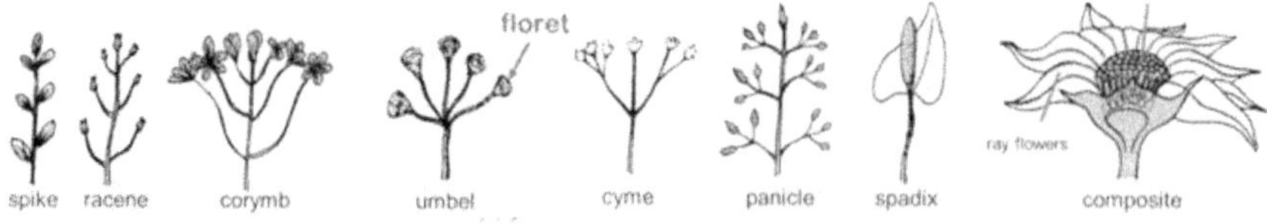

Corymb [KAWR-IMB] - a form of inflorescence in which the flowers form a flat-topped or convex cluster, the outermost flowers being the first to open.

Composite - is characterized by alternate, opposite, or *whorled* leaves and a whorl of bracts surrounding its flower heads. These flower heads typically extend from a disk containing tiny petal-less flowers and from the disk's rim to a ray of petals.

Cyme [SAHYM] - an inflorescence in which the primary axis bears a single central or terminal flower that blooms first.

Inflorescence [IN-FLAW-RES-*UH*NS] - the complete flower head of a plant, including stems, stalks, bracts, and flowers.

Panicle [PAN-I-K*UH*L] - any loose, diversely branching flower cluster.

Raceme [REY-SEEM] - a flower cluster with separate flowers attached by short equal stalks at equal distances along a central stem. The flowers at the base of the main stem develop first.

Spike - a type of racemose inflorescence.

Spadix [SPEY-DIKS] - an inflorescence consisting of a spike with a fleshy or thickened axis, usually enclosed in a spathe.

Umbel or Subumbel [UHM-BUHL] - consisting of several short flower stalks that spread from a common point, like umbrella ribs.

Seaweed

Blade - refers to the flattened and elongated portion of the seaweed that is similar to a leaf. The blade is the main photosynthetic organ of seaweed and is responsible for capturing light energy for photosynthesis.

Float - refers to a gas-filled bladder or sac that helps the seaweed stay afloat and near the water's surface, where it can receive maximum sunlight for photosynthesis.

Stipe - the stem-like structure that supports the leafy fronds. It is the main axis of the seaweed body and is analogous to the stem of a land plant.

Holdfast - a structure that anchors the seaweed to a solid surface, such as a rock or the ocean floor. Holdfasts are a critical part of the seaweed's anatomy as they provide stability and allow the seaweed to withstand the strong currents and waves of the ocean.

Fruit/Berry

Aggregate fruit [AG-RI-GIT FROOT] - composed of a cluster of carpels belonging to the same flower as the raspberry.

Dehiscent [DIH-HIS-UHNT] - opens to release seeds or pollen

Drupe [DROOP] - a fleshy fruit with thin skin and a central stone containing the seed, e.g., a plum, cherry, almond, or olive.

Globoid [GLOH-BOID] - approximately globular. Globe-shaped; spherical.

Infructescence [IN-FRUC-TES-CENCE] - an aggregate fruit.

Syconium [SAHY-KOH-NEE-UHM] - a fleshy hollow receptacle that develops into a multifruit.

Bark

Acaulescent [AK-AW-LES-UHNT] - stemless

Lenticel [LEN-TUH-SEL] - One of the many holes in a woody plant's stem that allows air to exchange between the inside and outside.

Myrmecochory [MUR-MUH-KOH-REE]- the dispersal of fruits and seeds by ants.

Elaiosome [IH-LAY-UH-SOHM] - an oil-rich body on seeds or fruits that attract ants and act as dispersal agents.

Medical Terms

Amygdalin [UH-MIG-DUH-LIN] - White, bitter-tasting glycosidic powder usually obtained from the leaves and seeds of plants of the genus Prunus and related genera: used mainly as an expectorant in medicine.

Anthocyanins [AN-THUH-SAHY-UH-NIN] - These flavonoids are known for their pigmentation properties, responsible for fruits, vegetables, flowers, and cereals' red, purple, and blue colors.

Astringent [UH-STRIN-JUHNT] - Contracting the body's tissues or canals reduces mucus or blood discharges.

Berberine [BUR-BUH-REEN] - Known as an antipyretic, antibacterial, and stomachic, this crystalline, water-soluble alkaloid is derived from barberry or goldenseal.

Carotenoid [KUH-ROT-N-OID] - Red or yellow pigments, similar to carotene, found in animal fat and some plants.

Cyanogenic glycosides - chemical compounds contained in foods that release hydrogen cyanide when chewed or digested.

Demulcent [DIH-MUHL-SUHNT] - a substance that relieves irritation of the mucous membranes in the mouth by forming a protective film.

Depurative [DEP-YUH-REY-TIV] - herbs considered to have purifying and detoxifying effects.

Flavonoids [FLEY-VUH-NOID] - An antioxidant, antiviral, anticancer, anti-inflammatory, and anti-allergenic group of water-soluble polyphenols found in plants.

Hydrocyanic acid - scientific word for cyanide.

Lutein [LOO-TEEN] - is known to have anti-inflammatory and immune-boosting properties and is important for maintaining healthy eyes and skin.

Lycopene [LAHY-KUH-PEEN] - Red crystalline substance found in some fruits, including tomatoes and paprika.

Odontalgic [OH-DON-TAL-JUH] - toothache.

Prunasin [PROO-NUH-SIN] - A cyanogenic glucoside related to amygdalin found in Prunus species.

Urolithiasis [YOOR-OH-LI-THAHY-UH-SIS] - A disease where stones form in the urinary tract.

Urushiol [OO-ROO-SHEE-AWL] - The active irritant principle in several plant species in the Rhus genus.

Zeaxanthin [ZEE-UH-ZAN-THIN] - is found in the macula of the eye, where it plays a role in protecting the eye from oxidative damage and age-related macular degeneration.

General definitions

Anthropogenic [AN-THRUH-PUH-JEN-IK] - caused by humans.

Decoction - concentrated herbal extracts that are made by boiling the plant material in water.

Glaucous [GLAW-KUHS] - covered with a whitish bloom, as a plum.

Siliceous [SUH-LISH-UHS] - growing in soil rich in silica.

Calcareous [KAL-KAIR-EE-UHS] - occurring on chalk or limestone.

Monoecious [MUH-NEE-SHUHS] - The stamens and pistils are in separate flowers on the same plant.

Mucilaginous [MYOO-SUH-LAJ-UH-NUHS] - having a viscous or gelatinous consistency.

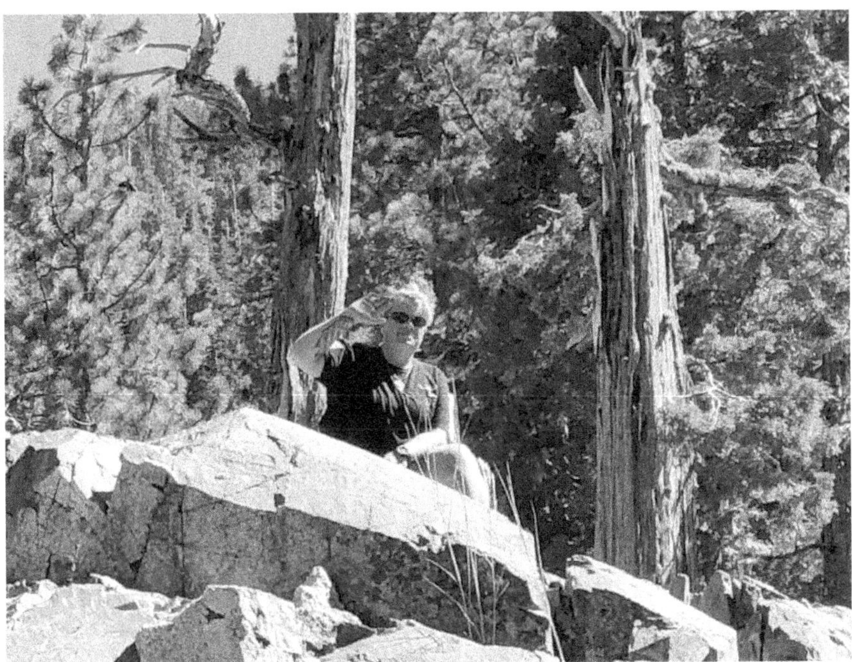

Shannon Warner is a long-time forager and survivalist with a deep love for the outdoors. She has spent countless hours exploring the wilderness, learning about the plants and animals that inhabit it, and honing her skills in sustainable harvesting and ethical foraging. She has embarked on many adventures with her two loyal dogs by her side, from hiking and camping to hunting and fishing.

One of her core beliefs is in sustainable harvesting and ethical foraging. She firmly believes that it is possible to enjoy the bounty of nature without causing harm to the environment or depleting its resources. In her books, she provides practical tips and advice on how to forage in a way that is both sustainable and respectful of the natural world.

Whether you are an experienced forager or a beginner looking to learn more about the plants that grow in your backyard, Shannon's books are an invaluable resource that will inspire and inform you. With her expert guidance, you, too, can discover the many benefits of wild edible plants and unlock the secrets of the natural world.

BIBLIOGRAPHY

Photo Attributions

Ribes Nigrum observed by Maja Dumat (licensed under creativecommons.org/licenses/by/2.0/)

Ribes Nigrum observed by Malcolm Manners (licensed under creativecommons.org/licenses/by/2.0/)

Ribes Nigrum observed by Gertjan van Noord (licensed under creativecommons.org/licenses/by/2.0/)

Rubus chamaemorus observed by Donald Hampton (licensed under https://creativecommons.org/licenses/by-sa/4.0//)

Rubus chamaemorus observed by Jason Grant (licensed under https://creativecommons.org/licenses/by/4.0/)

Rubus flagellaris observed by Will McFarland (licensed under https://creativecommons.org/licenses/by/4.0/

Rubus flagellaris observed by Violet T. (licensed under https://creativecommons.org/licenses/by/4.0/)

Ribes uva-crispa observed by Sus scrofa (licensed under https://creativecommons.org/licenses/by/4.0/)

Amelanchier nantucketensis observed by Zihao Wang (licensed under https://creativecommons.org/licenses/by/4.0/)

Ribes rubrum observed by Gertjan van Noord (licensed under https://creativecommons.org/licenses/by-nd/2.0/)

Ribes rubrum observed by Gavin Slater (licensed under https://creativecommons.org/licenses/by/4.0/)

Hippophae rhamnoides observed by Andreas Rockstein (licensed under https://creativecommons.org/licenses/by-sa/2.0/)

Hippophae rhamnoides observed by Andreas Rockstein (licensed under https://creativecommons.org/licenses/by-sa/2.0/)

Vaccinium vitis idaea observed by NTNU, Faculty of Natural Sciences (licensed under http://creativecommons.org/licenses/by/2.0/)

Gaultheria procumbens L. observed by Kathy Hofmeyer Woughter (licensed under http://creativecommons.org/licenses/by/4.0/)

Gaultheria procumbens L. observed by Larry Jensen (licensed under http://creativecommons.org/licenses/by/4.0/)

Symphytum officinale L. observed in the United States of America by Laura J. Costello (licensed under http://creativecommons.org/licenses/by/4.0/)

Symphytum officinale L. observed in the United States of America by Sarah Johnson (licensed under http://creativecommons.org/licenses/by/4.0/)

Symphytum officinale L. observed in the United States of America by Cullen Hanks (licensed under http://creativecommons.org/licenses/by/4.0/)

Danthonia spicata (L.) Roem. & Schult. observed in the United States of America by Derek (licensed under http://creativecommons.org/licenses/by/4.0/)

Danthonia spicata (L.) Roem. & Schult. observed in the United States of America by Brian Finzel (licensed under http://creativecommons.org/licenses/by/4.0/)

Dichanthelium clandestinum (L.) Gould observed in the United States of America by Sandy Wolkenberg (licensed under http://creativecommons.org/licenses/by/4.0/)

Dichanthelium clandestinum (L.) Gould observed in the United States of America by Violet T. (licensed under http://creativecommons.org/licenses/by/4.0/

Dichanthelium clandestinum (L.) Gould observed in the United States of America by mjpapay (licensed under http://creativecommons.org/licenses/by/4.0/)

Schoenoplectus tabernaemontani (C.C.Gmel.) Palla observed in the United States of America by Santiago Martín-Bravo (licensed under http://creativecommons.org/licenses/by/4.0/)

Schoenoplectus tabernaemontani (C.C.Gmel.) Palla observed in the United States of America by Zihao Wang (licensed under http://creativecommons.org/licenses/by/4.0/)

Tsuga canadensis (L.) Carrière observed in the United States of America by Sus scrofa (licensed under http://creativecommons.org/licenses/by/4.0/)

Betula alleghaniensis Britton observed in the United States of America by Jaime McGuigan (licensed under http://creativecommons.org/licenses/by/4.0/)

Betula alleghaniensis Britton observed in the United States of America by Rachel Stringham (licensed under http://creativecommons.org/licenses/by/4.0/)

Sargassum natans observed in the United States of America by James St. John (licensed under https://creativecommons.org/licenses/by/2.0/

Tricholoma magnivelare observed in the United States of America by Alan Rockefeller (licensed under https://creativecommons.org/licenses/by-sa/4.0/)

Tricholoma magnivelare (Peck) Redhead observed in Canada by Sigrid Jakob (licensed under http://creativecommons.org/licenses/by/4.0/)

Lentinula edodes (Berk.) Pegler observed in the United States of America by mfeaver (licensed under http://creativecommons.org/licenses/by/4.0/)

Lentinula edodes (Berk.) Pegler observed in the United States of America by Scott Morris (licensed under http://creativecommons.org/licenses/by/4.0/)

Lentinula edodes (Berk.) Pegler observed in the United States of America by Alan Rockefeller (licensed under http://creativecommons.org/licenses/by/4.0/)

Podophyllum peltatum L. observed in the United States of America by tkr421 (licensed under http://creativecommons.org/licenses/by/4.0/)

Podophyllum peltatum L. observed in the United States of America by florawhite (licensed under http://creativecommons.org/licenses/by/4.0/)

Podophyllum peltatum L. observed in the United States of America by john_hall (licensed under http://creativecommons.org/licenses/by/4.0/)

Betula papyrifera observed in the United States of America by psweet (licensed under http://creativecommons.org/licenses/by/4.0/)

Toxicodendron vernix observed in the United States of America by psweet (licensed under http://creativecommons.org/licenses/by/4.0/)

Pastinaca sativa observed in the United States of America by Sandy Wolkenberg (licensed under http://creativecommons.org/licenses/by/4.0/)

Aconitum napellus observed by Joan Simon (licensed under https://creativecommons.org/licenses/by-sa/2.0/)

Aconitum napellus observed by Joan Simon (licensed under https://creativecommons.org/licenses/by-sa/2.0/)

Aconitum napellus observed by Gertjan van Noord (licensed under https://creativecommons.org/licenses/by-sa/2.0/)

Cantharellus cinnabarinus observed by Bob (licensed under http://creativecommons.org/licenses/by/4.0/)

Cantharellus cinnabarinus observed by Katja Schulz_(licensed under http://creativecommons.org/licenses/by/4.0/)

References

Petruzzello, M. (2023, July 15). *shiitake mushroom. Encyclopedia Britannica.* https://www.britannica.com/science/shiitake-mushroom

Acer saccharum (Hard Maple, Leucoderme, Northern Sugar Maple, Sugar Maple) | North Carolina Extension Gardener Plant Toolbox. (n.d.). https://plants.ces.ncsu.edu/plants/acer-saccharum/

Acer saccharum Sugar Maple, Florida Maple, Hard Maple, Rock Maple PFAF Plant Database. (n.d.). https://pfaf.org/user/Plant.aspx?LatinName=Acer+saccharum

Achillea millefolium (Common Yarrow, Devil's Nettle, Dog Daisy, Dog Fennel, Milfoil, Soldier's Woundwort, Thousandleaf, Westen Yarrow, Yarrow) | North Carolina Extension Gardener Plant Toolbox. (n.d.). https://plants.ces.ncsu.edu/plants/achillea-millefolium/

Achillea millefolium Yarrow, Boreal yarrow, California yarrow, Giant yarrow, Coast yarrow, Western yarrow, Pacific yarrow PFAF Plant Database. (n.d.). https://pfaf.org/user/plant.aspx?LatinName=Achillea+millefolium

Aconitum napellus Aconite, Venus' chariot, Wolfsbane Garden, Monk's Hood Garden PFAF Plant Database. (n.d.). https://pfaf.org/user/Plant.aspx?LatinName=Aconitum+napellus

Aconitum uncinatum ssp. muticum (Blue monkshood) | Native Plants of North America. (n.d.). https://www.wildflower.org/plants/result.php?id_plant=ACUNM

Actaea pachypoda (Baneberry, Doll's Eyes, Dolls-eyes, Necklace Weed, Toadroot, White Baneberry, White Beads, White-beads, White Cohosh) | North Carolina Extension Gardener Plant Toolbox. (n.d.). https://plants.ces.ncsu.edu/plants/actaea-pachypoda/

Actaea pachypoda White Baneberry PFAF Plant Database. (n.d.). https://pfaf.org/user/Plant.aspx?LatinName=Actaea+pachypoda

Arisaema triphyllum (Bog onion, Brown dragon, Common Jack-in-the-Pulpit, Devil's ear, Dragon root, Indian Cradle, Indian Jack in The Pulpit, Indian Turnip, Jack-in-the-pulpit, Lady-in-a-chaise, Lord-and-Lady, Memory root, Parson-in-the-Pulpit, Pepper turnip, Starch wort, Three-leaved indian turnip, Wake robin, Wild turnip) | North Carolina Extension Gardener Plant Toolbox. (n.d.). https://plants.ces.ncsu.edu/plants/arisaema-triphyllum/

Arisaema triphyllum Jack In The Pulpit, Dragonroot, Indian Turnip PFAF Plant Database. (n.d.). https://pfaf.org/user/Plant.aspx?LatinName=Arisaema+triphyllum

Asarum canadense (Canadian Wild Ginger, Common Wild Ginger, Wild Ginger) | North Carolina Extension Gardener Plant Toolbox. (n.d.). https://plants.ces.ncsu.edu/plants/asarum-canadense/

Asarum canadense Snake Root, Canadian wildginger, Canada Wild Ginger, Wild Ginger PFAF Plant Database. (n.d.). https://pfaf.org/user/plant.aspx?latinname=Asarum+canadense

Augliere, M. (2023, June 22). The 2023 Edible Seaweed Foraging Guide for New England. *SpearfishingRI.*

https://www.spearfishingri.com/post/foraging-seaweed#:~:text=Foraging%20seaweed%20is%20le-gal%20in,ensure%20you%20are%20not%20trespassing.

Betula alleghaniensis (Golden Birch, Swamp Birch, Yellow Birch) | North Carolina Extension Gardener Plant Toolbox. (n.d.). https://plants.ces.ncsu.edu/plants/betula-alleghaniensis/

Betula alleghaniensis Yellow Birch, Swamp Birch PFAF Plant Database. (n.d.). https://pfaf.org/user/Plant.aspx?LatinName=Betula+alleghaniensis

Betula papyrifera (Canoe Birch, Kenai Birch, Mountain Paper Birch, Paperbark birch, Paper Birch, White Birch) | North Carolina Extension Gardener Plant Toolbox. (n.d.). https://plants.ces.ncsu.edu/plants/betula-papyrifera/

Betula papyrifera Paper Birch, Mountain paper birch, Kenai birch PFAF Plant Database. (n.d.). https://pfaf.org/user/Plant.aspx?LatinName=Betula+papyrifera

Cicuta maculata (Beaver Poison, Cowbane, Poison Hemlock, Poison Parsnip, Spotted Cowbane, Spotted Hemlock, Spotted Water Hemlock, Water Hemlock) | North Carolina Extension Gardener Plant Toolbox. (n.d.). https://plants.ces.ncsu.edu/plants/cicuta-maculata/

Cicuta virosa Cowbane, Mackenzie's water hemlock PFAF Plant Database. (n.d.). https://pfaf.org/user/Plant.aspx?LatinName=Cicuta+virosa

Cornus canadensis (Bunchberry, Canadian Bunchberry, Canadian Dwarf Cornel, Dwarf Dogwood) | North Carolina Extension Gardener Plant Toolbox. (n.d.). https://plants.ces.ncsu.edu/plants/cornus-canadensis/

Cornus canadensis Creeping Dogwood, Bunchberry dogwood, Bunchberry PFAF Plant Database. (n.d.). https://pfaf.org/user/plant.aspx?latinname=Cornus+canadensis

Danthonia spicata (Poverty oatgrass) | Native Plants of North America. (n.d.). https://www.wildflower.org/plants/result.php?id_plant=DASP2

Datura stramonium (Datura, Jamestown Weed, Jimsonweed, Stinkweed, Thorn-apple) | North Carolina Extension Gardener Plant Toolbox. (n.d.). https://plants.ces.ncsu.edu/plants/datura-stramonium/

Datura stramonium Thorn Apple, Jimsonweed, Jamestown Weed PFAF Plant Database. (n.d.). https://pfaf.org/user/Plant.aspx?LatinName=Datura+stramonium

Dichanthelium clandestinum (Deertongue, Deer-tongue Witchgrass, Witch Grass) | North Carolina Extension Gardener Plant Toolbox. (n.d.). https://plants.ces.ncsu.edu/plants/dichanthelium-clandestinum/

Empetrum nigrum Crowberry, Black crowberry, Black Crowberry PFAF Plant Database. (n.d.). https://pfaf.org/user/plant.aspx?latinname=Empetrum+nigrum

Eupatorium perfoliatum (American Boneset, Boneset, Bonset, Feverwort, Thoroughwort) | North Carolina Extension Gardener Plant Toolbox. (n.d.). https://plants.ces.ncsu.edu/plants/eupatorium-perfoliatum/

Eupatorium perfoliatum Thoroughwort, Boneset, Common boneset PFAF Plant Database. (n.d.). https://pfaf.org/User/Plant.aspx?LatinName=Eupatorium+perfoliatum

Gaultheria procumbens (American Wintergreen, Boxberry, Checkerberry, Common Wintergreen, Creeping Wintergreen, Eastern teaberry, Spreading Wintergreen, Teaberry, Wintergreen) | North Carolina Extension Gardener Plant Toolbox. (n.d.). https://plants.ces.ncsu.edu/plants/gaultheria-procumbens/

Gaultheria procumbens Checkerberry, Eastern teaberry, Teaberry, Creeping Wintergreen PFAF Plant Database. (n.d.). https://pfaf.org/user/plant.aspx?LatinName=Gaultheria+procumbens

Gaylussacia baccata (Black Huckleberry) | North Carolina Extension Gardener Plant Toolbox. (n.d.). https://plants.ces.ncsu.edu/plants/gaylussacia-baccata/

Gaylussacia baccata Black Huckleberry PFAF Plant Database. (n.d.). https://pfaf.org/user/Plant.aspx?LatinName=Gaylussacia+baccata

Hippophae rhamnoides Sea Buckthorn, Seaberry PFAF Plant Database. (n.d.). https://pfaf.org/user/plant.aspx?LatinName=Hippophae+rhamnoides

Horsetail Kelp (Laminaria digitata) | Gulf Of Maine, Inc. (n.d.). Gulf of Maine, Inc. https://gulfofme.com/all-sea-life/horsetail-kelp-laminaria-digitata

Impatiens capensis (Jewelweed, Jewel Weed, Orange Jewelweed, Touch-me-not) | North Carolina Extension Gardener Plant Toolbox. (n.d.). https://plants.ces.ncsu.edu/plants/impatiens-capensis/

Impatiens capensis Jewelweed PFAF Plant Database. (n.d.). https://pfaf.org/user/Plant.aspx?LatinName=Impatiens+capensis

Lady Bird Johnson Wildflower Center - the University of Texas at Austin. (n.d.-a). https://www.wildflower.org/plants/result.php?id_plant=EMNI

Lady Bird Johnson Wildflower Center - the University of Texas at Austin. (n.d.-b). https://www.wildflower.org/plants/result.php?id_plant=RILA

Lady Bird Johnson Wildflower Center - the University of Texas at Austin. (n.d.-c). https://www.wildflower.org/plants/result.php?id_plant=RUCH

Lady Bird Johnson Wildflower Center - the University of Texas at Austin. (n.d.-d). https://www.wildflower.org/plants/result.php?id_plant=VAVI

Lady Bird Johnson Wildflower Center - the University of Texas at Austin. (n.d.-e). https://www.wildflower.org/plants/result.php?id_plant=AMNA2

Lady Bird Johnson Wildflower Center - the University of Texas at Austin. (n.d.-f). https://www.wildflower.org/plants/search.php?search_field=Hippophae+rhamnoides&family=Acanthaceae&newsearch=true&demo=

Lady Bird Johnson Wildflower Center - the University of Texas at Austin. (n.d.-g). https://www.wildflower.org/plants/result.php?id_plant=RITR

Lady Bird Johnson Wildflower Center - the University of Texas at Austin. (n.d.-h). https://www.wildflower.org/plants/result.php?id_plant=RUPA

Lobelia inflata (Indian tobacco) | Native Plants of North America. (n.d.). https://www.wildflower.org/plants/result.php?id_plant=LOIN

Lobelia inflata Indian Tobacco PFAF Plant Database. (n.d.). https://pfaf.org/User/Plant.aspx?LatinName=Lobelia+inflata

Melissa officinalis (Balm, Balm Mint, Common Balm, Lemon Balm) | North Carolina Extension Gardener Plant Toolbox. (n.d.). https://plants.ces.ncsu.edu/plants/melissa-officinalis/

Melissa officinalis Lemon Balm, Common balm, Bee Balm, Sweet Balm, Lemon Balm PFAF Plant Database. (n.d.-a). https://pfaf.org/user/Plant.aspx?LatinName=Melissa+officinalis

Melissa officinalis Lemon Balm, Common balm, Bee Balm, Sweet Balm, Lemon Balm PFAF Plant Database. (n.d.-b). https://pfaf.org/user/Plant.aspx?LatinName=Melissa+officinalis

Mentha arvensis Corn Mint, Wild mint PFAF Plant Database. (n.d.). https://pfaf.org/user/Plant.aspx?LatinName=Mentha+arvensis

Mentha arvensis (Wild mint) | Native Plants of North America. (n.d.). https://www.wildflower.org/plants/result.php?id_plant=MEAR4

MushroomExpert.Com. (n.d.-a). Amanita muscaria var. flavivolvata (MushroomExpert.Com). https://www.mushroomexpert.com/amanita_muscaria_flavivolvata.html

MushroomExpert.Com. (n.d.-b). Artomyces pyxidatus (MushroomExpert.Com). https://www.mushroomexpert.com/artomyces_pyxidatus.html

MushroomExpert.Com. (n.d.-c). Auricularia americana (MushroomExpert.Com). https://www.mushroomexpert.com/auricularia_americana.html

MushroomExpert.Com. (n.d.-d). Cantharellus cinnabarinus (MushroomExpert.Com). https://www.mushroomexpert.com/cantharellus_cinnabarinus.html

MushroomExpert.Com. (n.d.-e). Coprinus comatus: The Shaggy Mane (MushroomExpert.Com). https://www.mushroomexpert.com/coprinus_comatus.html

MushroomExpert.Com. (n.d.-f). Flammulina velutipes (MushroomExpert.Com). https://www.mushroomexpert.com/flammulina_velutipes.html

MushroomExpert.Com. (n.d.-g). Hericium americanum (MushroomExpert.Com). https://www.mushroomexpert.com/hericium_americanum.html

MushroomExpert.Com. (n.d.-h). Hericium erinaceus (MushroomExpert.Com). https://www.mushroomexpert.com/hericium_erinaceus.html

MushroomExpert.Com. (n.d.-i). Hydnum repandum (MushroomExpert.Com). https://www.mushroomexpert.com/hydnum_repandum.html

MushroomExpert.Com. (n.d.-j). Lactarius rubidus (MushroomExpert.Com). https://www.mushroomexpert.com/lactarius_rubidus.html

MushroomExpert.Com. (n.d.-k). Lentinus tigrinus (MushroomExpert.Com). https://www.mushroomexpert.com/lentinus_tigrinus.html

MushroomExpert.Com. (n.d.-l). Trametes versicolor: The Turkey Tail (MushroomExpert.Com). https://www.mushroomexpert.com/trametes_versicolor.html

MushroomExpert.Com. (n.d.-m). Tricholoma magnivelare (MushroomExpert.Com). https://www.mushroomexpert.com/tricholoma_magnivelare.html

Nepeta cataria (Catmint, Catnip, Catswort) | North Carolina Extension Gardener Plant Toolbox. (n.d.). https://plants.ces.ncsu.edu/plants/nepeta-cataria/

Nepeta cataria Catmint, Catnip PFAF Plant Database. (n.d.). https://pfaf.org/user/Plant.aspx?LatinName=Nepeta+cataria

Ostrya virginiana (American Hop-hornbeam, Eastern Hop Hornbeam, Hop Hornbeam, Hop Horn Beam, Ironwood, Leverwood, Wooly Hop hornbeam) | North Carolina Extension Gardener Plant Toolbox. (n.d.). https://plants.ces.ncsu.edu/plants/ostrya-virginiana/

Ostrya virginiana Ironwood, Hophornbeam, Hop Hornbeam American, Hop Hornbeam Eastern PFAF Plant Database. (n.d.). https://pfaf.org/user/Plant.aspx?LatinName=Ostrya+virginiana

Picea rubens (Eastern Spruce, He Balsam, Pocono, Red Spruce, West Virginia Spruce, Yellow Spruce) | North Carolina Extension Gardener Plant Toolbox. (n.d.). https://plants.ces.ncsu.edu/plants/picea-rubens/

Picea rubens Red Spruce PFAF Plant Database. (n.d.). https://pfaf.org/User/Plant.aspx?LatinName=Picea+rubens

Pinus strobus (Eastern White Pine, North American White Pine, Northern White Pine, Soft Pine, White Pine) | North Carolina Extension Gardener Plant Toolbox. (n.d.). https://plants.ces.ncsu.edu/plants/pinus-strobus/

Pinus strobus White Pine, Eastern white pine PFAF Plant Database. (n.d.). https://pfaf.org/User/Plant.aspx?LatinName=Pinus+strobus

Porphyra tenera (Kjellman, 1897) | Marine Agronomy. (n.d.). http://www.marineagronomy.org/node/57

Prunus americana American Plum, American Wild Plum, Wild Plum PFAF Plant Database. (n.d.). https://pfaf.org/User/Plant.aspx?LatinName=Prunus+americana

Prunus americana (American Plum, American Wild Plum, Wild Plum) | North Carolina Extension Gardener Plant Toolbox. (n.d.). https://plants.ces.ncsu.edu/plants/prunus-americana/

Quercus bicolor (Bicolor Oak, Oaks, Swamp White Oak) | North Carolina Extension Gardener Plant Toolbox. (n.d.). https://plants.ces.ncsu.edu/plants/quercus-bicolor/

Quercus bicolor Swamp White Oak PFAF Plant Database. (n.d.). https://pfaf.org/user/Plant.aspx?LatinName=Quercus+bicolor

Quercus rubra (American Red Oak, Eastern Red Oak, Mountain Red Oak, Northern Red Oak, Oaks, Red Oak) | North Carolina Extension Gardener Plant Toolbox. (n.d.). https://plants.ces.ncsu.edu/plants/quercus-rubra/

Quercus rubra Red Oak, Northern red oak PFAF Plant Database. (n.d.). https://pfaf.org/user/Plant.aspx?LatinName=Quercus+rubra

Ranunculus bulbosus Bulbous Buttercup, St. Anthony's turnip PFAF Plant Database. (n.d.). https://pfaf.org/User/Plant.aspx?LatinName=Ranunculus+bulbosus

Rhus vernix Poison Sumach PFAF Plant Database. (n.d.). https://pfaf.org/User/Plant.aspx?LatinName=Rhus+vernix

Ribes lacustre Prickly Blackcurrant, Prickly currant PFAF Plant Database. (n.d.). https://pfaf.org/user/Plant.aspx?LatinName=Ribes+lacustre

Ribes triste American Red Currant, Red currant PFAF Plant Database. (n.d.). https://pfaf.org/user/Plant.aspx?LatinName=Ribes+triste

Rubus chamaemorus Cloudberry PFAF Plant Database. (n.d.). https://pfaf.org/user/Plant.aspx?LatinName=Rubus+chamaemorus

Rubus flagellaris (Blackberry, Common Dewberry, Dewberry, Northern Blackberry, Northern Dewberry) | North Carolina Extension Gardener Plant Toolbox. (n.d.). https://plants.ces.ncsu.edu/plants/rubus-flagellaris/

Rubus flagellaris Northern Dewberry PFAF Plant Database. (n.d.). https://pfaf.org/User/Plant.aspx?LatinName=Rubus+flagellaris

Rubus parviflorus Thimbleberry PFAF Plant Database. (n.d.). https://pfaf.org/user/plant.aspx?LatinName=Rubus+parviflorus

Schoenoplectus tabernaemontani (Softstem bulrush) | Native Plants of North America. (n.d.). https://www.wildflower.org/plants/result.php?id_plant=SCTA2

Seaweed.ie :: Codium fragile. (n.d.). https://www.seaweed.ie/descriptions/Codium_fragile.html

Seaweed.ie :: Information on marine algae. (n.d.-a). https://www.seaweed.ie/descriptions/Fucus_vesiculosus.html

Seaweed.ie :: Information on marine algae. (n.d.-b). https://www.seaweed.ie/descriptions/Plocamium_cartilagineum.html

Seaweed.ie :: Ulva or Sea Lettuce. (n.d.). https://www.seaweed.ie/algae/ulva.html

Solanum dulcamara (Bitter Nightshade, Bittersweet, Bittersweet Nightshade, Blue Blindweed, Blue Nightshade, Climbing Nightshade, Devil's Apple, European Bittersweet, Fellonwort, Felonwood, Poisonous Nightshade, Scarlet Berry, Snakeberry, Soda Apple, Violet Bloom, Wolfgrape, Woody Nightshade) | North Carolina Extension Gardener Plant Toolbox. (n.d.). https://plants.ces.ncsu.edu/plants/solanum-dulcamara/

Solanum dulcamara Bittersweet. Bittersweet Nightshade, Climbing nightshade, Bittersweet, Deadly Nightshade, Poisonous PFAF Plant Database. (n.d.). https://pfaf.org/User/Plant.aspx?LatinName=Solanum+dulcamara

Solidago canadensis (Canada Goldenrod, Canadian Goldenrod, Common Goldenrod, Goldenrod, Meadow Goldenrod,, Tall Goldenrod) | North Carolina Extension Gardener Plant Toolbox. (n.d.). https://plants.ces.ncsu.edu/plants/solidago-canadensis/

Solidago canadensis Canadian Goldenrod, Shorthair goldenrod, Harger's goldenrod, Rough Canada goldenrod, Common Goldenro PFAF Plant Database. (n.d.). https://pfaf.org/User/Plant.aspx?LatinName=Solidago+canadensis

Stevens, M. W. &. F. (n.d.). *California Fungi: Tricholoma murrillianum*. https://www.mykoweb.com/CAF/species/Tricholoma_murrillianum.html

Symphytum officinale (Black wort, Boneset, Bruise wort, Comfrey, Common Comfrey, Consound, Cultivated Comfrey, Knitbone, Quaker Comfrey, Slippery-Root, True Comfrey) | North Carolina Extension Gardener Plant Toolbox. (n.d.). https://plants.ces.ncsu.edu/plants/symphytum-officinale/

Symphytum officinale Comfrey, Common comfrey PFAF Plant Database. (n.d.). https://pfaf.org/user/Plant.aspx?LatinName=Symphytum+officinale

The Genus Ganoderma (MushroomExpert.Com). (n.d.). https://www.mushroomexpert.com/ganoderma.html

The Genus Sparassis (MushroomExpert.Com). (n.d.). https://www.mushroomexpert.com/sparassis.html

Toxicodendron vernix (Poison Sumac, Swamp Sumac, Thunderwood) | North Carolina Extension Gardener Plant Toolbox. (n.d.). https://plants.ces.ncsu.edu/plants/toxicodendron-vernix/

Trifolium pratense (Cow Grass, Peavine Clover, Purple Clover, Red Clover) | North Carolina Extension Gardener Plant Toolbox. (n.d.). https://plants.ces.ncsu.edu/plants/trifolium-pratense/

Tsuga canadensis (Canada hemlock, Canadian Hemlock, Eastern Hemlock, Hemlock Spruce, Spruce Pine) | North Carolina Extension Gardener Plant Toolbox. (n.d.). https://plants.ces.ncsu.edu/plants/tsuga-canadensis/

Tsuga canadensis Canadian Hemlock, Eastern hemlock PFAF Plant Database. (n.d.). https://pfaf.org/User/Plant.aspx?LatinName=Tsuga+canadensis

Urtica dioica (Common Nettle, Stinging Nettle) | North Carolina Extension Gardener Plant Toolbox. (n.d.). https://plants.ces.ncsu.edu/plants/urtica-dioica/

Urtica dioica Stinging Nettle, California nettle PFAF Plant Database. (n.d.). https://pfaf.org/user/Plant.aspx?LatinName=Urtica+dioica

Vaccinium macrocarpon (American Cranberry, Bearberry, Cranberry, Large Cranberry) | North Carolina Extension Gardener Plant Toolbox. (n.d.). https://plants.ces.ncsu.edu/plants/vaccinium-macrocarpon/

Vaccinium macrocarpon American Cranberry, Cranberry PFAF Plant Database. (n.d.). https://pfaf.org/user/plant.aspx?latinname=Vaccinium+macrocarpon

Vaccinium vitis-idaea Cowberry, Lingonberry, Northern mountain cranberry, Cranberry PFAF Plant Database. (n.d.). https://pfaf.org/user/plant.aspx?latinname=Vaccinium+vitis-idaea

Valeriana officinalis (All-heal, Garden Heliotrope, Garden Valerian, Valerian) | North Carolina Extension Gardener Plant Toolbox. (n.d.). https://plants.ces.ncsu.edu/plants/valeriana-officinalis/

Valeriana officinalis Valerian, Garden valerian PFAF Plant Database. (n.d.). https://pfaf.org/user/Plant.aspx?LatinName=Valeriana+officinalis

Veratrum viride (American White Hellebore, Corn Lily, False Hellebore, Hellebore, Indian Poke) | North Carolina Extension Gardener Plant Toolbox. (n.d.). https://plants.ces.ncsu.edu/plants/veratrum-viride/

Veratrum viride Indian Poke, American Hellebore PFAF Plant Database. (n.d.). https://pfaf.org/user/Plant.aspx?LatinName=Veratrum+viride

Verbena hastata American Blue Vervain, Swamp verbena PFAF Plant Database. (n.d.). https://pfaf.org/User/Plant.aspx?LatinName=Verbena+hastata

Verbena hastata (Blue Verbena, Blue Vervain, Simpler's Joy, Swamp Verbena, Swamp Vervain) | North Carolina Extension Gardener Plant Toolbox. (n.d.). https://plants.ces.ncsu.edu/plants/verbena-hastata/

What is Rockweed Seaweed? Ecology and Human History of Ascophyllum nod. (n.d.). Maine Coast Sea Vegetables. https://seaveg.com/pages/what-is-rockweed

What is Sugar Kelp Seaweed? Ecology and Human History of Saccharina la. (n.d.). Maine Coast Sea Vegetables. https://seaveg.com/pages/what-is-sugar-kelp

WoRMS - World Register of Marine Species - Turbinaria ornata (Turner) J.Agardh, 1848. (n.d.). https://www.marinespecies.org/aphia.php?p=taxdetails&id=221490

www.ingramcontent.com/pod-product-compliance
Lightning Source LLC
Chambersburg PA
CBHW070508160726
48003CB00004B/1483